Desire and Anxiety

In both feminist theory and Shakespearean criticism, questions of sexuality have consistently been conflated with questions of gender. This book refuses this all too common approach by instead detailing the intersections and contradictions between sexuality and gender in the early modern period. It argues that desire and anxiety together constitute the erotic in Shakespearean drama – circulating throughout the dramatic texts, traversing 'masculine' and 'feminine' sites, eliciting and expressing heterosexual and homoerotic fantasies, embodiments, and fears.

Taking heterosexuality and homoeroticism equally seriously, this is the first book to present a non-normalizing account of the unconscious and the institutional prerogatives that comprise the erotics of Shakespearean drama. Employing feminist, psychoanalytic, and new historical methods, using each to interrogate the other, the book implements a long overdue synthesis of the psychic and the social, the individual and the institutional.

Valerie Traub is Assistant Professor of Renaissance Drama and Gender Studies at Vanderbilt University.

Gender, Culture, Difference
General editor: Catherine Belsey

In the same series:

Signs of Cleopatra
History, politics, representation
Mary Hamer

Desire and Anxiety
Circulations of sexuality
in Shakespearean drama

Valerie Traub

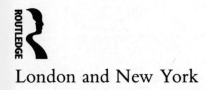

London and New York

First published 1992
by Routledge
11 New Fetter Lane, London EC4P 4EE

Simultaneously published in the USA and Canada
by Routledge
a division of Routledge, Chapman and Hall, Inc.
29 West 35th Street, New York, NY 10001

Typeset in 10/12pt Bembo by
Falcon Typographic Art Ltd, Fife, Scotland
Printed and bound in Great Britain by
T. J. Press (Padstow) Ltd, Padstow, Cornwall

British Library Cataloguing in Publication Data
Traub, Valerie
  Desire and anxiety: circulations of sexuality
  in Shakespearean drama.
  I. Title
  822.33

Library of Congress Cataloging in Publication Data
available on request.

ISBN 0-415-05526-1
      0-415-05527-X (pbk)

Books are gifts –
and I dedicate this one to the man who gave me many:
Joseph R. Traub

Contents

General editor's preface

Feminism has now reached a point where it is possible to produce a series of books written with the explicit aim of bringing together the politics of gender, cultural analysis and theoretically informed ways of reading. *Gender, Culture, Difference* offers a new kind of cultural history, which investigates the topics feminism has foregrounded, and takes the full range of cultural documents as its material.

GENDER

Feminism attends to the power relations inscribed in the areas patriarchal history treats as incidental: sexuality, private life and personal relations, cultural difference itself. At the same time, it also recognizes transgression of the existing conventions as a mode of resistance, and therefore takes an interest in behavior traditionally classified as perverse or dangerous. Above all, it is able to identify the differences within the relationships and practices it explores, treating them not as unified and homogeneous, but as contradictory to the degree that they participate in the uncertainties, incoherences, and instabilities of the cultures where they are found. The series addresses the topics politicized by feminism, analyzing them as sites where power is contested.

CULTURE

It is in culture that hierachies of power are defined and specified. Recent theory urges that the material of cultural analysis is always textual. We have no access to "experience," past or present, but only to the differential meanings in circulation within a culture. And these meanings reside in the existing documents, which can be read in order to make a history that refuses the injustices perpetrated by conventional patriarchal histories.

The documents of culture include, of course, every kind of material that it is possible to interpret: images, design and fashion, maps and domestic architecture, as well as philosophy, law, medicine. . . . But the project also involves attention, perhaps special attention, to fiction, since it is in stories, legends, plays, and poems that many cultures have tended to treat most freely and most precisely the relations between the sexes. (This in itself is a matter of some interest to feminism: fiction is what a patriarchal culture identified as "not true," not serious, not real and important. But to the extent that life follows art, in practice fiction returns to haunt the "real" history which marginalizes it.)

DIFFERENCE

Cultural contradictions, incoherences, and instabilities are pressure points for feminism, because they constitute evidence that existing power relations are always precarious. In this respect the interests of feminism coincide with recent modes of interpretation which specifically seek out instances of uncertainty, of difference within the text. For this reason, the series takes advantage of a range of theoretical developments which promote a differential practice of reading.

At the same time, feminism avoids the closed mode of address which sets out to deflect criticism and forestall debate. *Gender, Culture, Difference* is a speculative series that sets out to enlist readers in the process of discussion, and does not hesitate to engage with questions to which it has no final answers.

A NEW DIRECTION

The series brings together a differential reading practice and the construction of a cultural history which celebrates difference. In this respect *Gender, Culture, Difference* also offers a new model for literary studies. The epoch of the Author is over; few teachers and virtually no students now want to hear about maturity and the organic society, or about ambiguity and balance; and Elizabethan and other world pictures are totally played out. Meanwhile, English departments are looking for a way forward. It would not be at all surprising if feminism proved itself to be responsible for identifying one of the most exciting among the possible new directions.

Catherine Belsey

Acknowledgements

The Vanderbilt University Research Council provided me with a Summer Grant to support the completion of this manuscript. The debts I've incurred of a more personal nature are more numerous. Murray Schwartz, Arthur Kinney, and Lee Edwards encouraged the project from its beginning, and provided critical expertise as each early draft drastically redefined the book's scope. Abbe Blum, Peter Erickson, Barbara Mowat, Phyllis Rackin, and Valerie Wayne were generous with their time and responses to various parts of the manuscript. I have benefited enormously from conversations about feminism, desire, and the theater with Jean Howard and Susan Zimmerman. William Slights and Donald Foster commented perceptively on the Shakespeare Association of America seminar papers that formed the skeleton of later chapters. Jay Clayton responded thoughtfully and generously to almost all that I have written. The Introduction was given a rigorous reading by Mark Schoenfield, and it is far better because of it. Ann MacDonald's careful work on the manuscript meant that I had one less thing to worry about at a time that was particularly stressful. I owe a large debt of gratitude to R. Radhakrishnan for his impassioned introduction to post-structuralist theory and his example as a political activist within the university. Carol Batker, Ellen Garvey, and Alice Moore not only made graduate studies more a cooperative than competitive venture, and provided friendship both personal and intellectual, but also commented on the early essays that became the seed of this work. Catherine Belsey's comments always pushed me to think beyond the boundaries of my prior knowledge, and Janice Price's patience and enthusiasm have helped to still demons in my head. Peter Stallybrass deserves a special thank you, not only for his always brilliant, always detailed, and always challenging responses to my work, but for a generosity of spirit and intellect far beyond what I had been led to expect by the term "collegiality." He has not only welcomed me into an intellectual milieu that is as alive with pleasure as it is with demands, but has figured as a model for the integration of emotional, intellectual, and political commitment. Warm thanks to Barbara Michaelson for her exceptional thinking about me and my life's work during the early stages of this project. Susanna DesMarais' appreciation of literary endeavors, and Linda Wells' thirteen-year belief in the integrity of my choices formed a significant backdrop for the work that went into this project. The emotional support I've received from Teresa, Carolyn, and Michael Traub has been more important than they probably know. Teresa Goddu and Vereen Bell provided timely assistance in the final hours. And endless thanks to Brenda Marshall for sharing with me her insight into, and her delight about, language and sexuality.

Early versions of Chapters 1 and 2 appeared, respectively, in *Shakespeare Studies* 20 (Winter 1988) and *Shakespeare Quarterly* 40:4 (Winter 1989). Portions of the Introduction, Chapters 4 and 5 appear as "Desire and the Differences It Makes" in *The Matter of Difference: Materialist Feminist Criticism of Shakespeare*, ed. Valerie Wayne (Harvester and Cornell University Press, 1991).

Introduction
Talking about sexuality in Shakespeare

> It's natural
> It's chemical (let's do it)
> It's logical
> Habitual (can we do it?)
> It's sensual
> But most of all . . .
> Sex is something we should do
> Sex is something for me and you
> Sex is natural – sex is good
> Not everybody does it
> But everybody should
> Sex is natural – sex is fun
> Sex is best when it's . . . one on one
>   one on one
>   ("I want your Sex – Monogamy Mix"
>   George Michael, *Faith*)

I begin this book with the lyrics of a popular song because pop music functions in our own cultural milieu in a way analogous to public performances of Shakespeare's plays: both art forms reproduce and intervene in dominant ideologies, subtly transforming them through particular organizations of (aural and/or visual) pleasure; both are directed toward a mass audience that cuts across class and gender lines; and both exhibit a keen investment in eroticized bodies in order to deliver the pleasure they promise. And yet, insofar as George Michael's 1987 rock revision of the *carpe diem* tradition insists not only that "sex is natural – sex is good," but that sex is "logical" and "chemical," it demonstrates its embeddedness within a specifically *modern* conceptual paradigm.

That is, for Michael the meaning of "sex" is so self-evident that it requires no definition, merely repetition, for its erotic effects.

But has "sex" always been conceived as "natural"? "Fun"? "Good"? Something everyone should do, and best when performed "one on one"? From whose perspective and with whose pleasure in mind? The following book is written in the belief that this seemingly commonsensical view of "sex" is historically relatively recent, and had not emerged fully in the discourses of sexuality in the sixteenth and early seventeenth centuries. More specifically, I present Shakespearean drama as a contested site for the reproduction or interrogation of precisely the "essentialist" view of sexuality to which Michael and we are heir. Because of their embeddedness within modern discourses of sexuality, many literary critics, intent on celebrating Shakespeare's depiction of romantic love, have failed to see the extent to which Shakespearean drama represents erotic desire as *constituted* within a complex and contradictory social field. However much the plays endorse the view that "sex is natural" – and they do so whenever they assert the transcendence of romantic, sexual love over the tortured (or sordid) worlds of family or politics – they also structure those desires in irredeemably social, relational, hierarchical, and hence, political contexts. A contradiction thus fractures the Shakespearean terrain: on one side, an elevated, naturalized, transcendent "sexuality" coincident to and synonymous with a historically incipient ideology of romantic love; on the other side, a politicized "sexuality" simultaneously physical and psychological, often bawdy, and constituted as much by anxiety as by desire.

Plays, of course, do not neatly line up along one side or the other; each play is itself a site of struggle between the transcendent and the political. *Romeo and Juliet*, for instance, highlights the contradiction: the two lovers attempt to forge an erotic alliance beyond the physical and ideological constraints of the feuding houses of Capulet and Montague. To the extent that their erotic love is given expression in spheres untouched by the feud – the balcony, the bedroom, the abbey, the tomb – they succeed. But the tragedy of the play is precisely the futility of such a desire: each space of transcendent love is ultimately shown to be contained within, and even invaded by, the dominant ideology and effects of masculine violence.[1] Romeo and Juliet's erotic love, while liberated through the expression of spiritualized poetry, is ultimately doomed precisely because it attempts to exist outside of the material, political world. At the same time, the play demonstrates the impossibility of thinking of eroticism outside of these binary terms and their negation.

That Romeo and Juliet as lovers are positioned against the patriarchal houses of their fathers indicates further a historical tension between emergent and receding ideologies of "sexuality." The concept represented by the lovers' desire is our legacy: an individual, monogamous, heterosexual romantic love that finds its fulfillment in mutual physical passion – i.e., Michael's "one on one." Coincident with the rise of Puritanism, the post-Renaissance period witnessed an increase of ideological investment in just such "companionate marriages."[2] But the play just as insistently depicts an equally compelling desire: for family, name, property, rank, lineage – all those social statuses gathered together in the early modern term "house." Shakespearean drama thus marks within itself a struggle over the meaning of desire, as the process begins of separating off and mystifying the context in which sexuality is experienced.

This book is structured as an investigation of one problematic: the relation between erotic desire and its corollary, anxiety, and their role in the construction of male and female subjects in Shakespearean drama. Shakespeare's representations of erotic desire can be understood in relation to the anxieties and fantasies they occasion, and this point generates a number of correlates: that the plays' predominantly masculine perspective of desire expresses an attitude toward female bodies that, in its most potent form, is revealingly paranoid; that the conceptual grids of "heterosexuality" and "homoeroticism" in the early modern period differ significantly from their contemporary significations; that questions of sexuality cannot be divorced from issues of subjectivity – and that analyses of subjectivity should not subordinate erotic concerns.

The focus of each chapter represents a major strain in Shakespeare's representation of sexuality: the deadly importance of female chastity; the horrors associated with a fantasy of the female reproductive body; the disgust about erotic relations which finds its most extreme manifestation in the equation between desire and disease; and the pleasures and anxieties occasioned by homoerotic desire. Five fantasized bodily figures are deconstructed and reconstructed: an oedipal male, heterosexual body; a "grotesque" female reproductive body; the body as site of disease; and male and female homoerotic bodies. I have not covered the Shakespearean erotic field comprehensively; any such attempt would necessarily involve, for instance, a more thoroughgoing analysis of prostitution and the language of bawdy, attention to specifically class-bound sexualities, and far more emphasis on the desires of the theater audience. But, to the extent that I have analyzed a particular problem, I intend my treatment to suggest linkages throughout the Shakespearean corpus.

Two Anglo-American intellectual traditions present themselves as useful to the theorist of erotic desire: object-relations psycho-analysis and feminist theory. However, both offer limited explanatory models of the interactions between texts, psyches, bodies, and cultures during specific moments in time. This book thus charts a critical movement in reaction to these two paradigms, moving both toward a greater inclusion of historical specificity and toward a deconstructive questioning of the terms of my inquiry: sex, desire, power, man, woman, subject. It also progresses from a strictly feminist perspective – concerned with male anxiety toward women's eroticism and the maternal body in the first two chapters – to a gay and lesbian critical theory in the subsequent chapters. Additionally, the most rigorous attempt to integrate psychoanalytic and historical methods occurs in Chapters 3 through 5. The book thus represents not only the evolution of my thinking, but also an archaeology of contemporary theorizing about the relation between the psychic and the social, as I move farther from a psychoanalytic model of character to a psychoanalytic interrogation of culture, and from an emphasis on individual neurosis to a focus on cultural structure. As the chapters proceed, "identity" and "agency" are increasingly conceived in relation to determinate social structures; by Chapter 2, identity and the mechanisms associated with the psyche – notably, repression and displacement – are located less in character and author, and more diffusely in text and culture. Through this broader focus on repression and displacement, I analyze the ways subjects are variously constructed and positioned in the social field. As I attempt to bypass the anthropomorphic fallacy – the tendency to treat dramatic characters as "real" people rather than highly mediated representations – my analysis of the textual circulation of desire still maintains the possibility of a limited "agency": defined not as the clear, unhampered prerogative of characters conceived as individuals-generating-culture, but as the circumscribed negotiation of beings granted subjectivity *within* their culture.

What further links these chapters is the concept of displacement

– whether it be the displacement of erotic anxiety into a dramatic strategy (Chapter 1), the displacement of the "grotesque" by the "classical" body (Chapter 2), the displacement of disease through the mechanism of projection (Chapter 3), the displacement of erotic desire from one character to another (Chapter 5), or the displacement of sexuality into a critical discourse on gender (Chapter 4). Implicit in the psychoanalytic concept of displacement is the new historicist notion of containment: each displacement is motivated by an effort to contain a force unconsciously perceived as threatening; both displacement and containment are implicitly aspects of a mechanics of repression, once conceived not only in subjective but in socio-political terms.

Such displacements, different in type and moving across various registers, exist within one critical frame of reference: a model of cultural negotiation. Cultural negotiation concerns the ways social energies circulate through multiple domains as subjects and groups struggle for power and representation. The notion of the circulation of social energy – the ideological exchanges that occur along lines of social fracture and cohesion – has come to the study of literature via the emerging field of "cultural studies," especially through cultural materialism and new historicism. My subtitle, "Circulations of sexuality in Shakespearean drama," obviously is indebted to Stephen Greenblatt's *Shakespearean Negotiations: The Circulation of Social Energy in Renaissance England*.[3] In his first chapter, Greenblatt revises his previous model of power, in which he "had tried to organize the mixed motives of Tudor and Stuart culture" in favor of a less deterministic model of "cultural transactions through which great works of art are empowered."[4] Although I too am engaged in a "poetics of culture," I am less interested in the ways works of art are empowered than in the ways characters are represented as negotiating and struggling *for* power, the extent to which they are granted or denied agency – in short, the ways their subjectivity is constructed through representational means.

In *Desire and Anxiety*, such negotiation and struggle converge on the erotic: the ways the erotic is produced, the processes that define it, the ideological and institutional constraints placed on its activity, and the pleasures it affords or promises. I am interested, in David Halperin's useful revision of Greenblatt's phrase, in a "cultural poetics of desire," in detailing the "processes whereby sexual desires are constructed, mass-produced, and distributed."[5] The question motivating my book as a whole is, "What are the modalities of desire available to early modern subjects?", and the book's strategy is to trace the circulation of desire as it traverses dramatic texts. By "circulation" I refer to the expression of erotic energy as desire or anxiety, the object upon which desire or anxiety is projected, the movements of desire or anxiety through the social polity, and the ways in which anxiety is mediated or assuaged (whether by repression, containment, or displacement). This circulation of desire is less accurately viewed as a characteristic inhering within a given psyche than as a relation of exchange, an always potentially dynamic position from which subjects negotiate for pleasure. One way of visualizing the circulation of desire can be gleaned from the dramatic high jinks of *A Midsummer Night's Dream*: under the magical influence of Oberon and Puck, the desires of Hermia, Helena, Lysander, Demetrius, and Titania are passed from one erotic object to the next, as their gazes converge first on this, and then on that potential lover. It is almost as if desire is tossed around like a ball in some chaotic, yet impersonal game, as each character repudiates – represses – what s/he previously wanted. That this desire is manipulated by an external force – the magical flower juice appropriated by Oberon – highlights the extent to which desire itself is anonymous, without content, existing only in the context of a relation which gives it shape and meaning.

In the specific context of the Shakespearean theater, the circulation of desire is complicated by the gender asymmetry of patriarchal representation: female characters are conceived, interpreted, and (originally) acted by men; as mediated representations, they are in a complex relationship to early modern and postmodern women. To the extent that all representations are cultural fantasies, they inevitably involve projection, compensation, and wish-fulfillment, on the part of both author and audience or reader.

The effort to analyze the erotic must begin definitionally. In contemporary critical discussions, sexuality is variously perceived as an immanent, essential, biological drive or, conversely, as a mere "subjectivity effect"; the individual's "truth-in-being" or a studied theatrical performance; inherently (or constructed as) violent when male and inherently (or constructed as) passive or resistant when female. Everywhere it is equated with gender role.

To my mind, sexuality has no inherent meaning. We have no unmediated access to our bodies; our bodies, our subjectivities, our desires and anxieties, are constituted in relation to social processes. There is no "Ur-desire" that we can apprehend; sexuality comes to mean, to signify. And yet, sexuality is not a mere effect of cultural determinations. Each infant is born with polymorphous "desires" – how those desires are organized, regulated, incited, and disciplined is the province of culture.

My notion of desire is indebted to a particular reading of the works of Sigmund Freud, Jacques Lacan, and Michel Foucault. Lacan's revision of Freud systematically reopens the question of desire by insisting on the endless deferral of desire's fulfillment, and hence, its structural impossibility. Foucault, in contrast, draws desire back to the material domain of discourses and practices. Despite their differences, both Lacan and Foucault tie desire to the linguistic realm: whereas psychoanalysis contends that sexuality is the truth of discourse, Foucault reverses this relation by posing sexuality as the strategy for the incitement to discourse; and whereas Lacan views the linguistic as primarily a symbolic relation, for Foucault it is primarily a matter of force relations. It is within the gap between their theories that the following work finds its proper place and trajectory. For, as the following pages will demonstrate, I not only conceive of desire as a function of both the symbolic order and discursive practices, but I view the separation between the psychic and the material as a false dichotomy. For me, the contradiction between Foucault and Lacan is not paralyzing but enabling, enjoining me to strategically synthesize disparate ideas in the form of the following postulates: desire is always (1) a matter of both bodies and minds; (2) implicated in interpretative networks, signifying systems, discursive fields; and (3) substitutive, founded on a lack, and hence, always the desire of an other. Desire and anxiety thus involve *fantasies* of the other, fantasies that transform and recombine elements of the existing social formation. Desire is thus not a dyadic relation, but is always mediated through a third term – not, as in the work of René Girard, as a matter of individual rivalries, but in reference to the powerful ideologies that shape cultural possibilities.[6] And, insofar as our early infantile experiences of desire take place in the denial of our needs by someone more powerful than us, desire and power become intimately cathected, and indeed, by our adult years, inseparable.

By proposing this framework of desire and anxiety, I attempt to link together the mutually constitutive aspects of one problematic – sexuality – in hopes of bypassing two dominant frameworks commonly employed in discussing the erotic: the "normal" and the "latent." Despite Freud's efforts to denormalize the normal and insist on the existence of repressed elements in *every* unconscious, recourse to a dichotomy of normal and pathological, manifest and latent, as descriptive or analytical categories has more often than not served coercive ideological purposes. By referring erotic desire and anxiety back to an illusory myth of origin, appeals to the normal and the latent obscure their constructedness within and by ideological processes. Rather than assume a binary division between normality and the pathological, the manifest and the latent, I propose instead a mutually interactive dialectic: wherever there is desire, there is anxiety; wherever there is anxiety, there is desire. Like idealization and debasement, they are two sides of the same coin.

The danger of this model, however, is that it can reproduce past essentialisms, taking desire (in any of its forms) as a given, reifying it to the status of an ontological fact. Likewise, in detailing the presence of certain forms of anxiety – misogyny or homophobia, for instance – anxiety may appear transhistorical. In order to resist essentialism in this guise, I attempt to contextualize the desires and anxieties I decode, demonstrating the ways they are elicited and repressed, both psychically and culturally, within their historical moment.

Freud linked anxiety with sexual repression, arguing that lack of orgasmic release creates a state of free-floating anxiety.[7] But, whereas Freud viewed anxiety as a result of inescapable and transhistorical dictates of biology and culture (prohibitions on incest or homosexuality, for instance), I see such dictates as arbitrary political constructs, and thus open to transformation. Mine is not, however, a utopian project, wherein all anxiety or repression would be eradicated, for all societies depend on such basic structuring mechanisms as language, kinship and social networks, and political hierarchies. Rather, I hope to contribute modestly to the project of carving out space within the social structure for greater erotic variety by deconstructing and refiguring the anxieties that regulate and discipline erotic life.

Recent research in the field of gay and lesbian history demonstrates that the psychosexual developmental imperatives described (and defended) by Freud have been only tenuously hegemonic. For instance, the work of anthropologists and historians suggests that a significant proportion of men and women have engaged in same-gender erotic activities throughout history. A reversion to Freud's radical insight about the polymorphous potential of desire, combined with a rejection of the patriarchal imperatives that have legislated against "deviancy" or "perversion" leads us, not to an utopian impossibility, but to a redefinition of culture as such.[8] Many of the repressions which Freud argued were necessary to culture in *Civilization and its Discontents* are necessary only within the context of patriarchal and heterosexist ideologies.[9]

As my reference to Freud highlights, since the beginning of this century the primary method for analyzing sexuality has been psychoanalysis. In recent years, however, psychoanalysis has faced a major challenge posed by "social constructivism," those feminist, materialist, gay and lesbian, African-American, anthropological and Foucauldian discourses that detail the ways psychic and behavioral experience are constructed differentially across time and culture. In terms of sexuality, social constructivism demonstrates that whereas "sexuality" exists in all cultures, its signification is variously conceived as reproduction, ritual, pleasure for pleasure's sake, locus of self-discipline, mode of symbolic or political exchange, and/or key to identity. The importance of sexuality thus lies, not in some intrinsic meaning or value, but in the experience of sexuality as, in the words of Michel Foucault,

> an especially dense transfer point for relations of power . . . endowed with the greatest instrumentality: useful for the greatest number of maneuvers and capable of serving as a point of support, as a linchpin, for the most varied strategies.[10]

Sexuality is, in itself, an empty construct, a kind of power vacuum that acts, in the words of Jeffrey Weeks, "as a crossover point for a number of tensions whose origins are elsewhere: of class, gender, and racial location, of intergenerational conflict, moral acceptability, and medical definition."[11]

If sexuality is an ideological vacuum that is also a domain of power, then the erotic body is a material site for inscriptions of ideology and power. Dominant social formations not only manipulate but produce erotic desire through ideological and institutional means. Sexuality thus embodies (in the dual sense of inhering in the body and bodying forth) a power relation, not only for those members of erotic minorities who are positioned so as to feel most overtly the effects of institutionalized oppression, but for all sexual subjects (perhaps most insidiously for those who do not recognize the extent to which they are ideologically incited to act/think/fantasize erotically in prescribed ways). Sexuality as a crux of contemporary women's oppression has long been acknowledged, especially in its more violent or physically intrusive aspects – rape, battering, incest, pornography, advertising, constraints on reproductive rights. But that sexuality in its more benign manifestations – marriage, monogamy, the desire for particular genres of pleasure – is also a matter of ideological and institutional investments is an insight more difficult to sustain, perhaps because these practices implicate people where change is most difficult, in our erotic propensities and love relationships.

The result of such inscriptions is that erotic practice is material practice. Not only do physical bodies materially relate to one another, but more to the point, erotic choices position human beings in material (including, but not limited to, economic) ways. The *difference* between erotic choices is thus a palpable determinant of power. Unfortunately, the insertion of minority erotic practice into critical discussion often results in its annexation – to too many readers, the automatic response is "oh, that refers to them, not me." However, a guiding premise of this book, and a major argument of Chapter 3, is the need to deconstruct this Us/Them dichotomy, by which people are not only differentiated, but positioned in relations of dominance and subordination. Insofar as gay and lesbian theory foregrounds the possibility of erotic agency within a determinate field of constraints, it offers a mode of analysis applicable to erotic practice in general.

Precisely because sexuality is socially constructed, erotic practices and ideologies are open to transformation, however difficult such change in practice. Therefore, while recognizing the dominance of particular erotic ideologies, I am most interested in highlighting the slippages between ideological prescription and social practice, the ways individuals negotiate within ideological matrices to satisfy their complex needs and desires. This premise of limited agency refuses to view individuals as fully subjugated victims of their culture and recognizes the import of subjective, psychic experience as well – for it is within the unconscious (itself a social product) that the possibility of erotic disruption is born.

The appeal to the agency of the unconscious cuts against the grain of much feminist, materialist, and constructivist thinking. Citing the psychoanalytic assertion of a transhistorical human nature and its repressive policies toward "deviant" individuals, many critics indict psychoanalysis as a mechanism of social control, a form of power-knowledge that creates, organizes, and subjugates subjects in the interests of white, Western, phallocentric, heterosexist ideologies. However, despite some sympathy with this perspective, I believe that the theory of the unconscious is crucial to an understanding of erotic fantasies, preferences, and practices.[12] As Robert Stoller demonstrates, the construction of each individual's erotic "script" is an intricate, tangled process, involving "impulses, desires, defenses, falsifications, truths avoided, and memories of past events, erotic and nonerotic, going back to infancy."[13] Stoller calls the moment of erotic excitement "a piece of theatre" in which one's erotic script is rehearsed, revised, and performed.[14] That much psychoanalytic work ignores the location of each erotic "drama" within a larger theater of ideological codes does not obviate the existence of unconscious impulses. Although the unconscious is culturally constructed, it is not a rigid or predetermined totalization, but a flexible mechanism that uniquely influences and adapts to each subject's lived experience. Therefore, the psychic mechanisms of condensation, displacement, introjection, projection, substitution, splitting, and reversal may be useful vehicles for describing intra- and inter-psychic relationships as they exist within a cultural field. In the following pages, my examination of the way dominant modes of psychoanalysis construct male subjectivity, the maternal body, homoeroticism, and "desire" itself guides my attempt to develop a psycho-historical cultural and literary analysis, as I employ psychoanalytic concepts for the purpose of deconstructive resistance to normalizing narratives.

Because sexuality finds its signification at the intersection of multiple "private" and "public" pleasures and disciplines, because it exists only within relations – between bodies, between psyches, between institutions and bodies and psyches – the erotic is a privileged site of investigation of the interaction of the social and the psychic, the institutional and the subjective. Accordingly, the following chapters attempt to demonstrate the extent to which these "poles" of human experience are mutually implicated, mutually constitutive. Much of this book was written in unspoken dialogue with those feminist, psychoanalytic, new historical, materialist, and constructivist critics who conceive of their mutual projects in antipathetic terms. As I highlight the roles of these critical methods in reproducing erotic ideology, I also suggest the ways they can benefit from one another, with an eye toward disturbing their boundaries, and facilitating a strategic alliance for the collective transformation of the erotic system.

These critical methodologies often share a common failing: they tend to unthinkingly conflate gender and sexuality – as if, because gender and sexuality are constituted simultaneously, they are identical, as if sexuality flows unproblematically from gender role. An underlying premise of the following chapters, and the detailed focus of Chapter 4, is the attempt to chart both the articulations and disarticulations of gender and sexuality, and in particular to examine the disturbance of gender by its non-correspondence to sexuality. This involves the attempt to separate temporarily sexuality from gender in the interest of gaining greater specificity in our conceptual categories. Whereas this may appear similar to some currently fashionable attempts to "move beyond" gender in a "post-feminist" direction, my aim is different: rather than subsume gender under a larger rubric (subjectivity or power, for instance), the separation I advocate is intended to create greater clarification of both gender and sexuality.

Despite my indebtedness to the work of Michel Foucault, in at least three important respects my approach differs significantly from his. First, I emphasize the agency of the unconscious in affecting erotic life, while Foucault is antipathetic to all psychoanalytic projects. Second, I rigorously maintain the importance of locating and analyzing gender asymmetries – structural inequalities and individual anxieties – in erotic discourses and practices, whereas Foucault tends to elide the specificity of female experience. And third, I would like to render in more subtle terms than does Foucault the difference between a culture's discursive practices and that culture's production of *meanings*. Not only are dominant discourses an inadequate measure of erotic significations and practices, but the relation between discourse and meaning is more complicated than Foucault's polemical rhetoric of historical difference admits. Taken literally, Foucault implies that because neither sexuality nor its subsets (homosexuality, heterosexuality) were available in the early modern discursive field, no correlation exists between early modern erotic practices and modern significations. I would argue, however, that despite the absence of a specific discourse of sexuality, within early modern culture there circulated significations that, however incommensurate, can be usefully brought in tension with modern meanings.

Shakespeare's language metaphorizes and materializes desire;

within his drama, such terms as "blood," "flesh," "heart," "appetite," "passion," and "death" locate desire in a dispersed corporeal body. This discursive indeterminacy is foreign to our own reliance on a unitary abstraction, "sex," and foreign also to our romantic mystification, "make love." The drama's fascination with and dependence on body parts ("mammets" and "pricks," as well as "thing," "piece," "pit," "hell") reiterates what I shall call his propensity toward "metaphorizing materialization." More often than not Shakespeare's language connotes moral *judgments* (e.g., lust, lechery, luxury, corruption, pollution, vice, sin) or focuses on social *effects* (e.g., cuckoldry, effeminacy), rather than detailing the object of many post-Freudians: the psychological *origin* of desire. That Shakespearean erotic language not only defies our modern lexicon, but is foreign to the Freudian "depth model" of sexuality and subjectivity, does not obviate the persistent interest of his drama in the material and relational contexts in which "desire" is produced, sustained, and displaced.

Within the field of early modern studies, perhaps the most influential critic of the use of depth models is Stephen Greenblatt. His analysis of the "impersonation" of Martin Guerre is a "case history" of the early modern subject that utterly redefines the genre by demonstrating the irrelevance of psychoanalysis to that subject's world. He argues that

> what is at stake in this case is not psychic experience at all but rather communal judgment that must . . . be clarified and secured by legal authority. . . . At issue is not Martin Guerre as subject but Martin Guerre as object, the placeholder in a complex system of possessions, kinship bonds, contractual relationships, customary rights, and ethical obligations. . . . Martin's subjectivity . . . does not any the less exist, but it seems peripheral, or rather, it seems to be the *product* of the relations, material objects, and judgments exposed in the case rather than the *producer* of these relations, objects, and judgments.[15]

Greenblatt's is a boundary-marking discourse: object is demarcated from subject, surface from depth, communal judgment and legal authority from psychic experience, producer from product of social relations. It is also a hierarchical discourse, privileging external force relations over interiority to the point that Greenblatt can assert, in a later essay, "Fiction and Friction," that "individual identity in the early modern period served less as a final goal than as a way station on the road to a firm and decisive identification with normative structures."[16]

What concerns me here is not so much Greenblatt's insistence on the subordination of the subject-of-consciousness to pervasive systems of power and signification, but his assumption that "normative structures" are themselves a given. With difference reduced to a transitory moment in an overdetermined teleology, all possibility of resistance to these putative norms is denied. Norms in Greenblatt's analysis emerge as internally unified, cohesive, and above all, certain.

Yet, as Greenblatt would recognize, the notion of norms is a nineteenth-century concept that did not take on the evaluative valence of "normal" until the discourses of natural history, medicine, and sexology began to differentiate between, and thereby produce, those subjects who acquiesced to and those who deviated from a commonly held standard. If "normality" was not produced as a social category until the 1840s, then we need to ask again what "normative structures" meant in a culture as fractured, inconsistent, and internally riven as was that of the early modern period. I do not mean to suggest that difference was never demarcated – certainly, the categories of the "unnatural" and the "criminal" played a significant part in ritualistic and dramatic scapegoating. Nonetheless, although appeals to nature often underscore assertions of norms, there is no *necessary* relation between the two. Norms may *appear* to be "natural," but when did "nature" become "normal"?

The discourse of norms is complexly related to the discourse of the subject. For if the subject is constituted through social processes, the internalization of norms would appear to be a crucial moment in that process. This is, in fact, Greenblatt's premise. But *is* subjectivity only achieved through the adoption of norms? An affirmative answer would imply that those who bypass, manipulate, or defy norms lack even that modicum of subjectivity that Greenblatt concedes. Clearly, we need a more dynamic understanding of the way norms themselves are culturally negotiated.

Such an understanding, I want to suggest, is not only dependent upon viewing ideology as heterogeneous and contradictory, as Louis Adrian Montrose suggests,[17] but by revisioning the subject as bounded by a permeable membrane, through which cultural-psychic osmosis occurs. Here, I take as my guiding image Natalie

Zemon Davis's comment that we should examine the "apertures in the boundary of the person as important conditions in defining the self."[18] In fact, I want to amend her remark to suggest that we reconceptualize such boundaries *as* apertures. Teresa de Lauretis provides a useful visual metaphor for this reconceptualization: "Like the river between two cities, two countries, two histories . . . [borders] mark difference itself; a difference that is not just in one or in the other, but between them and in both."[19] As mutually interfacing and constitutive *spaces* rather than inflexible demarcations functioning to restrain movement and exchange, boundaries become permeable sites of interchange and circulation. If boundaries are apertures, the subject inhabits a logical space of "in betweenness," becoming a moving matrix of multiple, heteronomous, contradictory attributes, impulses, and positions which find no proper place or name within binary distinctions. If boundaries are apertures, norms are neither repressively imposed from without nor dutifully internalized from within, but produced by the ever-active combination and recombination of only temporarily dominant and always contestatory discourses.

This fluid relationship between subject and structure is materially manifested in the body – specifically, in the orifices through which food passes, language flows, and eroticism circulates. Without slipping into biologism, we can see that the body provides an analogy for the criss-crossings of cultural exchange. In particular, the *erotic* body metaphorically figures precisely the permeability that is constitutive of the early modern subject, its apertures palpably embodying social relations as linguistic and bodily intercourse. Even at its most solitary, sexuality never occurs in a vacuum – bodily exchanges, withholdings, and negotiations situate sexuality as a crucial site of cultural and psychic osmosis. And everyday "ways of using" the body, to invoke the terms of Michel de Certeau, provide instances of "tactical" resistance – isolated, improvisational, provisional – that defy the dominance of putative norms.[20]

Greenblatt's influence on the investigation of the erotic has been considerable, largely because of his insistence on the constitutive import of erotic friction to the Shakespearean stage. Despite his emphasis on the flexible indeterminacy and improvisational quality of Shakespearean and cultural constructions of gender and sexuality, however, the erotic in Greenblatt's work finally comes to rest in the biological body – which, despite its plasticity, is ultimately fixed, codified, and normalized. The early, article form of "Fiction and Friction," for instance, concludes with a parting gesture toward "the ultimate sexual reality" of the male body underneath the actors' costume.[21] But, by Greenblatt's own logic, the status of any "sexual reality" – even one as seemingly essential as biological embodiment – is a matter of constant renegotiation.

I focus on Greenblatt's work not only because it has been so enabling to many critics, including myself – indeed, its influence is pervasive in the following pages – but because the normalizing tendency it enacts circulates throughout critical discourse. I want to suggest at the onset that Shakespearean drama represents sexuality as even less determinant, and the status of normative structures even less clear, than most critics assume. The significations of sexuality in the early modern period were not self-evident, nor was erotic practice a primary means of identification of the self. As Chapter 4 will argue in some detail, no such category as homosexuality operated in early modern culture; and insofar as the entire erotic system seemed relatively fluid and continuous, we need to entertain the related proposition that the early modern construction of heterosexuality was neither as unified nor as codified as it was to later become. The erotic matrix of early modern culture seems to have been remarkably incoherent and open; its tensions, shifts, and accommodations produced erotic positionalities which defy our attempts to define them.

Deriving a methodological direction from a historical matrix of erotic indeterminacy necessitates avoiding the essentialism of those critical models in which sexuality is the defining characteristic of individuals, and instead involves tracing the textual circulation of erotic energy. Rather than inhering in the psyche of characters, sexuality in Shakespearean drama anonymously traverses the text. Characters in these plays do not so much possess sexuality as inhabit it; eroticism is an aperture, a permeable space of exchange, a position from which negotiations for pleasure take place. And, as I argue at some length in Chapter 5, certain characters inhabit more than one erotic mode.

Shakespearean drama registers countless instances of resistance to dominant discourses: the harsh or merry "shrew" whose mobile body and tongue defy efforts to contain them (*The Taming of the Shrew, Much Ado About Nothing*); the French princess who (mal)- appropriates the English language to assert her own knowledge of the bawdy/body (*Henry V*); the sodomitical male who temporarily refuses to engage in the militarism that defines masculinity (*Troilus and Cressida*); the cross-dressed heroine who elicits and enjoys multiple erotic investments (*As You Like It, Twelfth Night*). Each of these figures of resistance embodies a relationship of permeability, their desires for linguistic and erotic power and mobility exceeding, bypassing, and defying the dictates of their culture. To the extent that the sexuality of Shakespearean drama emphasizes the provisional, polymorphous creativity of the pursuit of pleasure, it is "tactical" in de Certeau's sense, rather than "strategic."[22] There is no overarching plan in Shakespeare's work, no theory comprising an ideological platform; there is only an exploration of dramatic and social possibilities. The eroticism of Shakespearean comedy, in particular, is consistently experimental, as plays exploit erotic resistance in order to generate dramatic conflict, pursuing a plurality of possible pleasures before the seemingly inevitable capitulation to the dominant ideologies of heterosexual closure and ritualized marriage. De Certeau's linguistic analogue for resistance, "the *construction* of individual sentences with an *established* vocabulary and syntax,"[23] coincides with how resistance in Shakespearean drama is *framed* by the dominant discourse of heterosexuality; resistance is a matter of improvising from within in order to generate unforeseen alternatives. In the tension between experimentation and capitulation, however, "norms" are reconfigured, the vocabulary of erotic desire broadened, sexual syntax stretched. The homoeroticism of Shakespearean comedy, in particular, traverses "masculine" and "feminine" sites, challenging the binary language of identity by which *we* normalize erotic desire. And, in those plays in which the imposition of heterosexual closure is even less certain – for instance, when the boy actor dressed in wedding drag leaps the bound of *As You Like It* to erotically tease male and female spectators – resistance approaches something akin to rebellion.

Which is not to say, however, that all of Shakespeare's plays highlight erotic resistance. In fact, the first part of this book focuses not only on the extent to which dominant erotic ideologies determine erotic life, but on the way such ideologies are pushed to their dramatic extremes, in an intense manifestation of erotic paranoia. If the book is structured in the form of a movement from a claustrophobically closed erotic system to a relatively more open one, it is not only because Shakespearean genres reflect tonal differences in erotic attitude, but because my critical practice has changed as I have learned from the play of differences animating the Shakespearean corpus.

Within the methodology I have outlined exists an unresolved tension between my emphasis on erotic resistance – which is located in a limited form of subjective agency – and the multiple desires that anonymously circulate through texts. But what this model makes, at least provisionally, *tactically* possible, is an alternative way of posing the question of the erotic. If one's starting point is not the assumption or assertion of normative heterosexuality, but the possibility of tactical improvisations, the guiding question becomes not whether representations of sexuality in Shakespearean drama ultimately reinscribe an alleged norm, but whether and how the possible repertoire of erotic modalities is put into play. I thus activate an obsolete definition of "apertures" as "the *process* of opening up what is involved, intricate, restricted," to suggest that *that* is exactly what is at stake in analyzing the economy of early modern desire.

The book, briefly outlined, proceeds in this way: Chapter 1, "Jewels, statues, and corpses: containment of female erotic power," argues that the strategies of containment of female erotic power employed in the tragedies *Hamlet* and *Othello* are evident as well in the romance, *The Winter's Tale*. Metaphorically and dramatically, women who are perceived by men as erotically threatening are monumentalized, their erotic warmth transformed into the cold, static form of jewels, statues, and corpses. Such a reading challenges the dominant psychoanalytic interpretation of the romance genre as reconstituting the broken families of the tragedies, and instead argues that the restraints of genre do not contain the erotic anxieties of gender.

In Chapter 2, "Prince Hal"s Falstaff: positioning psychoanalysis and the female reproductive body," I analyze the parallel construction of male subjectivity and sexuality in the *Henriad* and in psychoanalytic theory. I argue that Shakespeare's history plays and psychoanalysis perpetrate similar repressions of the fantasized female reproductive body, upon which "normative" male development depends. The drama enacted by Prince Hal and narrativized by Freud provides a telling instance of the mechanisms by which patriarchal relations reproduce themselves. The female body, first constructed as a "grotesque" maternal body (Falstaff) which must be repudiated, is displaced by the closed "classical" body (Katharine) which must be subjugated for Prince Hal to assume phallocratic control as King Henry V. To intervene in this continuing course of events, the fantasized maternal must be refigured from the perspective of the "experience" of maternal desires.

The movement from Chapter 1 to Chapter 2 marks a transition from the containment of the female erotic body (cold, closed, still) to the transgressions of a male body *figured* as female. It marks a shift from the imposition of the dead "classical body" on those women conceived as threateningly "grotesque," to the examination of a fantasy of the female "grotesque body" as embodied by a man. We move from one cultural polarity (virgin/whore) to another (virgin/mother). Both chapters are concerned with the threat that a particular fantasy of female sexuality poses to the male subject; both explore the eventual dramatic containment of that threat. At the same time, both chapters argue that the ideological work of their plays is not captured by reference to the formal closure of the ending; it is equally at work in the process of the play. "Containment" is thus problematized, even in some sense subverted, by the play's process.

Chapter 3, "Invading bodies/bawdy exchanges: disease, desire, and representation," examines *Troilus and Cressida* from a perspective born of reflection on the current AIDS crisis. Locating in Thersites and Pandarus, respectively, the psychic mechanisms of projection and internalization, this chapter describes recurring defensive strategies operating against the recognition that the "venereal" *is* disease. With the play's representation of syphilis which, in its circulation through the body mimes its circulation throughout society, we return to the "grotesque body" of Chapter 2, only with a heavier burden of disgust layered on the female contaminant. Part I ends, as well, with the most material and paranoid manifestation of the circulation of sexuality.

With Part II we move to a less paranoiac erotic sphere, as comedic possibility takes center stage. Whereas the chapters in Part I examine the rigid, contracted erotic perspectives of tragedy, history, and romance, the essays in Part II suggest a more flexible, expansive, comedic mode. Both within the plays and within my critical practice, the emphasis shifts from dramatic and political containment to the possibilities of resistance. That this marks a shift too from an emphasis on heterosexuality to homoeroticism is not coincidental; these two modes of erotic experience were, in Shakespearean drama, cathected quite differently.

The division between Part I's emphasis on the threat the female (hetero)sexual body poses to the male subject, and Part II's focus on the affirmative possibilities afforded by a homoerotic alternative is not necessitated by anything intrinsic to either erotic mode, but by the shape and meaning each mode took in Shakespeare's cultural situation and imagination. I do not mean to imply that Shakespeare's plays celebrate homoeroticism and denigrate hetero-sexuality. As the following chapters evidence, the drama's position *vis-à-vis* erotic life is far more complicated and multivalent than any mere opposition between object choices would suggest. But what seems clear is that the early modern intersection of gender and sexuality posed dramatic problems based, at least in part, in the contradiction between women's inferior social status and inordinate (fantasized) erotic power. Conversely, the congruency of men's social and erotic statuses may have made them less problematic erotic objects for other men. (The power differences between adult and youth may have contributed to adolescent boys' attractiveness as "intermediary" objects in the power hierarchy.) Whether Shakespeare himself was erotically attracted primarily to men, women, or boys, I have no idea – but that both males and females posed particular pleasures and problems for his dramatic practice, that his drama displays *interest* in the possible erotic positions of each (including women's erotic investment in one another) is a major premise of this book.

Before turning to Shakespeare's dramatic practice, however, Chapter 4 argues that in much contemporary criticism, gender is misrecognized as a signifier for sexuality in such a way that erotic practice is conveniently forgotten. Continuing the critique of psychoanalysis begun in Chapter 2, this chapter focuses on the reification of the critical construct "desire" though which subjec-tivity, sexuality, and gender are conflated. This conflation is traced first in our contemporary critical practice, in which the formula "feminine desire" is shown to unwittingly recapitulate phallocentric logic; it is then historicized by an examination of Freud's account of homosexuality. Despite Freud's criticism of the previous sexolo-gists' notion of "inversion," and his own attempt to divide sexual orientation into independent variables, his work remains caught within the paradigm which assumes that "normal" heterosexuality follows unproblematically from ascribed gender role, and that disruptions in gender identity result in deviancy in object choice. Via a historical account of the early modern discourses and practices of male and female homoeroticism, Chapter 4 moves toward deconstructing the Freudian sexual taxonomy – the binary, gen-dered oppositions upon which currently dominant notions of desire depend – and reconstructing sexuality in terms of the fluidity and polyvalence of erotic fantasies, practices, and subject positions. This deconstruction of categories, however, is itself dependent upon the Freudian notion of the polymorphous perverse.

Through a comparative analysis of *As You Like It* and *Twelfth Night*, Chapter 5, "The homoerotics of Shakespearean comedy," applies the historical information provided in Chapter 4, arguing that a circulation of homoerotic desire in these plays transgresses the binary logic upon which patriarchal mandates depend. In *As You Like It* Orlando's effusion of desire toward Rosalind/Ganymede, an object simultaneously heterosexual and homoerotic, prevents the stable reinstitution of heterosexuality, upon which the conventional marriage plot depends. However, in *Twelfth Night* anxiety about exclusive homoeroticism is conflated with anxiety about generational reproduction, with the result that the male homoerotic position is scapegoated at the same time that the female gender is resecured into a patriarchal economy.

A word about nomenclature. Insofar as this book's purpose is to question some basic "truths" about erotic relations, it must necessarily question too the vocabulary by which we reproduce erotic significations. As Chapter 4 argues in some detail, many standard usages which are currently available fail to provide enough specification and differentiation of erotic experience. But before that argument is made in full, the reader should be alerted to my usage of the following terms: "sex" will refer exclusively to those anatomical, biological distinctions by which cultures differentiate between males and females; it will not be used in the sense of "to have sex" or "to make love," nor will it be used synonymously with "gender". "Gender" denotes the culturally prescribed roles and behaviors available to the two "sexes"; its ideologically freighted outcome is a "masculinity" and "femininity" correlated with "males" and "females," but its instability is underscored by the cross-gendered presence, for instance, of "effeminate" men and "butch" women. "Sexuality" refers to erotic desires and practices, including but not limited to the direction and scope of erotic preferences (i.e., object choice). The purpose of such precise definitions is to put into play a refusal of the following commonsense suppositions: that each sex has a necessary gender (e.g., to be male means to be "masculine"); that each gender has a corresponding, "natural" sexuality (e.g., that "femininity" implies passivity); and that the purposes and functions of sexuality are confined by biology.

Secondly, by "homosocial" I refer to social bonds, animated by social energies, which may or may not intersect with erotic bonds and erotic desire. By "homoerotic" I refer to erotic bonds animated by specifically erotic desire, though that desire may not be fully conscious to or accepted by the desiring subject. And finally, I reserve the use of "homosexual" to refer to the relatively recent phenomena of erotic bonds and desires which simultaneously confer a social identity. Along a continuum of social determinants, "homosexual" has been for the most part a label ascribed by others (usually within legal, medical, or psychological domains), and is an authoritative category only by means of the "sciences" of erotic discipline; whereas historically, "gay" and "lesbian" are labels (sometimes reluctantly) attached to the self in an effort toward self-determination, a gesture made possible only by an intervention in the political economy of desire.

In addition, I refer to the period in which Shakespeare wrote as "early modern" rather than the "Renaissance" or the "Elizabethan" or "Jacobean" era. Through this terminology, I gesture toward the following recognitions: (1) that the figurations of subjectivity in the later years of the sixteenth century are precursors to our own; (2) that the number of subjects experiencing a renaissance of learning and opportunities was relatively limited (especially by gender); and (3) that to call a period after its reigning monarch is too hastily to privilege the dominant ideology, and specifically, the court, as arbiter of social practice.

Finally, although it is common practice to capitalize "Other" when referring to an identity constructed according to oppositional difference, I use *other* in order to distinguish my usage from that of Lacan. Although Lacan does not hold the mandate for its use, his distinction is a helpful one: the other (*objet petite a*) is the object of desire (a person, a fetish), whereas the Other (*grande autre*) is not a physical object at all but the source of meaning, the locus of speech, the symbolic order. Desire, for Lacan, always ultimately refers back to the Other; and while this conception of the impossibility of desire underpins my analysis, it is not ultimately what is at stake in my argument.[24]

Desire and Anxiety is animated by my agreement with Gayle Rubin that "sex is always political. But there are also historical periods in which sexuality is more sharply contested and more overtly politicized. In such periods, the domain of erotic life is, in effect, renegotiated."[25] The possibility of this book suggests that we live in such a time of renegotiation.

Part I

Erotic paranoia

Chapter 1

Jewels, statues and corpses: containment of female erotic power

Hamlet: What man dost thou dig it for?
First Clown: For no man, sir.
Hamlet: What woman, then?
First Clown: For none, neither.
Hamlet: Who is to be buried in't?
First Clown: One that was a woman, sir, but, rest
    her soul, she's dead.

(V.i.130–6)

This moment in *Hamlet* – a macabre instance of comedy that presumes and enacts the effacement of "woman" – figuratively points to gender as a site of inquiry and definition. Having refused the generic "man" as an inadequate description of the body for whom he is digging a grave, the Clown would seem to be making room for, indeed, insisting on, that body's feminine specificity. But no, both the Clown and Hamlet insist – Ophelia, being dead, is no longer a woman. Whatever it is that gendered Ophelia is ungendered by her death.

In Shakespearean drama what engenders the female body is her sexuality. As the drama positions the female gender within its psychic and narrative frame, "woman" becomes synonymous with the presence or absence of chastity. This statement may seem innocuously self-evident, until one considers that at its theatrical extreme, the presence or absence of chastity arbitrates life and death. To Ruth Kelso's dictum in *Doctrine for the Lady of the Renaissance*, "let a woman have chastity, she has all. Let her lack chastity and she has nothing," I would add: let her lack chastity, she *is* nothing.[1] To be a woman in Shakespearean drama means to embody a sexuality that often finds its ultimate expression in death.

Maid, wife, widow, whore: these are the positions accorded to women in early modern society. They are specifically *erotic* positions, locating women, via an erotic sphere of activity and signification, within the economy of patriarchal heterosexuality. By definition, a maid is virginal, a whore promiscuous; widows and wives can be either lusty or abstinent; all are defined, not merely by their biological sex, but by their sexual activity. The exceptional Queen Elizabeth only proves the rule, securing her power through the strategic manipulation of her virginity, raising it to an iconic level surpassed only by that of the Virgin Mary. As a defining characteristic, chastity renders woman's specifically *erotic* power incommensurate with her place in early modern gender and class hierarchies; the social importance accorded to chastity renders woman's erotic power inordinate, even excessive.

The Clown's burial of the female body, or more precisely, his interpretative designation of the body he is burying, metonymically signifies the psychic impulse and narrative teleology of three of Shakespeare's most compelling plays. In *Hamlet* (1600–1), *Othello* (1604), and *The Winter's Tale* (1610–11), male anxiety toward female erotic power is channeled into a strategy of containment; the erotic threat of the female body is psychically contained by means of a metaphoric and dramatic transformation of women into jewels, statues, and corpses. Indeed, together, the plays seem motivated toward this end: to give women speech only to silence them; to make women move only to still them; to represent their bodies on stage only to enclose them; to infuse their bodies with warmth only to coldly "encorpse" them.

What is crucial about these plays, however, is not so much the eventual status of women as reified objects (that, after all, is hardly unique to Shakespeare), but the *process* by which the drama renders them as such, the *transformation* that occurs as the motive and telos of dramatic action. Ophelia, Desdemona, and Hermione are not *essentially* objectified; rather, the plays enact the *process* of female objectification *as* the dramatic process. Inviting our complicity with this process as the very terms of their intelligibility, these plays seduce us with the promise of theatrical pleasure – either in the form of catharsis (tragedy) or heterosexual closure (romance) – actively *working* to obscure the possibility of female erotic agency.

Shakespeare's preoccupation with the uncontrollability of women's sexuality – witness the many plots concerning the need to prove female chastity, the threat of adultery, and references to cuckoldry in songs, jokes, and passing remarks – was not individual to him, but a shared vulnerability of men in his intensely patriarchal and patrilineal culture. Socially and psychologically, early modern men's erotic vulnerability was overdetermined: their infantile dependence on women, the development of their subjectivity in relation to "femininity," and their adult dependence on women's word for paternity of children all secure the importance of female chastity for the early modern male subject. Conversely, the psychic centrality of male vulnerability gives rise to defensive strategies to deny it. As Carol Cook's analysis of cuckoldry emphasizes, male power is restored through such mechanisms as cuckold jokes; by means of the vilification of women upon which cuckold jokes depend, female erotic autonomy is reduced to silence and absence.[2]

This masculine imposition of silence, and more particularly of stasis, on women is connected in the plays I shall be examining with a fear of chaos associated with heterosexual intercourse. Whereas phallic penetration in Shakespearean drama is rigorously upheld as the apex of masculine identity and power, the orgasm which follows is imagined in terms of dispersion, a psychic dissolution of power and identity. Sonnet 129 sums up this bifurcation and dispersal in temporal terms: "A bliss in proof, and prov'd, a very woe;/ Before, a joy propos'd; behind, a dream." As many critics have argued, masculine identity in the early modern period is constructed in relation to a fantasy of the female body as different, oppositional, other.[3] However, in the act of orgasm, male experience of the female body is not so much that of an object to be penetrated and possessed, but of an enclosure into which the male subject merges, dissolves, and in the early modern pun, dies. Orgasm within the body of a woman calls attention to – makes palpable – the myth of the unity and self-identity of the masculine subject: orgasmic release is precisely too much a release of the self. Insofar as women act as mirrors for the development of male subjectivity, female erotic mobility threatens the process by which male subjectivity is secured.[4] For men to achieve the fantasy of full subjectivity, women must remain still.

It is this fear, ultimately, of the subject's demise that leads Hamlet, Othello, and Leontes to long for stasis, for a reprieve from the excitations and anxieties of erotic life. In response to their fear that such security and calm are not forthcoming, they displace their desire for stasis onto the women with whom they are most intimate. The result is what Abbe Blum has aptly termed the "monumentalizing" of woman:[5] the fetishization of the dead, virginal Ophelia, the eroticized death of Desdemona, and the transformation of Hermione into a living but static form, a statue.

Within these plays, dominant metaphors set up a series of correspondences between temporal, sensate, and spatial experience. Within a rigid system of dichotomies – mobility/stasis, heat/cold, open/closed – bodily movement, heat, and integrity define the "erotic" in early modern terms.[6] Stephen Greenblatt's notion of the erotic "friction" animating the early modern stage celebrates the affirmative aspect of this dichotomy;[7] monumentalizing, on the other hand, is the strategy by which female erotic energy is disciplined and denied. For women in Shakespearean drama, "chastity" requires being still, cold, and closed; to be "unchaste" is to be mobile, hot, open. What is striking is the minimal room within which to maneuver; even a minimum of erotic "warmth" is quickly transmogrified into intemperate heat. Indeed, what the drama enacts is the disappearance of any middle ground, with the rigidity of this bifurcation following a unidirectional narrative: from a projection of too much movement, warmth, openness, to an enclosing fantasy of no movement or heat at all. As a strategy of containment, monumentalizing is itself excessive.

The metaphorical displacement of women into static objects takes various forms according to the requirements of genre; the specific strategy of monumentalizing is modified as Shakespeare's art uncovers, releases, and then reorganizes masculine anxieties into new modes of expression. According to Joel Fineman, "plays are not only a means of representative expression but as such constitute strategies of psychological defense, defending, that is, against the very fantasies they represent."[8] My attempt is not to explicate *Hamlet*, *Othello*, or *The Winter's Tale*, but rather to analyze the multiple deployments of a recurring anxiety and the means by which the plays exorcise or assuage it. These plays demonstrate a progressive reworking of monumentalizing which challenges the benign developmental progression presumed to organize Shakespeare's own movement from tragedy to romance.

★

As many critics have noted, in *Hamlet*, Gertrude's adultery and incest – the uncontrollability, in short, of her sexuality – are, in Hamlet's mind, projected outward to encompass the potential of such contamination in all heterosexual liaisons.[9] As Gertrude's adultery turns all women into prostitutes and all men into potential cuckolds, Hamlet's world is contracted into "an unweeded garden/ That grows to seed. Things rank and gross in nature/ Possess it merely".[10] In this vile yet seductive garden, sexually threatening women poison vulnerable and unwitting men. Thus, through their erotic power, women are seen to adjudicate life and death – a connection summed up by the "Mousetrap" player who reads the speech inserted by Hamlet in the play performed to "catch the conscience of the King": "A second time I kill my husband dead,/ When second husband kisses me in bed" (II.ii.606; III.ii.182–3).

The threat posed by Gertrude's sexuality is paranoiacally projected onto Ophelia, whom Hamlet exhorts: "Get thee to a nunn'ry. Why wouldst thou be a breeder of sinners? . . . I could accuse me of such things that it were better my mother had not borne me" (III.i.122–5). As the culmination of this speech makes clear, those things of which Hamlet could accuse himself are less the pride, ambition, and knavery that he mentions, as his suspicion that he, like his father before him, will be cuckolded: "Get thee to a nunn'ry, farewell. Or, if thou wilt needs marry, marry a fool, for wise men know well enough what monsters you make of them" (III.i.138–41). As the pun on nunnery and brothel makes clear, Hamlet is not concerned with Ophelia's ability to contaminate other men; trapped as he is within the boundaries of an oedipal relation, Hamlet's paranoia extends only to himself and his beloved father.[11] Women make men into monsters, the early modern euphemism for cuckolds, because they deceive:

> I have heard of your paintings too, well enough. God hath given you one face, and you make yourselves another. You jig, you amble, and you lisp, you nickname God's creatures, and make your wantonness your ignorance. Go to, I'll no more on't; it hath made me mad. I say, we will have no moe marriage.
>
> (III.i.144–50)

No more marriage because all marriage is madness and whoredom – degrading to both parties, but especially to the man who never knows who else has slept between his sheets. And not only is marriage likened to whoredom, but Hamlet himself self-identifies as a whore as he, unable to carry out the revenge thrust upon him by his father's Ghost, "Must, like a whore, unpack [his] heart with words,/ And fall a-cursing, like a very drab,/ A stallion" [male prostitute] (II.ii.586–8).

However potent Hamlet's fear of cuckoldry, one senses something else behind his vituperation of Ophelia: an anxiety associated with sexual activity itself. The language with which Hamlet describes sexuality is riddled throughout with metaphors of contagion and disease; his mother's hidden adultery and incest are imagined as an "ulcerous place" that "infects unseen" (III.iv.154–6). For Hamlet who early asks, "And shall I couple hell?" (I.v.94) – the phraseology of which suggests the possibility of coupling *with* hell – *all* sexuality is unnatural.

Hamlet's sexual nausea finds its antecedent in his father's Ghost, who characterizes Gertrude thus: "But virtue, as it never will be moved,/ Though lewdness court it in a shape of heaven,/ So lust, though to a radiant angel link'd,/ Will sate itself in a celestial bed,/ And prey on garbage" (I.v.54–8).[12] Here the dualistic ideology that divides women into lustful whores and radiant angels collapses upon itself, revealing the fear upon which it is based: women are imagined either as angels or whores as a psychological defense against the uncomfortable suspicion that underneath, the angel *is* a whore. The collapse of this defensive structure unleashes precisely the masculine aggression it was originally built to contain. Even the Ghost's ostensible protection of Gertrude from Hamlet's wrath is sexually sadistic: "Taint not thy mind, nor let thy soul contrive/ Against thy mother aught. Leave her to heaven/ And to those thorns that in her bosom lodge,/ To prick and sting her" (I.v.86–9). Gertrude's conscience is imagined as an aggressive phallus, pricking and stinging her female breasts, in an act that reinscribes Hamlet Sr. within Gertrude's body, and thereby reappropriates the alien serpent, Claudius, as the legitimate patriarch-within: the conscience. It is at once a repossession, replication, and reprojection of the action that simultaneously "effeminized" King Hamlet, and deprived him of his life and wife: "The serpent that did sting thy father's life/ Now wears his crown" (I.v.40–1), crown symbolizing both his kingship and his wife's genitalia.

Identified as he is with his father, Hamlet displaces disgust for the Queen's erotic mobility onto Ophelia, and adopts his father's strategy of aggression. Although his violence remains verbal rather than physical, Ophelia's death is as much an outcome of Hamlet's rage as it is an expression of her grief, madness, or self-destruction. Killed off before she can deceive or defile Hamlet, only in death can Ophelia-as-whore regain the other half of her dichotomized being: chaste virgin. Contaminated in life by the taint of Gertrude's adultery, Ophelia reclaims sexual desirability only as a dead, but perpetual, virgin.

In our first view of Ophelia, Laertes warns his sister of the unlikelihood of Hamlet's fulfilling her expectations of betrothal:

> Then weigh what loss your honor may sustain
> If with too credent ear you list his songs,
> Or lose your heart, or your chaste treasure open
> To his unmast'red importunity.
> Fear it, Ophelia, fear it, my dear sister,
> And keep you in the rear of your affection,
> Out of the shot and danger of desire.
> The chariest maid is prodigal enough
> If she unmask her beauty to the moon.
> Virtue itself 'scapes not calumnious strokes.
> The canker galls the infants of the spring
> Too oft before their buttons be disclos'd,
> And in the morn and liquid dew of youth
> Contagious blastments are most imminent.
>
> (I.iii.29–42)

As imagined by Laertes, Ophelia's genitalia are a "chaste treasure," a "button," that must be clasped shut against the "unmast'red importunity," the "contagious blastments," the "shot and danger" of masculine desire. Laertes' language interweaves Hamlet's equation of sexuality and disease (canker, contagion) with his own view of sexuality as masculine aggression (importunity, shot and danger, strokes, blastments). Ophelia's reply, "'Tis in my memory lock'd,/ And you yourself shall keep the key of it" (I.iii.86–7), suggests not only that Laertes' advice is "lock'd" in her memory, but also that Laertes alone possesses the key to her properly immured "chaste treasure."

As if to underscore the importance of Laertes' warning, Ophelia is next interrogated by Polonius, who is similarly concerned with the status of his daughter's chastity. Polonius too views Hamlet's erotic intent with suspicion – only his fear is not of masculine violence but of the possible prostitution of the female body: "Do not believe his vows, for they are brokers. . . ./ Breathing like sanctified and pious bawds,/ The better to beguile" (I.iii.128–32). His accusation, that "you yourself/ Have of your audience been most free and bounteous" (I.iii.93–4) links Ophelia's personhood (her audience) with the sign of her femaleness (her genitalia) through the reiteration of Laertes' spatial metaphors. To be "free and bounteous" with one's person is to risk opening one's "chaste treasure." When Claudius later asks Polonius to repeat the advice he gave to Ophelia regarding Hamlet's advances, Polonius replies: "That she should lock herself from his resort" (II.ii.143). The message of father and son is clear: the proper female sexuality is closed, contained, "lock'd."[13]

In the graveyard scene – the last scene in which her presence is required – Ophelia's dead, virginal body is fetishized by Hamlet and Laertes alike. As Ophelia's funeral procession reaches her newly dug grave, Laertes exclaims, "Lay her i' th' earth,/ And from her fair and unpolluted flesh/ May violets spring!" (V.i. 238–40). Soon thereafter he leaps on top of her casket: "Hold off the earth awhile,/ Till I have caught her once more in mine arms" (V.i.249–50). Such passion, of course, incites Hamlet to claim his place as chief mourner: "Dost thou come here to whine?/ To outface me with leaping in her grave?" (V.i.277–8).

Critics largely focus on the grave as a site of masculine competition, neglecting to mention that Ophelia's grave becomes the only "bed" upon which Hamlet is able to express his sexual desire.[14] And yet, it is neither the right to mourn Ophelia, nor the right to give her pleasure that is actually being contested; rather, Laertes and Hamlet fight over the right to Ophelia's chastity. Fetishized to the extent that it is utterly divorced from the rest of her being, Ophelia's chastity embodies, as it were, a masculine fantasy of a female essence wonderfully devoid of that which makes women so problematic: change, movement, inconstancy, unpredictability – in short, life. The conflict between Hamlet and Laertes is over the right and rite of sexual possession; it occurs only after Ophelia's transformation into a fully possessible object. The earlier punning of the gravedigger (with which I began this chapter) seems eerily premonitory as he responds to Hamlet's query regarding who is to be buried in the newly turned grave: "One that was a woman, sir, but, rest her soul, she's dead" (V.i.135–6). No longer a woman, or rather, a *perfect* woman because immutably pure, Ophelia is no longer likely to incite erotic anxiety; she is, however, a likely object to figure in erotic fantasies of masculine prowess. In addition to masculine competition, the conflict between Hamlet and Laertes

suggests an underlying necrophiliac fantasy, by which I mean
not so much a perversion, as a logical extension of the system
of sexualization in place. As an eroticized yet chaste corpse,
Ophelia signifies not only the connection between sexuality and
death evident in *Romeo and Juliet*, but also suggests that sexuality is finally safely engaged in only with the dead. Earlier,
Hamlet spoke of his own death as "a consummation/ Devoutly
to be wish'd" (III.i.64–5), narcissistically linking his own death
with sexual intercourse, and imagining both as the perfection of
his desire.[15] Here, the fear shared by Hamlet and Laertes of a
dynamic, expressive female sexuality culminates in the imposition
of stasis on that which threatens to bring sexual (and for Hamlet,
metaphysical) chaos, and in the desire, having acquired a fully
immobile object, to possess her fully. Claudius' exit from this
scene with the words "This grave shall have a living monument"
(V.i.297) explicitly articulates the monumentalizing impulse behind
the men's collective desires, for Ophelia is immortalized only as she
is immobilized.

In *Othello*, the need to suppress the anxieties that female sexuality engenders is tragically manipulated into the murder of the
woman who elicits those anxieties. As critics have noted, Othello
is both emotionally vulnerable to Desdemona and ambivalent
about women in general, and it is precisely because his anxieties are multivalent and mutually reinforcing that Othello is
susceptible to Iago's murderous seduction. Like Brabantio's pre-
monition of Desdemona's elopement – "This accident is not unlike
my dream;/ Belief of it oppresses me already" (I.i.144–5) – and
Hamlet's suspicion of Gertrude's crimes – "O, my prophetic
soul!" (I.v.42) – Othello's belief in woman's power of deception
lies just under the surface of his idolization. Othello himself
exclaims in reaction to Iago's intimations, "Think, my lord? By
heaven, *he echoes me,*/ As if there were some monster in his
thought/ Too hideous to be shown" (III.iii.111–13, my emphasis),
suggesting that Iago echoes not merely Othello's words, but his
thoughts. Indeed, having betrayed her father, Desdemona is suspect
to all men except the similarly manipulated Cassio. Brabantio
warns: "Look to her, Moor, if thou hast eyes to see./ She has
deceiv'd her father, and may thee" (I.iii.295–6). And Iago voices
the same refrain: "She did deceive her father, marrying you" (III.
iii.211).

That a woman may "seem" to be one erotic thing and yet may "be" another comes to signify, in the masculine mind of *Othello*, woman's very existence. Underneath the dichotomization of women into virgins or whores, *Othello* implies, lies the belief that women may simultaneously appear as virginal and yet *be* promiscuous. In *Hamlet*, we have seen that the breakdown of the carefully contrived sexual dichotomy (wherein virgin and whore are mutually exclusive terms) unleashes Hamlet's aggression toward Gertrude and Ophelia. Importantly, however, Hamlet's suspicions never obtain the status of existential Truth; they never assume the posture of irrevocable judgment. Gertrude, though an adulteress in Hamlet's mind, may be redeemed if she avoids the marriage bed. And Ophelia's madness and death rectify her virginity, as Laertes testifies: "Lay her i' th' earth,/ And from her fair and unpolluted flesh/ May violets spring! I tell thee, churlish priest,/ A minist'ring angel shall my sister be/ When thou liest howling" (V.i.238–42).

The price of such redemption, however, is a complete capitulation to masculine terms as well as the resurrection of the faulty structure of sexual dualism. Hamlet explicitly instructs his mother to re-form her being in the shape of a virgin:

> *Hamlet*: Confess yourself to heaven,
>   Repent what's past, avoid what is to come,
>   And do not spread the compost on the weeds
>   To make them ranker. . . .
> *Queen*: O Hamlet, thou hast cleft my heart in twain.
> *Hamlet*: O, throw away the worser part of it,
>   And live the purer with the other half.
>   Good night. But go not to my uncle's bed;
>   Assume a virtue, if you have it not.
>
> (III.iv.156–67)

In order to allay masculine suspicions and anxieties – in order to not "be" a whore – Gertrude must throw away her "worser" part, her sexuality, and assume celibacy, an appropriate response to Hamlet's call for "no moe marriage."

Such redemption, equivocal though it may be, is not offered in *Othello* because here suspicion quickly takes on the irrevocable status of Truth, and female deception becomes, not a hideous possibility, but a damned certainty. Othello complains: "O curse of marriage,/ That we can call these delicate creatures ours,/ And not their appetites!" (III.iii.274–6). As the ambiguous syntax of the first line shows, marriage is not only cursed by women's sexual appetites and deception, marriage is itself a curse. Unlike Hamlet, for whom women's deception is cause for the abolition of marriage, for Othello women's inconstancy comes to signify the *very foundation* of the marriage relation, its hidden source and origin.

As Peter Stallybrass has noted, Iago succeeds in manipulating Othello because "his is the voice of 'common sense,' the cease- less repetition of the always-already 'known,' the culturally 'given'."[16] He seduces Othello in multiple ways. By pouring "this pestilence into his ear,/ That she repeals him for her body's lust" (II.iii.350–1), Iago invokes the cultural suspicion that all women are whores. In this respect, according to Edward Snow, Othello's fear of adultery masks a more basic castration anxiety, a fear of "thralldom to the demands of an unsatisfiable sexual appetite in woman," brought on by the consummation of his marriage.[17] Othello's murder of Desdemona, then, is a ritualistic effort to repeat and undo his own sexual complicity. Secondly, as Stephen Greenblatt demonstrates, in abusing "Othello's ears/ That he is too familiar with his wife" (I.iii.396–7), Iago manipulates the Christian doctrine of sexuality that posits even marital sexuality as sinful.[18] Thirdly, Othello's ambivalent relation to Christian society as Moor and alien creates the conditions for internalized racial self-hatred, the logical outcome of the play's representation of the "Moor's" sexuality as "lascivious" (I.i.127), even "monstrous."[19]

The racial dynamics of the play are crucial to any understanding of Othello's subjectivity, for, although the primary spokesmen of racist ideologies are Iago, Roderigo, and Brabantio, one of the tragedies of the play is the extent to which Othello internalizes their negative representations of his race. In the first three scenes, the discourses of Iago, Roderigo, and Brabantio set up the following dichotomy: black, dark, evil, animal, hyper-sexual, versus white, fair, virtue, human, chastity.[20] The terms by which Brabantio expresses his refusal to believe in Desdemona's willing love for Othello – "For nature so preposterously to err" (I.iii.64) – under- scores their culture's appeal to "nature" as the causal basis of these dualisms. As Martin Orkin argues, much of the play resists these "natural" categories, not the least of which is Desdemona's love and Othello's spiritual nobility.[21] However, these racist dualisms are reinscribed all the more forcefully by being expressed in Act

III, scene iii by Othello himself. His meditative response to Iago's intimations of Desdemona's infidelity, "And yet, how nature erring from itself" (234), credits Desdemona's choice of mate as unnatural, a recognition that permeates Othello's final conclusion, "Her name, that was as fresh/ As Dian's visage, is now begrim'd and black/ As mine own face" (391–3). At that moment, Othello marks his acceptance of the racist categories which correlate skin color with the presence or absence of virtue. His inability to maintain trust in Desdemona is directly related to his inability to trust his own racial identity and self-worth.

After Desdemona's murder, Othello's response to Lodovico's query as to his whereabouts, "That's he that was Othello. Here I am" (V.ii.292), signals his acceptance of the split identity that has in fact been his implicit "subject position" all along. His further attempt to narrativize his life-story in his final speech – "Speak of me as I am" (351) – serves to metaphorize his identity to the point that it loses all grounding. Othello becomes a signifier only of another signifier: the "base Indian," and the "I" who murders the "turban'd Turk," the "circumcised dog" that is himself. Having internalized the racist tensions of his culture, he must play them out within his own being, ultimately commanding his Venetian "civilized" self to kill the "uncivilized" "animal" he has "become."

In short, Othello's anxiety is culturally and psychosexually over determined by erotic, gender, and racial anxieties, including, I now want to argue, the fear of chaos he associates with sexual activity. In his confession to the Venetian senators – "I do confess the vices of my blood" (I.iii.125) – Othello dismisses consummation and orgasm as an aspect of his desire, declaring himself to be impotent:

> Vouch with me, heaven, I therefore beg it not
> To please the palate of my appetite,
> Nor to comply with heat – the young affects
> In me defunct – and proper satisfaction,
> But to be free and bounteous to her mind.
>
> (I.iii.264–8)

The halting measure of the first four lines contrasts sharply with the lyrical expansion of the final line, suggesting that erotic matters evoke in Othello an anxiety that is abated only by idealizing speeches that lift, as it were, sexuality from the earth and into the heavens that would "vouch" for him. Prior to consummation, the image of a "free and bounteous" Desdemona helps Othello to cerebralize and desexualize their relationship. Equally comforting is Brabantio's early description of his daughter: "A maiden never bold;/ Of spirit so still and quiet that her motion/ Blush'd at herself" (I.iii.96–8). After consummation, however, Desdemona's "fruitfulness and liberal heart" are signs of a "hot and moist" sexuality which must be "sequester[ed] from liberty" (III.iv.38–40). At this point Othello shares with Hamlet, Laertes, Polonius, and Brabantio the sense that women's sexuality should be locked up.

As a military officer who makes crucial decisions regarding war and peace, life and death, Othello's subjectivity is predicated upon an absolute dichotomy between chaos and stasis. He characterizes all relations – within himself and between self and other – by means of these terms. Othello associates romantic love with calm and "content[ment]" and, as the following quote makes clear, the loss of that love with chaos: "Excellent wretch! Perdition catch my soul/ But I do love thee! And when I love thee not,/ Chaos is come again" (III.iii.92–4). Woman has a metaphysical responsibility to represent and maintain peace – a responsibility that correlates with her function as stable mirror of masculine subjectivity. However, throughout the play, Othello also equates Desdemona's sexuality with chaos and violence. A disjuncture thus exists within Othello's psyche between romantic love (associated with stasis and calm) and sexuality (associated with chaotic violence). Such hostilities, brought to a head by the consummation of his marriage, between the psychic structures necessary to his sense of self and those related to his sexuality must ultimately be reconciled if Othello is not to go mad. The means for such reintegration? Employing violence to achieve stasis.

The equation between Desdemona's sexuality and stormy violence is first forged by her frank admission of erotic desire: "That I did love the Moor to live with him,/ My downright violence and storm of fortunes/ May trumpet to the world" (I.iii.251–3).[22] The syntax of her speech equates her sexual desire with "downright violence" that may be "trumpeted" to the world by her "storm of fortunes," as well as characterizing her sexuality as a "storm of fortunes" – a storm that may trumpet *itself* to the world – as Desdemona is doing in front of the senate at that moment. In addition, the linguistic proximity of "storm" and "trumpet" allows a conflation of consonants, producing "strumpet" – exactly the charge Othello makes in Act V.

Even earlier, however, Othello likens Desdemona's sexuality to a storm, but to him the equation is troubling rather than exciting – or perhaps troubling because exciting. Upon their victorious reunion in Cyprus, Othello holds forth:

> It gives me wonder great as my content
> To see you here before me. O my soul's joy!
> If after every tempest come such calms
> May the winds blow till they have waken'd death!
> And let the labouring bark climb hills of seas
> Olympus-high and duck again as low
> As hell's from heaven! If it were now to die,
> 'Twere now to be most happy; for, I fear,
> My soul hath her content so absolute
> That not another comfort like to this
> Succeeds in unknown fate. . . .
> I cannot speak enough of this content;
> It stops me here; it is too much of joy.
> And this, and this, the greatest discords be
> [*Kissing her*]
> That e'er our hearts shall make!
>
> (II.i.181–98)

Othello's "content" – his peace of mind and the very fabric of his being – is permeated throughout with a sense of *dis*content, of dangers barely escaped, and his longing for stasis seems more internally motivated than a desire for land after a sea battle.[23] Or, more precisely, for Othello the consummation of sexuality *is* a battle after which he is quite ready to die (pun intended) – but not to rise up again, rather, to escape the turbulence of future storms. For Othello, as was true of Hamlet, sexual gratification is likened to the threat of dissolution. As his speech concludes with a conjunction of discord (violence) and desire, Othello's consciousness of sexuality causes him to falter, to halt, so that he swallows his words just when he asserts that he cannot refrain from speaking: "I cannot speak enough of this content;/ It stops me here."

Othello's "content" does indeed stop him, for his desire for calm fixates his gaze on that which threatens to disrupt his tranquility: Desdemona's passionate movements on behalf of Cassio. The myopia of that gaze works counter to its own best interest for Othello never again achieves a "content so absolute": "I had been happy if the general camp,/ Pioners and all, had tasted her sweet body,/ So I had nothing known. O, now, forever/ Farewell the tranquil mind! Farewell content!" (III.iii.350–3). As the ambiguous syntax suggests, as much as Othello wishes he had remained ignorant of Desdemona's betrayal, he also regrets having "tasted her sweet body," a regret explicitly linked to his loss of repose.

And, having "tasted her sweet body," Othello is, as Iago suggests, "eaten up with passion" (III.iii.396), and as such, Othello becomes more victim than connoisseur of an act that metaphorically connotes the dissolution of boundary distinctions. The love that promised calm and repose actually sparks erotic arousal, and with it the fear of complete chaos: "Get me some poison, Iago; this night. I'll not expostulate with her, lest her body and beauty unprovide my mind again. This night, Iago" (IV.i.203–5). The only protection against "unprovision" is to project onto the loved one the tranquility that she is supposed to (but because of her mobile sexuality, fails to) create. Paradoxically, that imposition of stasis can be achieved only through violent means, imaginatively linked for Othello with the tempestuous sea that he seeks to escape:

> Like to the Pontic sea,
> Whose icy current and compulsive course
> Nev'r feels retiring ebb, but keeps due on
> To the Propontic and the Hellespont,
> Even so my bloody thoughts, with violent pace,
> Shall nev'r look back, nev'r ebb to humble love,
> Till that a capable and wide revenge
> Swallow them up.
>
> (III.iii.457–64)

The imposition of calm on Desdemona is explicitly offered as a remedy for the "hot, and moist" palms of her excessively sexual body (III.iv.39). Just prior to the murder, Desdemona's moistness and heat are replaced in Othello's imagination by the cool, dry, immobile image of "monumental alabaster" (V.ii.5). Once dead, Desdemona is compared to "another world/ Of one entire and perfect chrysolite" for which Othello would not have sold her, if only she had been true (V.ii.149–50). After having realized his error, Othello compares himself to a "base Indian" who "threw a pearl away/ Richer than all his tribe" (V.ii.356–7). Despite the value such idealization appears to ascribe, the comparison of Desdemona to jewels is part of Othello's strategy for containing her distressing erotic mobility. By imaginatively transforming Desdemona into a jewel – hard, cold, static, silent, yet also adored and desired – Othello is able to maintain both his distance from and his idealization of her. By reducing a warm, living body to a static yet idealized object, Othello hopes to master the situation that threatens him, just as Hamlet defends against the image of Gertrude's incest by projecting Claudius as a "cutpurse" who stole the queen, a "precious diadem" (III.iv.102–3).

The equation of women and jewels within the poetic catalogue of feminine attributes is a standard Petrarchan convention. I maintain, however, that the equation of female body parts with precious gems – the body metaphorically revealed, undressed, and dismembered through the poet-lover's voyeuristic gaze – is a crucial strategy in the attempt both to construct a masculine subjectivity and to exert control over a situation in which the poet-lover's power is limited and secondary. Insofar as masculine subjectivity is developed and asserted through conflict with a feminine other, the poet-lover masters his lady by inscribing her in a text, constructing and dismembering her, part by body part.

This strategy of mastery is constitutive of *Othello*. However, the intensely insecure and ambivalent Othello cannot wholly depend upon metaphorical objectification. Instead, he must fulfill the promise, only nascent in Petrarchanism, of fully containing the love-object. In Othello's defensive strategy, what is idealized becomes sacramentalized, and objectification finds its final expression as religious sacrifice. As Othello assumes the role of priest – invulnerable, omnipotent, and supremely justified – his strategies of idealization and objectification are conjoined and elevated in a powerful synthesis: sacramentalized murder.

"Peace, and be still" becomes the one cry of the increasingly urgent and obsessive Othello (V.ii.48), as he seeks to quiet the woman whose "bold motion" is stilled, but only temporarily, in sleep. Kissing the slumbering Desdemona, Othello murmurs: "One more, one more./ Be thus when thou art dead, and I will kill thee,/ And love thee after" (V.ii.17–19). Although Othello believes her kisses to be fatal to *him* – "So sweet was ne'er so fatal" (V.ii.20) – it is Desdemona who dies because of her sexuality. The terms by which he earlier mourned his cuckoldry, "'Tis destiny unshunnable, like death" (III.iii.281), signify the intertwining of sexuality and death in his mind; but rather than experience the death that *is* desire, he imposes death *on* desire. Like Hamlet, who idealizes *and* eroticizes Ophelia's corpse, Othello may safely sexualize Desdemona only posthumously, after she is permanently immobilized and sacramentally elevated.

Othello's strategy, of course, provides him with only a temporary measure of safety. The unified image of male subjectivity which Desdemona's still body would seem to guarantee is shown to be fractured as soon as the illusion of her guilt is challenged. The terms of self-loathing by which Othello describes and inflicts his own death demonstrate a self-recognition of fragmentation made more devastating because so utterly constituted by racist categories. As the valiant Christian warrior smites the Turkish "circumcised dog" (V.ii.361–4), Othello demonstrates the price for men of woman's failure to comply with her mirroring function: psychic disintegration and death.

Paradoxically, the need to discipline women is both the "cause" and the "cure" that is offered throughout *Othello*. Though Othello exceeds the boundaries of his culture's notion of suitable "taming," to discipline an erring wife is entirely appropriate within the play's ethos. For Desdemona to have ventured beyond the bounds of patriarchal dictates would have been axiomatic evidence of guilt. Though Desdemona's tarnished reputation is burnished by the end of the play, the play's valorization of chastity registers the impossibility of her innocence beyond the masculinist ethos. In one moment Desdemona is vindicated *and* reinserted securely within masculine control.

The erotic anxieties of which *Othello* is a particularly vehement testament are to be found throughout the Shakespearean canon. Othello's strategies of containment, for example, form a part of the earlier play, *Much Ado About Nothing* (1598–9). In fact, it is as if the Hero/Claudio plot of *Much Ado About Nothing* were split into two parts, each trajectory followed to a different destination in *Othello* (1604) and *The Winter's Tale* (1610–11). The fraught courtship of Claudio and Hero is replicated in Othello's marriage to Desdemona, whereas Hero's semblance of death for restorative purposes is, even in the failure of its ritual resolution, reproduced in *The Winter's Tale*.[24] Like Othello, Claudio first idealizes the object of his affection, using similar metaphors – "Can the world buy such a jewel?" (I.i.174) – and Claudio's readiness to suspect Hero's infidelity matches Othello's susceptibility to Iago's allegations. Like Ophelia and Desdemona, Hero is divided into virgin and whore, a "Dian . . ./ As chaste as is the bud ere it be blown" and an "intemperate . . . Venus" or animal that "rage[s] in savage sensuality" (IV.i.56–60). The flip side of Claudio's romantic idealism is his misogyny, and both stem from a fear of female erotic power.

The tragic brutality of *Othello*, however, seems to have operated as a kind of exorcism. Although fear of women's sexual power dominates *King Lear* (1605) and *Macbeth* (1606), never again are the strategies employed to combat those fears so vitriolic and vituperative – or so horrifyingly final. Rather, Lear and Macbeth are themselves victimized by the sexual power wielded by commanding and evil women. With *The Winter's Tale*, however, Shakespeare returns to his previous paradigm, as if in an effort to moderate both its ferocity and efficacy.

According to most critics, *The Winter's Tale* reintroduces the possibility of mutuality in the Shakespearean canon; and, insofar as the second generation is allowed to renegotiate the terms of heterosexual alliance, and generational continuity succeeds over filial rupture, *The Winter's Tale* does amend the tragic vision of *Hamlet* and *Othello*.[25] In addition, the communal vitality and playfulness of Bohemia, and Hermione's magical reappearance, broaden the previously contracted and paranoid world of Leontes' Sicilia. As much as such reformations relieve psychic stress, however, they do not resolve the primary conflict posed by the fear of woman's erotic betrayal. What is commonly accepted as the play's essential reparative act – Hermione's transformation, first into a statue, and then back into a woman – is inspired nonetheless by the threat Hermione's sexuality poses to Leontes.

The Winter's Tale retraces the pattern of erotic anxiety in *Hamlet* and *Othello*. All of the men in Leontes' court depend upon sexual dualism to mediate their relations with women. Polixenes' narration of the kings' shared boyhood ambivalently projects women as simultaneously sacred and sexually seductive: "O my most sacred lady,/ Temptations have since then been born to 's, for/ In those unfledg'd days was my wife a girl;/ Your precious self had then not cross'd the eyes/ Of my young playfellow" (I.ii.76–9). Underneath the idealized appellations is the unconsciously felt danger of the temptation. Leontes' ostensible compliment to Hermione in the story of their betrothal – "Why, that was when/ Three crabbed months had sour'd themselves to death/ Ere I could make thee open thy white hand/ And clap thyself my love" (I.ii.101–4) – replicates three of Hamlet's and Othello's most potent associations: the link between eroticism and death, the image of women's sexuality as an opening, and the use of hands as an erotic emblem. Opening her hand, a woman gives herself in marriage; but that gesture conjures up for Leontes other kinds of giving: for women to possess and use their hands suggests that they can give *of themselves* rather than *be* the gifts of men. If in the context of courtship, Hermione's open hand is a positive image, just a few lines later it becomes a prostitute's "paddling palm"; and her "free face" that derives a "liberty/ From heartiness" signifies whorish behavior (I.ii.112–15).[26] As Leontes' metaphors make clear, Hermione's sexuality has become too open and "Too hot, too hot!" (I.ii.108).

In a reworking of Hamlet's and Othello's objectification of women, Leontes imagines Hermione as a "medal, hanging/ About [Polixenes'] neck" (I.ii.306–7), a medal representing, even more explicitly than jewels, the power and prestige of the male. In a powerful reversal of Othello's moral absolutism – "My life upon her faith!" (I.iii.297) – Leontes bases everything upon his fantasy of Hermione's infidelity: "Is this nothing?/ Why, then the world and all that's in't is nothing,/ The covering sky is nothing, Bohemia nothing,/ My wife is nothing, nor nothing have these nothings,/ If this be nothing" (I.ii.291–4). Paranoia and projection become the order of the day, as even Antigonus, in his ambivalent effort to defend the honor of his queen, projects Leontes' accusations onto his daughters:

> Be she honor-flaw'd,
> I have three daughters – the eldest is eleven,
> The second and the third, nine, and some five –
> If this prove true, they'll pay for 't. By mine honor,
> I'll geld 'em all; fourteen they shall not see
> To bring false generations.
>
> (II.i.144–9)

In its explicit clarity, Antigonus' verbal violence invites a comparison to Leontes' increasingly vituperative, yet confused, sexual disgust:

> And many a man there is, even at this present,
> Now while I speak this, holds his wife by th 'arm,
> That little thinks she has been sluic'd in 's absence
> And his pond fish'd by his next neighbor, by
> Sir Smile, his neighbor. Nay, there's comfort in't,

>   Whiles other men have gates and those gates open'd
>   As mine, against their will.
>
>   (I.ii.192–8)

As Murray Schwartz points out, Leontes not only rages against cuckoldry, but his ambiguous syntax suggests that he does so through a confused identification with the woman: "The genital violation of the woman-as-property is equivalent to homosexual assault."[27] Both Hermione's and Leontes' "gates" are "open'd" in what must be for Leontes a doubly terrifying loss of sexual control.[28]

Many critics have attempted to pinpoint the reasons for Leontes' fantastic jealousy, and the motivations animating his subsequent harsh treatment. To my mind, it is less profitable to locate Leontes' anxieties psychoanalytically than to ask what nexus of cultural relations creates the conditions for such a paranoiac reaction. The anxieties of Leontes are the anxieties of a masculinist culture in which women's bodies possess enormous powers of signification. Hermione's pregnant body, as much as it is a signifier of maternal fecundity and hereditary lineage, is a palpable reminder of erotic activity: to Leontes, her pregnancy visually re-presents the consequences of heterosexual intercourse. In reaction to this excess of signification, Leontes not only psychically kills Hermione,[29] but also the child Mamillus who not only represents the product of her sexual congress, but, through his Latin name, her female breast. Indeed, confining Hermione to prison is not sufficient; only the fantasy of her death brings Leontes psychic calm: "say that she were gone,/ Given to the fire, a moiety of my rest/ Might come to me again" (II.iii.7–9). Like Othello, Leontes imagines Hermione's death to be a sacrifice: "Given to the fire," Hermione is an offering made in hopes of reconstituting Leontes' sacred, desexualized feminine ideal.

In contrast to Ophelia and Desdemona, of course, Hermione is not literally killed, nor does Leontes himself turn her into a monument. Indeed, it is Paulina who, after Hermione faints at the news of her son's death, fabricates the fiction of Hermione's death; and she acts to help, not hinder, her beloved friend and queen. And, Leontes quickly (almost too quickly?) repents: "Apollo, pardon/ My great profaneness 'gainst thine oracle!/ I'll reconcile me to Polixenes,/ New woo my queen" (III.ii.153–7). Why then, is Hermione whisked off to seclusion? Why the sixteen-year delay in reconciliation? Why the superfluous, albeit spectacular, transformation of Hermione into a statue? Exigencies of plot, of course, require that time pass: Perdita and Florizel must meet, woo, and marry, and Leontes must demonstrate devotion to his dead wife. For "tyranny [to]/ Tremble at patience" (III.ii.31–2), Hermione's patience must be given dramatic form. I would argue that, in addition, Leontes must experience a reprieve from the exigencies of female erotic life before he can re-enter marriage with any degree of psychic comfort; and, most importantly, that Hermione's "unmanageable" sexuality must be metaphorically contained and psychically disarmed.

Thus, the strategy of containment begun in the subplots of *Much Ado About Nothing* and *Hamlet*, and given its most extreme form in *Othello*, progresses through *The Winter's Tale*. Out of cultural anxieties regarding women's erotic power, Leontes fantasizes Hermione's adultery, and the projection of those anxieties leads to her metaphorical death. That death is reversed only when another symbolic form of stasis and control is imposed: Hermione's "dead likeness" (V.iii.15) re-presents her living body through the illusion of preserved feminine integrity. "[W]arm" but not hot (V.iii.110), Hermione is chastened (made chaste), her erotic power curtailed. Upon her revivification, Hermione is granted one speech of eight lines, and this speech a maternal blessing and query directed toward her daughter. Her silence toward Leontes bespeaks a submissiveness, or perhaps an emotional distancing, most unlike her previous animation. Rather than a victory for the wronged heroine, the final scene works as wish-fulfillment for Leontes, who not only regains his virtuous wife and loses his burden of guilt, but also reassumes his kingly command of all social relations, represented by his deft matchmaking and integration of the two remaining isolated figures, Paulina and Camillo.

Hermione's monumentalization, of course, also commemorates her worth; as a statue, she "Strike[s] all that look upon with marvel" (V.iii.100), the pun on marble implying the temporary transformation of spectators into stone. But, as much as Hermione is reinfused with value, the terms of that valuation have not altered since Leontes' first fit of jealousy. In speaking of monumentalization in *Antony and Cleopatra*, Jonathan Dollimore writes: "the statue is a literal, material embodiment of a respect for its subject which is inseparable from the obsolesence of that subject."[30] The logic crucial to *The Winter's Tale*, I submit, is respect *because* obsolete: Hermione can be sacramentalized because the threat she represented has been psychically encased in stone. To the extent that a statue's function is commemorative, Hermione-as-statue safely re-members, but does not em-body, the threat of female erotic power.

Leontes has come to terms with his specific anxieties *vis-à-vis* Hermione's alleged adultery with Polixenes, but the wish-fulfillment that constitutes the play's close does not substantially alter the relation of Hermione to Leontes within the heterosexual economy. The conflicts ostensibly resolved by the "new marriage" still lurk in the background, temporarily abated, but able to create instability at any time. Had Hermione actually exceeded the bounds of patriarchal dictates, she never would have been revivified. Hermione herself gestures toward the containments of masculinist discourse in her refusal to defend herself in Leontes' terms:

> Since what I am to say must be but that
> Which contradicts my accusation, and
> The testimony on my part no other
> But what comes from myself, it shall scarce boot me
> To say "Not guilty".

>   (III. ii. 22–6)

Within the dualistic logic which governs chastity, there are no terms of defense available other than the assertion of innocence, which Hermione recognizes as the flip side of her projected guilt. Cook's comments in regard to *Much Ado About Nothing* ring equally true of *The Winter's Tale*: "the play masks, as well as exposes, the mechanisms of masculine power and that insofar as it avoids what is crucial to its conflicts, the explicitly offered comic [or romance] resolution is something of an artful dodge."[31]

Many feminist critics would argue that Leontes' repentance, Hermione's forgiveness, and Paulina's unifying role illustrate a victory of "feminine" over "masculine" values, and further, that because of this privileging of "feminine values," Shakespeare can be appropriated to feminist ends.[32] Like the Clown in *Hamlet*, Shakespeare, these critics imply, would seem to dramatically represent, even insist on, a feminine specificity. Other feminist critics, however, demonstrate that such an expression of "feminine values" ultimately may perpetuate patriarchal gender distinction.[33] In this respect, Shakespeare is, again like *Hamlet*'s Clown, taking away as much as he gives. Others still reject the possibility of feminine representation within the masculinist discourses of early modern England. Carol Cook, for example, maintains

that the phallocentric bias of all patriarchal discourse, including Shakespeare's, precludes the possibility of positive "feminine
values":

> The construction of femininity within an economy of repre-
> sentation governed by the phallus – a construction in which
> women mirror masculine identity by their own lack – obviates
> the possibility of "feminine values" or of a feminine alternative
> to the "predominately masculine ethos." Alternatives cannot be
> generated from within the binary structures by which patriarchy
> figures gender.[34]

Within Lacanian terms, insofar as "feminine values" exist, they are
merely the figuration of the reduced other of full, masculine presence. Finally, Kathleen McLuskie rejects a "feminist Shakespeare"
as historically anachronistic, arguing that feminist criticism must
subvert rather than assimilate the "patriarchal Bard."[35] Through
the radically different auspices of materialist and psychoanalytic
methods, McLuskie and Cook reach the same conclusion: representing female power is an impossibility within the early modern
ideological configuration of which Shakespeare was a part. In the
terms implied by the Clown, early modern woman is always
already dead.

Although the final destination of my argument coincides with
that of McLuskie and Cook, distinguishing between our methods
creates a crucial shift in emphasis. McLuskie charges feminist
psychoanalytic criticism with "mimetic essentialism" – that is,
with accepting a mimetic model of the relation between ideas
and drama, and believing in an ahistorical, essential gender difference. Indeed, the weakness in Cook's argument seems to be
precisely the ahistoricism McLuskie decries: Cook's subscription
to a culturally determining logic poses patriarchy as a monolithic, transhistorical entity that can be transformed only with the
destruction of phallocentrism. The implication of her perspective is
that all patriarchal societies have identical interests in maintaining
phallocentrism. On the other hand, my analysis, I hope, demonstrates that early modern patriarchy was a profoundly unstable
structure and ideology: the *work* involved in Shakespeare's representation of monumentalization discloses an intense investment in
staging the impossibility of female erotic agency in order to contain
it more fully. In this sense, the inaccessibility of female erotic power
is not inherent in a totalizing phallocentrism, but quite literally is

imposed precisely because such erotic power constitutes a threat to a historically constituted patriarchal masculine subjectivity.

Insofar as the dramatization of this impossibility reveals its own constructed nature, the plays disclose the possibility of their deconstruction. Indeed, shifting the critical emphasis away from the structural oppositions that figure gender distinctions, and toward the cultural anxieties generated by those structures creates a space for resistance. Whatever the cause of masculine fears – most likely the fact that men's first and most intense dependency is upon their mothers, whom patriarchy demands they must renounce in favor of paternal identification[36] – Shakespearean drama exposes the mechanisms by which they are legitimized and reproduced.

Shakespearean tragedy and romance not only depend upon but are constituted by masculine anxieties; those anxieties circumscribe and delimit the entire dramatic action. Not even in Cleopatra's Egypt do we step outside of a masculine psychic economy. Indeed, despite the depiction of more flexible and mutual gender roles in *Antony and Cleopatra* and *Romeo and Juliet*, the intensification of the desirability of sexual activity seems to induce an even greater internalization of male codes on the part of the female hero; witness Cleopatra's repudiation of female mobility and inconstancy before committing the suicide that will turn her into a tableau: "I have nothing/ Of woman in me. Now from head to foot/ I am marble-constant; now the fleeting moon/ No planet is of mine" (V.ii.238–41). In addition, exigencies of masculinity, represented by Antony's ties to Rome and Romeo's involvement in the feud,[37] intervene in the pleasures of the body, as both men come to fear the supposed "effeminacy" brought on by erotic excess. Here, male characters do not impose stasis; Cleopatra and Juliet impose it on themselves.

While dramatically exploring masculine anxieties, and even presenting the crisis of masculinist values, Shakespearean drama nonetheless perpetuates defensive structures of dominance instituted by men. A reconciliation with any of the wronged heroines of *Hamlet*, *Othello*, or *The Winter's Tale* is imaginable only *within* the territory of masculine prerogatives. Once dead, Ophelia becomes an angel: a status as imbued with masculine anxiety as was her previous degradation. Gertrude is granted the possibility of redemption, but only at the cost of her sexuality. Desdemona is declared innocent after death, but exists thereafter only as a jewel in the masculine imagination – the tragedy being less the murder of her innocence than the justification her guilt would have given to such violence. Hermione is reunited with her husband, but the anxieties that incited the imposition of stasis upon her are still immanent, indeed, inherent, in their relationship. Insofar as Shakespeare's theater serves as a projective or transitional space in which to articulate and thereby assuage psychic concerns, the dramatization of *Hamlet*, *Othello*, and *The Winter's Tale* may act as a temporary exorcism of masculine anxieties. However, the metaphorical displacement of sexually threatening women into jewels, statues, and corpses perpetuates the containment and vilification of female erotic power.

At the time I first wrote and published a version of this chapter, my private subtitle was: "Or – the only good woman is a dead virgin." Such was the extent of my belief in the containing power of masculine discourse *vis-à-vis* female erotic agency. The controlling gaze of the male subject, which totalized the object of desire, was for me the only possible position from which to view the action of the play. In designating the woman as monument, I unwittingly adopted the viewpoint of Hamlet, Othello, Leontes.[38]

Focusing on the seemingly relentless power of containment, I failed to see the possibility of female agency in excess of masculine control. Desdemona and Ophelia die; but, at least in the case of Desdemona, a female voice – that of Emilia – resists her death, proclaiming it murder. Likewise, in her bawdy songs, Ophelia asserts a measure of erotic agency before her death. And Hermione finally does move off her pedestal, does speak, and is directed in her movements, not by her husband but by her female friend.

Yet each of these assertions of agency is still circumscribed by a patriarchal discourse that terms Ophelia's tuneful accusations of sexual infidelity "mad," and places Emilia's and Paulina's resistance to oppression within the iconography of "shrew." In its ambiguous troping on spatial and erotic metaphors, Ophelia's song eerily gestures toward the containments of this discourse:

> Then up he rose, and donn'd his clo'es,
> And dupp'd the chamber-door,
> Let in the maid, that out a maid
> Never departed more.

> (IV.v.52–5)

Chapter 2

Prince Hal's Falstaff: positioning psychoanalysis and the female reproductive body

Despite the specific meanings we may ascribe to the female reproductive body historically, whether they derive from an Aristotelian,
Galenic, or modern gynecological paradigm, the bare fact of biological reproduction remains irrefutable, ineffable. In our own cultural tradition the figure of the maternal is simultaneously an object
of terror (fears of maternal engulfment) and idealization (the Virgin
Mother). That "dark continent" traversed by every infant, where we
are conceived and from which we are delivered, the maternal figure
exists in our pre-natal memories – before culture, language, law,
before knowledge of the father, before the Law of the Father.

Psychoanalysis offers a brilliant reading of the enculturation of
the infant who is expelled from this body into the social order,
of the simultaneous development of its subjectivity, gender, and
sexuality. But, as feminist critics have made abundantly clear,
the psychoanalytic narrative of psychic development is predicated
upon a male subject. Not only is the trajectory of the male
posited as normative, but that subject is constituted in relation to
a fantasized other – an other that is at once engendered as "woman"
and eroticized in reference to female reproductive functions.

The reflexivity and redundancy of the psychoanalytic narrative of
psychic development also characterize its analysis of literary texts:
it generally tells the same tale, a story of "real" or fantasized loss,
with all psychic conflict organized around the threat of castration. Despite the variety of literary plot, image, and metaphor,
psychoanalytic criticism tends to rehearse a drama of the same,
seeing only its own image in the face of the other.

In an attempt to break out of this circle, I pose the female reproductive body as the repressed figure upon which two paradigmatic
narratives of male subjectivity depend: Lacan's revision of the

Freudian oedipal drama as the subject's entrance into the symbolic order, and Shakespeare's drama of the development of a
"prototypical" male subject in the *Henriad*. In a recursive reading of
drama through psychoanalysis, and psychoanalysis through drama,
I argue that despite significant differences in family and social structure between late-sixteenth-century England and twentieth-century
Vienna and Paris, Shakespearean drama and psychoanalytic theory
share in a cultural estimation of the female reproductive body as a
Bakhtinian "grotesque body," and that they repress this figure in
their narratives of psychic development.[1]

I am interested not so much in posing the *Henriad* as case history,
applying psychoanalytic terminology to individual characters, but
in the interrogation of persistent repetitions of psychoanalytic and
dramatic narratives, repetitions that demonstrate their cohabita-
tion within a dominant structure of gender. The *Henriad* and
psychoanalysis are parallel narratives, similarly positioning male
subjectivity and the female reproductive body, staging a conflict
between "paternal authority and maternal priority."[2] By using the
terms "drama" and "narrative" in reference to both, I mean to stress
that psychoanalytic theory is as shaped by the politics of narrative
convention and the constraints of a historically constructed cultural
unconscious as is early modern drama.

In asserting such a connection between Shakespearean and
psychoanalytic texts, I acknowledge the risk of effacing historical
differences in ideology and representation. However, early modern
texts in fact demonstrate indigenous cultural rationales that, as
today, construct the maternal as a locus of profound ambivalence. If,
as Thomas Laqueur argues, the Galenic paradigm which dominated
sixteenth- and seventeenth-century medicine understood men to
originate as female, then the fear of a reverse teleology – of
being turned back into a woman – may have been a common
masculine fantasy.[3] And if "lust" was seen as effeminizing in its
power to subordinate men to women by making men more
"like" women, then anxiety about desire itself obviously infused
and structured heterosexual relations.[4] Finally, if the practice of
wet-nursing caused not only early separation of the infant from
the biological mother, but competition for maternal nurturance
and subsequent ambivalence in object-relations (and perhaps in
class identifications as well),[5] then "getting back to the mother" was
not only massively prohibited, but enormously problematical.[6] For
aristocratic children especially, mothering itself was so much a field

of dispersal that one hardly knows who the "mother" is. In addition, insofar as children of most classes and both genders were kept in an almost exclusively female world, wearing skirt-like dress until the age of seven,[7] the moment of boys' "breeching" instances not only a delayed physical separation, but an enforced conceptual dichoto-mization, of male from female. Indeed, that men were perceived to originate as female, and that infant and toddler boys were dressed as "girls" does not obviate the centrality of the cultural opposition of male and female; on the contrary, these practices suggest a psychic rationale for the dualism defensively and reactively enforced by the adult system of gender evidenced in Shakespeare's plays. Material practices and their psychological corollaries converge to render women generally, and mothers specifically, as objects to be desired, resented, and most importantly, feared.

In noting the similarities that exist despite historical differences in family and social structure, I do not propose that the line between Shakespeare and Freud is direct or continuous. Clearly, as the Victorian idealization of the maternal attests, the female reproductive body has been variously constructed and valued within different periods. Rather, I mean to suggest that in respect to the female reproductive body and its influence on male subjectivity, Shakespearean drama and psychoanalytic theory share in a cultural moment, in much the same way as we can say that the narrative strategies of *Tristram Shandy* or *Don Quixote* share in those of a "postmodern moment." History is neither smooth teleology nor total disruption. It may repeat itself – but always with a difference. The salient difference between the *Henriad* and psychoanalysis is, I would argue, less ideological than stylistic, less political than performative.

The relationship of feminist critics to Shakespeare's history plays has until recently been one of not-so-benign neglect. For many feminists, the lack of powerful female characters in the histories forecloses the critical questions they bring to Shakespearean drama. "Women don't figure" seems to sum up the stance of many critics who turn their analyses of gender and power to the greater presence of women, and the themes of chastity, courtship, marriage, and adultery in the comedies, tragedies, and romances.[8] In a recent article, Carol Thomas Neely takes this argument even further: she maintains that the focus of new historical critics on the histories is in part evidence of their antipathy to feminism.[9]

In arguing against this trend of dismissing the histories, I mean to suggest that the *Henriad* is a "seminal" point for an examination of the construction and maintenance of phallocentric ideology, particularly in regard to male subjectivity and sexuality. Although the histories depend on a resolutely hierarchical representation of gender difference, they do not merely exclude women; they *stage* the elimination of women from the historical process (an exclusion that *is* the historical process), thus exhibiting the kinds of repressions a phallocentric culture requires to maintain and reproduce itself. By means of this staged repudiation, the *Henriad* embodies a marginal, subversive discourse, if only to demonstrate the fantasized expulsion of that discourse. This expulsion, however, is neither final nor total; we thus see in the *Henriad* not only the "rehearsal" of power stressed by new historical critics, but also the possibility of the deconstruction of dominant sixteenth-century ideologies of gender, sexuality, and power.[10] In short, male dominated as it is, the *Henriad* contains within itself the means for its own meta-critique.

Access to this meta-critique is possible through a reading of the *Henriad* as paradigmatic of the gendered and erotic repressions upon which sixteenth-century male subjectivity depends. In psycho-dramatic terms, Prince Hal's subjectivity is constituted, first, in his relation to Falstaff, whose somatic iconography metonymically positions him as the fantasized pre-oedipal maternal, against whom Hal must differentiate; and, second, in relation to the French princess, Katharine, whose material and linguistic subjugation demonstrates the extent to which the male subject's (hetero)sexuality depends upon the repression and control of a female other.

My reading of the *Henriad* draws an explicit parallel with the Lacanian description of the development of subjectivity within phallocentric culture. In Lacanian psychoanalysis the individual is constituted simultaneously as a subject, a gender, and a sexuality through entrance into the symbolic order of language. With the insertion of the third term, the phallus, into the imaginary pre-oedipal relation of mother and child, the child loses its fantasized symbiosis with the mother, falling into a pre-existing order of culture that, through its endlessly substitutive chain of signification, enforces an always-divided subjectivity or "lack-in-being."[11] The signifier of this lack-in-being is the phallus: first, because by breaking the imaginary dyad, it inaugurates all subsequent desire as substitutive; and second, because all subjects, male and female, are psychically castrated, learning the meaning of separation and difference through their alienation into language.

The symbolic order governed by the Law of the Father is implicitly phallocentric, in part because of the resolutely hierarchical binaries by which it structures all categories of being and thought, beginning with gender: "The Father's Law enjoins the subject to line up according to an opposition, man/woman, to assume its place as 'he' or 'she' in a preexisting order of language and culture."[12] From this binarism of gender, all subsequent difference is defined as oppositional and hierarchical, leading to the ascription of a host of related oppositions: rational/irrational, strength/weakness, civilized/primitive.

Like Freud, Lacan describes a sequence of psychic events – the movement from the pre-oedipal through the oedipal – that is both constituted by and constitutive of patriarchal culture. For feminists, the value of Lacanian analysis is precisely in this description of how phallocentrism reproduces itself within and through a family structure that is inscribed by larger cultural codes. Despite its embeddedness in patriarchal ideology, Lacanian psychoanalysis provides the means for a critique of the pretensions of phallocentrism. As the signifier of the *fiction* of unmediated presence and integrated identity, as the metaphor for a fragmented and precarious subjectivity, the phallus exposes even as it upholds the artificiality of the division upon which gender and sexual identity are based. As Jane Gallop remarks, "The penis is what men have and women do not; the phallus is the attribute of power which neither men nor women have."[13]

As Gallop is well aware, however, the danger in this formulation is that historically the phallus has stood for precisely the kind of power men have had – as metaphor for their male identity and as figuration of their sexual, political, and economic power over women. A feminist psychoanalysis must therefore conscientiously resist subsuming gender hierarchies under the aegis of the radical instability of all speaking subjects.[14] While retaining the Lacanian description of the way gendered subjects are constituted by and through phallocentric culture, language, and logic, feminists will continue to intervene strategically in this course of events.

Psychoanalytic criticism of the *Henriad* has tended to perceive Prince Hal's developmental problem as a choice between two

fathers: a biological father, King Henry IV, standing for conviction, duty, and control, yet burdened by his guilty acquisition
of the crown; and a father substitute, Falstaff, whose hedonism,
lawlessness, and wit provide an attractive, if temporary, alternative.
In his classic 1952 formulation, Ernst Kris argued that Prince Hal
dissociates himself from the court both as protest against his father's
regicide, and to escape his own unconscious temptation to parri-
cide.[15] Upon his father's death, Hal ascends the throne, displacing
his parricidal impulses onto his father substitute; his harsh rejection
of Falstaff thus acts as a symbolic killing of the father.

Kris's normalizing account of psychosexuality celebrates the
successful reintegration of the wayward, unruly child into the
patrilineal order of kingship. The tetralogy ends as a comedy, with
the marriage of the newly crowned and martially victorious King
Henry V to the French princess Katharine ensuring the continued
generation of patriarchal power through the expectation of male
progeny.

More recently, Murray Schwartz and Peter Erickson also posit
Falstaff as a paternal figure, but they view with ambivalence
the tetralogy's close. In stressing that Falstaff represents in non-
legitimate, infantile ways adult male fantasies of omnipotence,
avarice, orality, and egotism, Schwartz argues that as low-life
"sport" is channeled into high-minded military exploits, the drama
expresses the cultural legitimation of infantile egotism.[16] And
Erickson's examination of male bonding suggests that the guilt
Hal feels toward both Henry IV and Falstaff prevents the *Henriad*
from reaching a clear resolution. Both father figures are "scapegoats
who refuse to stay away."[17]

I see Schwartz and Erickson as beginning a movement to
problematize psychoanalytically the *Henriad* from the perspective of a troubled masculinity, based in a flawed father–son
dynamic that replicates the larger problems of patriarchy. I want
to take their analyses of patriarchal relations one step further by
arguing that Falstaff represents to Hal not an alternative paternal
image but rather a projected fantasy of the pre-oedipal *maternal*,
whose rejection is the basis upon which patriarchal subjectivity
is predicated. I see in this process of the oedipal rejection of
the maternal and identification with the paternal not merely the
individual psychosexuality of one character, but a paradigm for
the cultural construction of early modern masculine subjectivity.
Furthermore, through his militaristic courtship of Katharine, Hal's

subjectivity is established as thoroughly phallocentric, depending upon the repression of the object of his erotic desire.

That Falstaff is figured in female terms is suggested first by his body, which is associated with the metaphors of women's bodies and carnality that Shakespeare elsewhere exploits in his denunciation of female eroticism. Physically, Falstaff is most like *The Comedy of Errors'* spherical, oily kitchen maid (variously referred to as Luce and Nell, who mistakenly attempts to seduce the Syracusian Dromio) and the bawdy Nurse of *Romeo and Juliet*, who, like Falstaff, huffs and puffs as she waddles on fat legs.[18] In contrast to the disembodied voices of Shakespeare's other fools, Falstaff's being is exceedingly corporeal; indeed, his corpulence is referred to constantly, invoking, in the emphasis on a swollen and distended belly, associations of pregnancy.[19] In the space of three scenes, Hal calls Falstaff "fat rogue" twice, "damn'd brawn" (pig or fatted swine), "fat-kidney'd rascal," "fat-guts," "whoreson round man," "clay-brain'd guts," "emboss'd [swollen] rascal," and "my sweet beef."[20] Not only fat Jack's gut, but also what goes in and comes out of his body is the object of constant discussion – especially sweat and oil: Falstaff is an "oily rascal," a "greasy tallow-catch" who "sweats to death,/ And lards the lean earth as he walks along."[21]

Such a focus on the bulging and the protuberant, the openings, permeabilities, and effusions of Falstaff's body situate him as a "grotesque body." According to Peter Stallybrass and Allon White, who reformulate Bakhtin's paradigm, early modern somatic concepts were organized into mutually exclusive iconographies of the low and high, the open and closed, the grotesque and the classical, with the grotesque body being

> an image of impure corporeal bulk with its orifices (mouth, flared nostrils, anus) yawning wide and its lower regions (belly, legs, feet, buttocks and genitals) given priority over its upper regions (head, "spirit", reason) . . . a subject of pleasure in processes of exchange . . . it is never closed off from either its social or ecosystemic context.[22]

When Hal calls Falstaff "gross as a mountain, open, palpable" (*H.IV, pt 1*, II.iv.224), or "this bed-presser, this horse-back-breaker, this huge hill of flesh" (*H.IV, pt 1*, II.iv.240–1), or a "tun of man," a "bolting-hutch of beastliness," a "swoll'n parcel of dropsies," a "huge bombard of sack," a "stuff'd cloak-bag of guts," a "Manningtree ox with the pudding in his belly" (*H.IV, pt 1*, II.iv.443–8), he instantiates Falstaff as a grotesque body.

The many references to Falstaff as a pig, including his self-identification as "a sow that hath overwhelm'd all her litter but one" (*H.IV, pt 2*, I.ii.11–12), not only further locate him as a grotesque body, but also create a web of associations that direct our attention to Falstaff's belly, which becomes increasingly feminized.[23] When, after he has had a scuffle with Pistol, Hostess Quickly asks Falstaff, "Are you not hurt i' th' groin? Methought 'a made a shrewd thrust at your belly" (*H.IV, pt 2*, II.iv.207–8), she shifts the linguistic emphasis from the masculine "groin" (in danger of castration) to the more feminine "belly," the "already castrated," vulnerable recipient and receptacle of a "shrewd thrust." False-staff becomes precisely a false phallus, in inverse relation to the Freudian declaration that, upon entry into the "phallic phase" of sexual development, "the little girl is a little man."[24] Falstaff himself makes the link between his belly, its "effeminacy," and his identity when, in response to the Knight Colevile's question, "Are you not Sir John Falstaff?" he replies, "I have a whole school of tongues in this belly of mine, and not a tongue of them all speaks any other word but my name. . . . My womb, my womb, my womb undoes me" (*H.IV, pt 2*, IV.iii.18–22).[25]

I will argue soon that his womb does indeed undo him. For now, I merely mean to suggest that the associational chain from pig, sow, groin, belly, to womb effects a transposition from the grotesque body to the female reproductive body. As Bakhtin has argued, sexual as well as excremental functions form the core of the category of the "grotesque" that was operative throughout early modern culture. Although Bakhtin elides gender specificity in his work, the symbolic functioning of the bodily processes of menstruation, pregnancy, childbearing, and lactation – which render women, particularly in respect to their genitals and breasts, open, protuberant, and never-quite-sealed-off – all metonymically instantiate the maternal body as "grotesque."[26]

Obviously, Falstaff could be analyzed as a "grotesque body" without specific reference to his maternal functions: many resonances echo between the Rabelaisian carnivalesque and Falstaff's gluttony and drunkenness, between the early modern marketplace and the Eastcheap tavern.[27] However, precisely because gender is repressed in Bakhtin's account, the demonstration of its salience is all the more pressing.

That the maternal was linked to the "grotesque body" in early modern societies is evidenced in part by the performance of certain pollution behaviors. The practice of "churching" women after menstruation and childbirth suggests that the products of women's sexual and reproductive bodies posed enough of a psychic threat to the social order to call for ritual purification.[28] I would argue, further, that the fantasy represented by the non-sexualized maternity of a Virgin Mary further manages anxieties about female reproducive corporeality. With the Reformation's institutionalized occlusion of Mariolatry, the social and psychic functions the Virgin performed were left with little institutional accommodation.[29] The symbolic complex of the "grotesque body" was one intervention in this social field, performing the psycho-social function of containing psychic phenomena perceived as threatening. The danger posed by the grotesque-body-as-maternal is the physical contamination which, by virtue of the birth process – "*inter urinas et faeces nascimur,*" to quote Freud, who was himself quoting St Augustine – the maternal body represents to early modern psyches, socially constructed as they were through a dualistic logic of mind over matter, spirit over body, or, to invoke Simone de Beauvoir, transcendence over immanence.[30] Hal's development as a male subject depends not only upon separation and differentiation from a state of physical dependency and a fantasized state of psychic symbiosis, but also on the exorcism of the figure responsible for and associated with that state: mother, *mater*, matter.[31] Hal's public disavowal and humiliation of Falstaff in *Henry IV, part 2* – "I know thee not, old man" (*H.IV, pt 2*, V.v.47) – suggest his need to externalize just such an intra-psychic threat.

The rejection of Falstaff, like the signification of his body, is overdetermined; within the absolutist paradigm of early modern rule and kingship, his transgressions are obviously dangerous. Yet, interestingly enough, Hal's statement of rejection likens his previous relationship with Falstaff to a dream, a pre-oedipal fantasy of nondifferentiation of boundaries: "I have long dreamt of such a kind of man,/ So surfeit-swell'd, so old, and so profane,/ But, being awak'd, I do despise my dream" (*H.IV, pt 2*, V.v.49–51). As C.L. Barber notes, "Elsewhere in Shakespeare, to dismiss dreams categorically is foolhardy."[32] Part of Hal's "dream" has included role playing such as that indicated by his statement, "I'll play Percy, and that damn'd brawn shall play Dame Mortimer his wife" (*H.IV, pt 1*, II.iv.109–10). Whereas the homoerotics of the

Henriad deserve fuller treatment than I can render here, it is apparent that homoerotic desire infuses the relationship of Falstaff and Hal, signaled both by Falstaff's "feminine" qualities and Hal's predominant lack of interest in women. Although Falstaff portrays himself as a womanizer, his relations with neither Mistress Quickly nor Doll Tearsheet carry the erotic impress and tenderness of his bond to Hal. Indeed, the connection between Falstaff and Hal seems to invert the power relations we so often assume structure male homoerotic relations: rather than involving a powerful older man who protects and mentors his young lover, the Falstaff/Hal relation concerns an older, less attractive, socially marginalized man who is emotionally and financially dependent on a younger, more attractive, increasingly independent and powerful aristocrat – the same asymmetry explored in greater detail in Shakespeare's sonnets.

Hal's rejection of Falstaff thus seems temporarily to assuage anxieties, first, about the intimacy of their homoerotic bond and, second, about the equation of woman and maternity. The repudiation simultaneously exorcises both possible threats to Hal's development of adult heterosexuality. Indeed, the threat of maternal power is mapped onto anxieties about homoerotic desire, insofar as Falstaff's eroticization is based precisely on the "grotesque body" (damn'd brawn) of the mature woman – "Dame Mortimer [my] wife." When Hal charges Falstaff to "Make less thy body hence, and more thy grace;/ Leave gormandizing. Know the grave doth gape/ For thee thrice wider than for other men" (*H.IV, pt 2*, V.v.52–4), he not only pointedly situates Falstaff's grotesque body as the problem, but metaphorically hurries this body off to its material end, Mother Earth's hungry maw.

Death holds specifically maternal associations for both Hal and his father. When a nobleman enters the tavern in quest of the prince, Hal retorts, "Send him back again to my mother" (*H.IV, pt 1*, II.iv.288). Insofar as the queen, Mary de Bohun, had long been laid to rest, the editor of the *Riverside Shakespeare* perceptively glosses this line as "get rid of him permanently."[33] *Henry IV, part 1* begins with the king imagining his country's recent period of war and destruction in maternal terms: "No more the thirsty entrance of this soil/ Shall daub her lips with her own children's blood" (*H.IV, pt 1*, I.i.5–6) – a projection of maternal destructiveness later repeated in Falstaff's description of himself as a sow that has devoured her litter (*H.IV, pt 2*, I.ii.11–12).[34]

That Hal is disturbed by precisely such associations between the "grotesque" maternal body and potential death is made evident by the language in which he voices his aspirations. He envisions his redemption in the eyes of men as a separation from "the base contagious clouds" that "smother up his beauty from the world." His maturity, identity, and freedom will be achieved by "breaking through the foul and ugly mists/ Of vapors that did seem to strangle him" (*H.IV, pt 1*, I.ii.192–7). Such suffocation anxiety takes on the configuration of a bloody birth fantasy during his later repetition of this vow. He tells his father:

> I will redeem all this on Percy's head,
> And in the closing of some glorious day
> Be bold to tell you that I am your son,
> When I will wear a garment all of blood
> And stain my favors in a bloody mask,
> Which, wash'd away, shall scour my shame with it.
> (*H.IV, pt 1*, III.ii.132–7)

The vapors that threatened to strangle him in the enclosure of the womb become the blood of birth that, when washed away, will scour off the filth of his maternal associations. Cleansed in a battle both martial and natal, the newborn babe will become simultaneously his father's son and his nation's hero.

Hal's escape from maternal suffocation, from threatened retention in the world of the mother – and thus his re-enactment of early modern boys' "breeching" – is predicated upon his assumption of martial arms and engagement in fraternal rivalry with a brother-surrogate, Hotspur.[35] Hotspur early provides both the opposition between femininity and militarism, and the equation of sexuality with violence, that will later designate Hal's assumption of the masculine role. As Hotspur says upon leaving his wife for battle: "This is no world/ To play with mammets and to tilt with lips./ We must have bloody noses and crack'd crowns" (*H.IV, pt 1*, II.iii.90–2). Heterosexuality not only gives way to male homosocial bonding and warfare, but is reconstituted through a military paradigm: that "this" is not a time to "tilt with lips" implies that there *is* a time for heterosexuality, but it is imaged in specifically militaristic terms.[36]

As if to underscore this relation between militarism and male maturity, *Henry IV, part 2* begins with the official separation of Falstaff from Hal on martial orders of the king; Falstaff is to join Hal's younger brother, John of Lancaster, while the Prince of

Wales asserts himself independently in battle. When the Lord Chief Justice comments to Falstaff, "the King hath sever'd you" (*H.IV, pt 2*, I.ii.201), he incisively indicates the necessity for the newly minted soldier-prince to renounce the maternal in favor of the Name-of-the-Father. That the motivation for such identification is based precisely on a connection between aggression and masculinity is clarified by Nancy Chodorow: "A boy gives up his mother in order to avoid punishment, but identifies with his father because he can then gain the benefits of being the one who gives punishment, of being masculine and superior."[37] Ironically, it is Falstaff's repeated use of the term "prick" to denote the selection of commoners for battle that enforces a chain of signification between military conscription, sharp weaponry, and the penis (*H.IV, pt 2*, III.ii).[38]

By the beginning of *Henry V*, the violence of war has thoroughly permeated male subjectivity and sexuality. Both on the military front and in the French court, Henry V's language demonstrates the extent to which the phallus and military might are mutually constitutive. Henry V threatens the citizens of Harfleur with phallic violence: "What is't to me . . .," he says, "If your pure maidens fall into the hand/ Of hot and forcing violation?" (*H.V*, III.iii.19–21) Invading a city is imagined as rape (*H.V*, III.iii.7–35), just as the object of Henry V's desire, Katharine, is figured by her father as virginal property, a city "all girdled with maiden walls that war hath never ent'red" (*H.V*, V.ii.321–2).

With the conquest of France, the time is right for Henry, if not Hotspur, to "play with mammets and to tilt with lips." The achieved heterosexualization of Henry is a "triumph" which is perversely fulfilled by his inability to woo Katharine except through military metaphors. Henry himself is aware of his inadequacies as a lover; he remarks,

> If I could win a lady at leap-frog, or by vaulting into my saddle with my armour on my back . . . I should quickly leap into a wife. Or if I might buffet [box] for my love, or bound my horse for her favors, I could lay on like a butcher and sit like a jack an apes, never off.
>
> (*H.V*, V.ii.138–43)

As Erickson notes, Henry's

> "speaking plain soldier" (V.ii.149) causes him to portray sexuality as a form of military aggression and conquest. Phrases like "I love

thee cruelly" and "I get thee with scamblin" [fighting] (202–3, 204–5) contain ironies the king cannot control.[39]

Henry is, even in courtship, "a soldier/ A name that in my thoughts becomes me best" (*H.V*, III.iii.5–6).

The military dimension of Henry's sexuality is paralleled by his linguistic domination of Katharine. When he asks her to "teach a soldier terms/ Such as will enter at a lady's ear" (*H.V*, V.ii.99–100), his subsequent behavior attests that the linguistic emphasis is more on penetration than the acquisition of a new language. As Henry says, "It is as easy for me, Kate, to conquer the kingdom as to speak so much more French" (*H.V*, V.ii.185–7). Like Lady Mortimer, who speaks only Welsh and thus relies on her father, Glendower, to translate even marital endearments, Katharine's linguistic status positions woman as a foreign language. It is she who must give up her native tongue – a French language and nationality that throughout the play are associated with the despised "effeminacy" of French nobles – for the "plain soldier" language and nationality of manly "Harry of England" (*H.V*, V.ii.248).

Thus far my analysis has suggested that insofar as Katharine is the object of Henry's discourse, *Henry's* subjectivity and sexuality are predicated upon his repression of Katharine's linguistic power. But what of Katharine as the subject of her own discourse? In the scene between Katharine and her lady-in-waiting (*H.V*, III.iv), in which Katharine not only learns English but metaphorically dismembers it – "d'hand, de fingres, de nails, de arm, d'elbow, de nick, de sin, de foot, le count" – we encounter a Katharine who skillfully engages in linguistic play.[40] Indeed, in this private scene between two women, Katharine takes control of the specifically erotic aspects of language; while asserting that "O Seigneur Dieu! Ils sont les mots de son mauvais, corruptible, gros, et impudique, et non pour les dames d'honneur d'user" (50–2), Katharine nonetheless continues to recite "une autre fois" her "leçon ensemble," including the offending "de foot and le count" (54–57). Insofar as this female appropriation of the sexual body directly follows Henry's threats of rape to the virgins of Harfleur, we are, I think, encouraged to see Katharine as temporarily subverting the play's overwhelmingly male representation of the proper role of female sexuality.

Despite her appropriation of linguistic and sexual power, however, Katharine fails to maintain such control once in the presence of Henry V. During the "wooing scene," her language is reduced to

24 short lines of maidenly embarrassment and deference compared to Henry's 150 lines of vigorous self-presentation. Listen to the tenor of her response to Henry's kissing of her hand, her longest speech (I follow the *Bevington* translation of her French): "don't, my lord, don't, don't; by my faith, I do not wish [you] to lower your greatness by kissing the hand of an – Our dear Lord! – unworthy servant; excuse me, I beg you, my most powerful lord" (*H.V*, V. ii.254–8n). Although, as Helen Ostovich points out, Katharine attempts to evade Henry's "battery of questions" and thus deflect his desire by answering him mainly through the negative ("I cannot tell what is dat", "I do not know dat"),[41] Katharine's predicament is structural; whatever her individual power, it is subsumed by her ideological, political, and economic function in the systematic exchange of women between men.[42] As Katharine says when Henry asks if she will have him: "Dat is as it sall please de roi mon pere" (*H.V*, V.ii.248).

That nationality in *Henry V* is gender marked is often noted. Less obvious is that women's bodies are figured as territory: when Henry describes Katharine as "our capital demand, compris'd/ Within the fore-rank of our articles" (*H.V*, V.ii.96–7), not only does the giving of her body symbolize the capitulation of French territory; her body *becomes* that territory. Once married to the masculine kingdom of England, the subservient state of France embodied by Katharine will be partially enclosed, its watery borders policed by British soldiers. At the same time, Falstaff's body, that unruly "globe of sinful continents" (*H.IV. pt 2*, II.iv.284), is tamed and appropriated through its transfiguration into a more manageable "state."[43]

The symbolic substitution of Falstaff by Katharine effects a strategic displacement and containment, as the debased maternal is replaced with an idealized woman, the "classical body," which, as Stallybrass and White note, is "elevated, static and monumental" with "no openings or orifices."[44] Katharine's virginal body, while presumably to be used for reproductive purposes, is yet in Henry V's fantasies free of implication in maternal bodily processes. As "fair Katharine," "dear Kate," "gentle Princess," "queen of all," "an angel," "my fair flower-de-luce," Katharine is positioned, in the space of a hundred lines, as far as possible from the "grotesque" maternal body (*H.V*, V.ii.104, 154, 203, 246, 110, 210–11).

Such a replacement of the "grotesque body" by the idealized "classical body" is an ambivalent and troubling resolution; for although Hal's psychic anxiety is transcoded into erotic desire, the "classical" and the "grotesque" are two sides of the same coin, arising from the same cultural/psychic complex. Because of our dualistic system of thought, all women, regardless of their individual maternal status, are implicated in male fantasies of maternal omnipotence, nurturance, seduction, engulfment, and betrayal. To the extent that they are gendered, both the "grotesque" and the "classical" body are masculine projections – one, an anxious debasement, the other, a defensive idealization of the physical body from which we are born and to which, in the Shakespearean (and Freudian) equation of womb and tomb, we return.[45]

The *Henriad*'s fantasies and anxieties about women revolve, not like *Othello* and *Hamlet*, around the virgin and the whore, but, like *Romeo and Juliet*, *Macbeth*, and *King Lear*, around the virgin and the mother. Despite this distinction, it is clear that Shakespearean anxieties about female promiscuity and maternity are mediated through fantasies of the grotesque body. Whores, like mothers, are agents of contamination – syphilitic, polluted, and corrosive. With the possible exception of Cleopatra, nowhere in Shakespearean drama does one meet the equivalent of the French or Italian courtesan – educated, politic, and refined – suggesting that the construction of female sexuality was always already preempted by fantasies and fears of the reproductive body.[46]

One of the unfortunate legacies of this conflation of sexuality and reproduction is the contemporary critical impulse to collapse the whole of female subjectivity into a maternal position defined by nurturance, fecundity, and non-differentiated access to the language of the body. This "resorption of femininity within the Maternal," in the words of Julia Kristeva,[47] while an attempt to revalue traditionally female activities, obscures the psychic pain and violence of infants' early object-relations, as well as the autonomous desires of mothers; it limits women's right to choose *not* to bear children or to structure their involvement with children in alternative ways. Reversing the value accorded to the maternal position simply re-enacts the same problematic from the side of idealization rather than debasement. The problem seems to be that the "pre-oedipal" can only with difficulty be divorced from our own adult fantasies and fears. Our understanding of that period is retrospective as we follow a trajectory back through our childhoods; it always involves the risk of nostalgia, of the projection of our unmet early needs.[48]

Recently, the "missing mother" has come into focus in Shake-spearean criticism.[49] On the surface, at least, mothers seem to be expendable in Shakespeare's drama in a way fathers are not. And yet, despite her seeming erasure, the maternal figure often returns: the more benign "resurrections" of the Abbess in *The Comedy of Errors*, of Thaisa in *Pericles*, and of Hermione in *The Winter's Tale* only serve to offset the anxiety embodied in other maternal returns; as Sycorax in *The Tempest* and the witches in *Macbeth* suggest, maternal erasures can also reproduce maternity in a monstrous, "grotesque" guise. Even Falstaff, resurrected in *The Merry Wives of Windsor* (according to legend, at Queen Elizabeth's behest), turns out to be unkillable. The desire to bypass the maternal, then, seems to be a doomed project; if anything, these texts demonstrate the inevitable return of the repressed – oftentimes with a vengeance.

And yet, the negation of the maternal body continues in our own cultural milieu, albeit in modified forms. One of the principal propagations of this erasure is that of psychoanalysis itself. Volumes such as *The (M)Other Tongue* and *In Dora's Case* show psychoanalysis to be, like the male subject, constituted on the basis of the repression of the maternal. As Shirley Garner, Claire Kahane, and Madelon Sprengnether write:

> Psychoanalysis, whether it posits in the beginning maternal presence or absence, has yet to develop a story of the mother as other than the object of the infant's desire or the matrix from which he or she develops an infant subjectivity. The mother herself as speaking subject, as author, is missing from these dramas.[50]

More recently, Sprengnether has argued that part of the problem is that, despite their differences, both object-relations and Lacanian analysis continue to relegate maternity to some place prior to and outside of culture. By maintaining the "Oedipal/preoedipal hierarchy established by Freud," by refusing to locate maternal functions within a cultural sphere, psychoanalysis reproduces the subordinate status of maternity.[51]

Whereas object-relations theory depends on an idealized maternal plentitude, the Lacanian figuration of the maternal is curiously devoid of corporeality: Lacan reduces the maternal to a position (the imaginary) taken in reference to the Law. In contrast to both, the Shakespearean "grotesque" suggests just how thoroughly the maternal can be saturated with specific bodily attributes. If Shakespeare persistently records the horror of an omnipresent maternal materiality, if object-relations indulges in a fantasy of the maternal embrace, Lacan just as assiduously denies the maternal as a *body*. Denial, idealization, and hyperbole are equally defensive reactions to a female biology that cannot be escaped, but whose meanings are not fixed or immutable.

The question to pose to both the *Henriad* and psychoanalysis is not who is the appropriate parent – the harsh, guilt-provoking father who administers gender and erotic difference through his Law, or the easy, libidinally free mother who signifies both nurturance and suffocation – as if, like judges in a custody battle, we are bent on determining which parent represents the best interests of the child. I am not advocating Falstaff as Woman of the Year, Mom of the Month, or Queen for a Day, nor do I mean to idealize his obvious faults: his greed, his egotism, his manipulation of others. Rather, what is at issue in both the Shakespearean and psychoanalytic dramas is why the parent who is rejected, metaphorically killed, is figured in the iconography of the female body, and why the mature heterosexuality of the male subject – the *Henriad*'s "star of England" (*H.V.* V Epilogue 6) – depends upon this repudiation.[52]

Psychoanalysis tells us that the mother is rejected in the "normal" course of individuation, the alternative being to remain neurotically attached to or dominated by her. But surely this narrative of the individuation process is defensive in its own right. As Chodorow writes:

> it is possible to be separate, to be differentiated, without caring about or emphasizing difference, without turning the cognitive fact into an emotional, moral, or political one. In fact, assimilating difference to differentiation is defensive and reactive, a reaction to not feeling separate enough.[53]

When it emphasizes the excessive, overwhelming, engulfing mother, psychoanalysis exposes its own paranoia that, were it not for the decisive entrance of the father, the contiguity of the pre-oedipal period would seductively go on and on. What such a suspicion disguises is the belief that women are incapable of defining, enforcing, and representing cultural exigencies. This relegation of women to a space and time prior to culture is both a defensive denial of the cultural work mothers perform daily, and a masking and projection of the longing to live outside the imperatives of the symbolic in an endless and seamless "semiotic."

To my mind, neither rigid adherence to the symbolic nor immersion in the semiotic are viable alternatives; posing the problem in these terms simply reproduces the gender system in place. Indeed, the maternal body is a nexus of ambivalence and radical instability: representative simultaneously of lack and excess, nurturance and betrayal, it encompasses the most basic poles of positivity and negativity within which our individual subjectivities are formed. Insofar as it inhabits both the semiotic and the symbolic, the maternal is a potentially privileged position from which to interrogate precisely the binarisms that constitute our apprehension of subjectivity. As Sprengnether writes, following Kristeva:

> The body of the (m)other provides its own sources of signification and ultimately a ground for reconciliation between the preoedipal (m)other and culture, between the (m)other and the Symbolic order. . . . The condition of pregnancy creates a radical paradox in terms of subjectivity. The mother is neither one nor two but two-in-one, her body the ground of an otherness that is nevertheless experienced as an aspect of self. . . . The function of the father . . . to divide the mother from her infant seems hardly necessary if division has already taken place, if division is somehow embedded in the process by which each individual consciousness emerges into being.[54]

And yet, the dangers of using the body (either the phallus or pregnancy) as the ground of signification of the subject is in essentializing and fixing the meaning of what is really a process. The body provides a *context* within which the development of subjectivity occurs, but it is neither source nor grounding of the subject. The status of the maternal body, like that of the phallus, cannot be rendered *as such*; known to us through our fantasies – of subjection, dependency, power, control – it doesn't signify outside of those social relations. Like history, the body is not so much a thing, an aggregate of facts, as a process which cannot be divorced from the intersubjective matrix from which it evolves.

Refiguring of the maternal, then, must give priority to the lived experience, the intersubjectivity, of mothers – the ones who predominantly carry out the demanding, crucial, if still devalued work of caring for children. Such a refiguration would begin with the refusal to conflate the maternal and the pre-oedipal, recognizing that maternal *desires*, including erotic desires, precede and continue long after the pre-oedipal dyad is dissolved. Reproductive capacity has no necessary relation to the use of that capacity; and the choice to reproduce has no necessary relation to the psychic relationship that may subsequently develop with the infant carried in the womb. As long as the actual experiences of mothering are ignored or, alternatively, mystified and idealized, the maternal will be vulnerable to the logic of the replacement of the "grotesque" by the "classical" body. The experience of mothers suggests that it is possible to negotiate between various cultural necessities – open/closed, inside/outside, the imaginary/the symbolic – without forming allegiances or hierarchizing value. Refiguring the maternal would not alter the disunification of all subjects in language – the replacement of the phallus as signifier of substitutive desire would not change the fact that all desire remains, in the words of Ellie Ragland-Sullivan, "a shadow pantomime of the primordial drama of Desire"[55] – but it would detach the pain of loss from real mothers, real women.

The *Henriad* gestures toward the possibility that the maternal body may possess desires of her own. Although Falstaff is contained within a paradigm of the grotesque body, his strategies of self-representation prefigure maternal agency. Such agency, however, is deeply compromised: not only enacted by a male actor, but figured through a male character, maternal desires in the *Henriad* are always already re-figured in the shape of masculine projections.[56]

In the *Henriad*, subjectivity, gender, and sexuality are inseparable. For Prince Hal, subjectivity is imaginable only in gendered terms: to be a person is to be his father's son, which is to be his father's heir, which is to be a soldier, which is to be a king whose gender identification is maintained by the homosocial exchange of women in heterosexual marriage. As Henry V says to Katharine: "If thou would have such a one, take me. And take me, take a soldier; take a soldier, take a king" (*H.V*, V.ii.166–8). And just as subjectivity is meaningful largely in terms of gender, so too is sexuality. To be masculine in Henry's world is to be the active subject of a sexualized violence and a violent sexuality. It is never clear which is cause and which effect: does the fantasized maternal *produce* a "grotesque" sexuality, or does a particular construction of sexuality trigger a fantasy of the grotesque maternal?

The unanswerability of these questions within the logic of the *Henriad* – the circuitous interdependency of subjectivity, sexuality, and gender – is, I believe, one of the most powerful legacies of Shakespeare's histories and tragedies, and is one reason why Shakespeare's plays so often seem a preview of the works of Freud. Both authors tend to view gender as a totalization; it subsumes whatever it touches. Most recently, the psychoanalytic infatuation with "desire," referring simultaneously to subjectivity, sexuality, and gender, replicates this totalizing impulse – as if, because gender and subjectivity are constituted contemporaneously they are identical, as if sexuality were reducible to gender roles. Interestingly enough, it is the *difference* between sexuality and gender that Shakespearean comedy explores – but that is the subject of the following chapters.

It would hardly be fitting to finish this discussion of the maternal in the *Henriad* without mentioning the two mothers to whom its fantasy of repression is implicitly addressed. Henry of Monmouth's mother, Mary de Bohun, conveniently died in 1394 when the prince was seven or eight, thus denying us her articulation of maternal desire, and doing her part to ensure the relative absence of women in Shakespeare's histories.

The other maternal figure was not so obliging. Indeed it is not, I think, fortuitous that the *Henriad*'s phallocentric representation of power and the corresponding repression of women were staged at the moment when the most powerful person in the country, Queen Elizabeth, a woman, was in her sixties, having given birth to no heir.[57] As the repeated interest in and intrigues surrounding Elizabeth's marriageability attest, hers was not only the body upon which power was anointed, but the body over which power was contested. To the extent that the *Henriad* limits the reign of power to the male subject, its compensatory function is complicated, doubling back upon itself in a negation of the Virgin Queen. Present in *Henry V* only as "our gracious Empress," Elizabeth I is supplanted by Henry V who, in his colonization of Katharine, decisively reverses Essex's subordinate position.[58]

And yet, as much as Elizabeth's rule might elicit such reactive textual strategies, as a historical agent she was not contained by phallic discourse. Indeed, as Louis Adrian Montrose has noted, her astute manipulation of virginal, phallic, maternal, and paternal metaphors transformed "the political liability of her gender to advantage for nearly half a century."[59] Elizabeth's own instantiation of the classical body – a secular Virgin Mary married to the Kingdom of England – allowed her to invest "her maternity in her political rather than in her natural body,"[60] while her adoption of the identities of Prince, Husband, and Shepherd underscored the particularly phallic pretensions of her rule.[61] Elizabeth's gradual assimilation of her father's kingly identity which, according to Leah Marcus, "allowed her finally to become free of it, to discard his effacement of her sex, his overbearing concern for the Tudor succession, his notion that royal authority had to be validated through the production of a masculine heir,"[62] is the obverse of Shakespeare's "feminization" of Falstaff: both strategies suggest the pervasiveness of the equation of masculinity and rule, as well as the possibility of that equation's deconstruction. As an aging, "grotesque" body, and as the "virginal mother" to whom the *Henriad*'s fantasy of repression is indirectly addressed, Queen Elizabeth acts simultaneously as inciter of male anxiety and model for its compensatory mediation. Indeed, her manipulation of gender and sexual ideologies shares with Shakespeare, Freud, and Lacan the pervasive circularity of phallocentric representation: not only is power constitutive of gender and sexuality, but so too are gender and sexuality constitutive of power.

Such a reading allows us to see that phallocentric culture is neither monolithic nor impregnable, in part because it stages its own necessary exclusions – the others, in diacritical opposition to whom its own identity is constructed. Those others are also historical actors who, like Queen Elizabeth and no doubt countless other early modern women, found their own space of power within a determinate field of constraints. Both Falstaff and Katharine are constructed in order to be repudiated or subjugated as the basis upon which Prince Hal assumes phallocentric control as King Henry V. But, to the extent that their exclusions are *enacted*, and to the extent that Falstaff "impregnates" the drama with maternal desire, Falstaff and Katharine suggest ways in which the phallocentric order might be undermined. I am arguing, then, not for Shakespeare as proto-feminist or the *Henriad* as *her*story, but rather for a recognition of the return of the repressed in the act of psychoanalyzing psychoanalysis and the Shakespearean text.

Chapter 3

Invading bodies/bawdy exchanges: disease, desire, and representation

The discourses that have contributed to the global crisis of AIDS demonstrate the extent to which the body can be constructed as a vulnerable enclosure, with its erotic apertures positioned as sites of and conduits for contamination. Representations of AIDS also testify to the tendency to place blame for epidemics on those others who are vulnerable by virtue of their erotic practice or racial/national origin.[1] Such twentieth-century preoccupations are prefigured by early modern constructs of venereal disease in which gender, erotic, and nationalist anxieties were managed by conferring blame on those who, by reference to their social status or geographical location, could be considered not merely inferior but inherently contaminated. The early modern terminology of syphilis, for instance, points to an endless deferral of origin and cause: in a dizzying displacement of culpability, syphilis made its way into the British vocabulary as the "French pox" or "morbus gallicus"; the Parisians alternately rerouted the disease to be Germanic or Italian in origin – "morbus Germanicus" or "la maladie Napolitiane"; the Germans placed the blame on the Italians and the French: "mal de Naples," "morbus gallicus," "malafranzcos" or "Franzosenkrankheit." The Turks pointed the finger to *their* others, "male dei cristiani," while Africans blamed the Jews who had been driven out of Spain.[2] In each case, xenophobia protected the nation, if not the nation's bodies, from disease. Itinerants – Jews and gypsies – were the primary focus of scapegoating until 1539, when the origin of syphilis was further displaced onto the New World: according to this new theory, the disease was introduced to Europe by Spanish sailors who engaged in sexual relations with Haitian women during the second of Columbus' voyages.[3] Whatever the possible facticity of the "Columbian hypothesis" –

and it remains a matter of debate in the medical community today – it is clear that early modern "America" functioned in the European imagination much as does "Africa" in some Western minds today: a foreign, "primitive" continent, inhabited by "savages" practicing exotic and diseased sexual behaviours.[4]

Many contemporary critics have argued that the orifices of the body metonymically figure the vulnerabilities of the gendered psyche and the nation.[5] The specific ways in which bodies are constructed can thus be read as maps of both the subject's and the state's self-representation. *Troilus and Cressida* provides a particularly telling rendition of the vulnerabilities of the erotic body and the body politic. In this play, faithlessness to nation is synonymous with faithlessness to love, as the position of Helen so palpably indicates: whether she remains in Troy or is forcibly carried back to Greece, her transfer of affection from Menelaus to Paris suggests that the mobility of her person goes hand in hand with the mobility of her desire. Likewise, erotic mobility is clearly the main stake in Cressida's movement from Trojan walls to Grecian camp, and the subsequent transformation of her identity from Trojan beauty to "The Troyans' [s]trumpet" (IV.v.64).[6] Within the nationalist framework of the play, at issue for both women is whether they are to be positioned as idealized or degraded objects of male desire – in the vernacular of the play, as "pearls" or "plackets"[7] – and the answer depends, in part, on which nation (and which man) claims their allegiance.[8]

Questions of nationalist and erotic identity, then, are consistently intertwined: it is those "merry Greeks", after all, defined as morally and sexually loose, who seek to penetrate the walls of a Troy also already defined via Paris' abduction of Helen as sexually licentious.[9] Much in the play contributes to a linking of war and sexuality: early on, Cressida quips that she will lie "Upon my back, to defend my belly" (I.ii.262), and she continues this line of reasoning when she tells Troilus she will "war with" him over the ability to remain honest (III.ii.169). On a more cynical level, Thersites sums up the Greek/Trojan conflict thus: "all the argument is a whore and a cuckold" and "war and lechery confound all" (II.iii.71–74). Indeed, René Girard argues that metaphorically embodied in the Greek/Trojan war is the very essence of sexuality: a "mimetic desire" for the object of one's rival, in which identity is constructed through the envious gaze of the other.[10] More recently, Linda Charnes intriguingly argues that within the play's circularity

of desire and aggression is a male homosocial ethos that produces a
myth of heterosexuality. Whereas many critics view the homoerotic
relation of Achilles and Patroclus as the ultimate corruption of sexuality, with sodomy carrying the signifying burden of the "unnatural,"
Charnes views male homoerotic aggression as one moment in an
endless cycle of exchange producing the Trojan war.[11]

To my mind, however, it is less male homoeroticism than sexual
exchange *per se* that signifies psychic dis-ease in this play, as literal
venereal disease is posed as the necessary outcome of all erotic
liaisons. That is, just as the equation between war and sexuality
sums up erotic relations in *Troilus and Cressida*, so too does a
further tropological substitution specify the empty content of
"sexuality." If war equals sexuality, then sexuality equals syphilis.
If state-sponsored masculine aggression fundamentally motivates
(and provides the appropriate metaphor for) erotic encounters, then
"penetration" is not merely represented by the "invading bodies" of
the Trojans, but also by the "invaded bodies" of those afflicted with
venereal disease.

"Diseases" is the final word of *Troilus and Cressida*, and metaphors
of disease are invoked to describe all the major problems in the play,
from Nestor's comment that "all our power is sick" (I.iii.139); to
the "infection" of "plaguy" self-pride charged against Achilles and
Ajax (I.iii.187, II.iii.176) and the "envious fever" of emulation
that spreads throughout the Grecian camp (I.iii.133); to Troilus'
characterization of his love for Cressida as "the open ulcer of my
heart" (I.i.55). Contagion is not only the imagistic base, but the
goal of Thersites' curses:

> the rotten diseases of the south, the guts-griping, ruptures,
> catarrhs, loads o' gravel i' the back, lethargies, cold palsies,
> raw eyes, dirt-rotten livers, wheezing lungs, bladders full of
> imposthume, sciaticas, limekilns i' th' palm, incurable bone-
> ache, and the rivell'd fee-simple of the tetter, take and take again
> such preposterous discoveries!
>
> (V.i.17–24)

A rhetoric of contagion not only "contaminates" the action of the
play, it supplies the central signifier of desire: desire *is* disease,
the play seems to say, and both are posed as a military problem,
defined in terms of attack and defense.[12] The play in fact presents
three interconnected fantasies of invasion: the prophesied (and, for
the audience, legendary) Greek penetration and destruction of the

walled city of Troy, the syphilitic infection of individual bodies, and the incursion of the "diseased" (Pandarus, Cressida, and prostitutes generally) into the body politic.[13] The multiple deployment of these fantasies renders desire not only contagious, but deadly.

Let us return to Thersites' remark in full: "All the argument is a whore and a cuckold, a good quarrel to draw emulous factions and bleed to death upon. [Now the dry serpigo on the subject, and war and lechery confound all.]" (II.iii.71–4). Syphilis – the "dry serpigo" – is invoked both as a description of the subject (the argument, the war) and as a curse upon it. Thersites is merely repeating what he said 50 lines earlier: "After this, the vengeance on the whole camp! Or rather, the Neapolitan bone-ache! For that, methinks, is the curse depending on those that war for a placket" (II.iii.17–19). Those that fight over a woman – woman defined as a "slit in the petticoat" and thereby through her genitals – deserve for their foolishness the "Neapolitan bone-ache." Here, aching bones becomes a symptom not only of disease but of male heterosexual desire and, in Charnes' terms, the male homosocial desire that fuels the continuation of the war. Thersites' use of the equivocal "depending on" suggests that disease not only *threatens* but *depends on* those who em-body the co-incidence of sexuality and war. Through such "bawdy exchanges," syphilis becomes a displaced signifier for the anxieties potentially inhering in *all* bodily exchanges.

The exchange of bodies is a primary thematic and structuring principle of the play: not only is Cressida traded "in right great exchange" for the Trojan prisoner Antenor (III.iii.21; IV.ii; IV.iv), and then passed from one kissing Greek to the next (IV.v), so too the possibility of giving Helen back to the Greeks is forcefully argued between Troilus and his brothers (II.ii). Not only does Cressida allegedly "substitute" Diomedes for Troilus (V.ii), but the entire war is fought over Helen's purported "exchange" of Menelaus for Paris.[14] And, what is war, if not the exchange of live bodies for dead? Bodily exchange forms the basis of the play's representation of both sexuality and war; it symbolizes, in fact, the interchange between sexuality and war that serves as the play's pretext.[15] In this context the bawdy exchanges about venereal disease take on a special significance, metaphorically and metonymically replicating and enhancing the play's irreducibly interwoven erotic and militaristic significations.

What is at stake, ultimately, in the mutual implication of disease, desire, and bodily exchange is the identity and relation of subject

and state. Insofar as the body metonymically represents the subject as a whole, the body's vulnerabilities to both disease and
desire demonstrate the tenuousness of a subjectivity constructed
in relation to social processes. Indeed, the intersection of desire and
disease intimates the extent to which subjectivity can be "spoiled"
by forces external to it. Not only does syphilis transform the body
into something alien, something repulsively other,[16] it introduces
a biological and social force into the state that could not, in those
days, be managed or contained.[17] Like those desires that initiate the
Greek/Trojan war, early modern syphilis seemed paradigmatically
excessive, not only in its ravages of the individual body, but in its
epidemic march across the polity. Like leprosy, syphilis was, in
Steven Mullaney's terms, an "incontinent disorder," an illness that
"exceeded the bounds of community and classification."[18] And like
the symptoms of leprosy in the culture at large, the symptoms of
syphilis in *Troilus and Cressida* function as

> manifestations of a disorder that [is] both particular and per-
> vasive, signs of disease in an individual body and signs whose
> frame of reference extend[s] to the culture as a whole, signaling
> on a figurative level a disorder to which the body politic itself
> [is] vulnerable.[19]

As invasion of body and state, as symbol of erotic and social
incontinence, syphilis demands, within the defensive logic of
Troilus and Cressida, corresponding military action.

In his assertion of "mimetic desire" as the primary mode of exchange
in *Troilus and Cressida*, René Girard remarks:

> Pandarus, the go-between, the *mediator* of desire . . . plays no
> political role but . . . nevertheless rightly appears as the symbol
> of everything in the play, the alpha and the omega of *Troilus
> and Cressida*. He is on stage at the beginning, and he is on stage
> again at the end. In his Rabelaisian epilogue he bequeaths to
> the spectators a venereal disease that had not been mentioned
> earlier, and that seems to turn him almost into an allegory of
> the contagious power of mimetic desire.[20]

Syphilis, however, *had* been alluded to earlier, not only in the
above statements of Thersites, but also in Hector's allegation that
Grecian women are "sunburnt" (I.iii.282), and in puns on "sodden

business" and "stew'd phrases" (III.i.41).[21] Girard's effacement of such references, and in particular references to the disease's vivid material reality, seems to serve his effort to translate syphilis into a disembodied allegory of mimetic desire. Contagion in Girard's schema is pre-eminently psychological, an epidemic of envy and emulation: "Emulation is mimetic rivalry itself. It creates many conflicts but it empties them of all content."[22] But what if we were not to allegorize Pandarus or syphilis, but to take both quite literally and materially, resisting the structuralist urge to empty the epidemic of content, and instead placing the dramatic representation of syphilis within the historical discourses of the sixteenth century? The epidemic of syphilis that "invaded" Europe a century before Shakespeare's play continued well into the Tudor period; and insofar as no cure had yet rendered the disease less fatal – Thersites calls it the "*incurable* bone-ache" (V.i.22) – it is likely that its ravages were the focus of considerable anxiety.

At the same time, the meaning of syphilis was, from its inception, ideologically constructed. Indeed, as Bruce Boehrer argues, the *discovery* of syphilis is also an *invention*.[23] That is, while it seems true that a possibly new disease emerged in epidemic form in Naples in 1494, and quickly made its deadly way across Europe (reaching England by 1498 and Japan about twenty years later), it is also true that the English discourses in which the symptoms and possible treatments of "morbus gallicus" were described worked as more than description: not only were the names given the disease a signifier of nationalist sentiment, but the terms by which the medical and legal discourses defined the victims, carriers, and healers of the scourge were also ideologically invested. Boehrer's analysis of early modern representations of syphilis concludes:

> syphilis is invented as a new medical category and various treatments are explored when the illness becomes a recognized challenge to the power elite. . . . [It] comes into being *as a treatable ailment* only when it is associated with those figures at the heart of the political and social order. . . . When identified with the poor and socially undistinguished, the disease almost ceases to be a disease at all; instead, it emerges in its concomitant character as an instrument of discipline and punishment – that is, as an appendage of government itself.[24]

Gender as well as nation and class affected the representation of syphilis: women were uniquely figured as carriers of the disease, perhaps because of their perceived immunity – a common belief supported by the less visible symptomology on female genitalia in comparison to the penile sores and painful urination of men.[25] More to the point, this positioning of women as vessels but not victims of syphilitic contamination draws upon the cultural reservoir of disgust which animates other early modern representations of women's erotic desire. Add to this disgust the image of syphilis as a threat not only to man, but ultimately to nation, and we find gender, nationalistic, and erotic anxieties converging in a powerful demonstration of othering: through a particular ideological slippage, the possibly diseased "woman" comes to equal the potentially invasive "foreigner."

The history of syphilis, then, is the history of the construction of various *boundaries* of disease, formulated along mutually reinforcing nation, class, and gender lines. These material boundaries served a psychological function of defense: by drawing lines of differentiation between victims and carriers, elite males both enhanced their own sense of medical emergency and freed themselves from responsibility for transmission.

If, as Boehrer argues, early modern syphilis emerges not simply as a medical crisis but as a "managed political event," then it makes sense to ask what ideological work Shakespeare's play performed in its own time.[26] It is hardly incidental that syphilis had from its inception been figured through literary constructs: many surgeons poeticized the disease, and in the sixteenth century the poet-surgeon Girolamo Fracastoro wrote the Latin poem whose depiction of the shepherd Sifilo gave the disease its modern name.[27] Indeed, this mutually sustaining relation between aesthetic, political, and medical events forms the basis of Shakespeare's representation of syphilis in *Troilus and Cressida*.

In a culture so dedicated to displacing blame for disease, and in a play so concerned with the need to affirm nationalist boundaries, it would not be surprising to see venereal disease projected onto the foreign others against whom the identity of the state is maintained. Although the Greek and Trojan warriors do not employ such metaphors, privileging instead the language of chivalry to mediate their conflict, the primary observer of and commentator on battle does, as Thersites indifferently heaps curses upon Greek and Trojan alike. As spokesman against lechery who imagines it lurking everywhere, Thersites embodies the quality of *projection*.[28] Since there is "nothing but lechery," "Lechery, lechery, still wars and lechery; nothing else holds fashion," he indifferently flings curses on both camps: "A burning devil [venereal disease] take them" (V.i.98; V.ii.198–200).[29] Finally, in a powerful conflation of the physical wasting of disease that owes much to the early modern confusion between syphilis and leprosy, he observes: "lechery eats itself" (V.iv.35).[30]

What is less expected, perhaps, is that as much as the disease is projected outward, the inverse is equally true: syphilis in *Troilus and Cressida* is the foreign disease that is paradoxically always already *within*. "Syphilis is Us," Pandarus intimates at the end of the play, as, having crossed over onto the liminal ground of the blood-soaked plains outside Troy, he invites the audience into a bawdy partnership of prostitution and venereal disease:

> A goodly medicine for my aching bones! O world, world, world! Thus is the poor agent despis'd! O traders and bawds, how earnestly are you set a-work, and how ill requited! Why should our endeavor be so lov'd and the performance so loath'd? What verse for it? What instance for it? Let me see:
>
>> Full merrily the humble-bee doth sing,
>> Till he hath lost his honey and his sting;
>> And being once subdu'd in armed tail,
>> Sweet honey and sweet notes together fail.
>
> Good traders in the flesh, set this in your painted cloths:
> As many as be here of Pandar's hall,
> Your eyes, half out, weep out at Pandar's fall;
> Or if you cannot weep, yet give some groans,
> Though not for me, yet for your aching bones.
> Brethren and sisters of the hold-door trade,
> Some two months hence my will shall here be made.
> It should be now, but that my fear is this,
> Some galled goose of Winchester would hiss.
> Till then I'll sweat and seek about for eases.
> And at that time bequeath you my diseases.
>
> (V.x.35–56)

How has the bee lost his phallic sting? His impotence, the rest of the passage implies, is caused by syphilis, its distressing material effects graphically represented in decaying eyes, aching bones, and the sweating cure.[31] Pandarus' repetition of venereal references constructs himself as a walking em-body-ment of syphilitic inter-change, while his construction of the audience-as-bawds (Brethren and sisters of the hold-door trade) assumes, indeed depends upon, their prior contamination. The "trader in the flesh" who constantly bewails his aching, syphilitic bones (V.iii.105) thus gives voice to the underlying anxiety of the play: we are all already infected.

This paranoid fantasy is related to the discourse of prostitution which "infects" the play, and of which Pandarus comprises a major part. In *Troilus and Cressida*, prostitutes are vessels and primary agents of disease;[32] they have presumably contracted their illness by some means, but that means is never specified, instead lurking murkily in the play's non-dramatized pre-history. This dramatic strategy reproduces the dominant paradigm of disease in which moral sign and physical manifestation are one: as agents of moral corruption, prostitutes are "naturally" agents of physical corruption as well. That this unidirectional causality is asymmetrical in its gender alignments is obvious: female prostitutes infect men, never the other way around, and men are uniquely vulnerable by means of their excessive lust. It is this vulnerability to lust and disease – or the lust that *is* disease – that is displaced onto Pandarus: as voyeur of and procurer for *other* men's lusts, he is implicated, not only in prurient pleasure at other men's pleasures, but in the infectious dangers to which their desires are subject. Add to this heterosexual vulnerability Pandarus' role as instigator of female corruption – his function as pimp – and he comes to represent simultaneously the male victim and the female cause of disease. The effect of this doubling is the enormous power of the horrific fantasy he expresses, a power incommensurate with his putative function in the plot.

Victim and agent, Pandarus represents both the manifest sign and the psychic *internalization* of the disease. By giving Pandarus the final say, the play, however uncomfortably, positions him as authority, summing up from the other side Thersites' denuncia-tions of war and lechery. By means of these characterizations, *Troilus and Cressida* holds in tension two fantasized trajectories: on the one hand, Thersites' representation of the Greek/Trojan conflict dramatizes the tendency to project outward the threat of contagion, to expel it and attach it to others. On the other hand, Pandarus gives voice to the fear that impels such projective desire: contamination already lurks within the perpetually vul-nerable body. Seemingly oppositional, these fantasies are in fact two aspects of a mutually sustaining mode of defense, each diacritically necessitating the other.[33] Despite their diametrical positioning as bawd and anti-bawd, Pandarus and Thersites are in essential agreement about the nature of desire. Any tension between their two responses collapses, as Pandarus and Thersites adopt opposite yet symmetrical strategies to psychically manage the threat that the "venereal" *is* disease. Between the articulations of these two spokesmen, *Troilus and Cressida* denies the possibility of "choosing" between alternative "viewpoints"; insofar as each term and each response is integrally constitutive of the other, the system of representation governing the play allows no escape from the circularity of disease and desire, projection and internalization. Hence the sense of suffocation, of claustrophobia we feel when reading or watching this play.

It is a claustrophobia which would have been experienced even more acutely by Shakespeare's audience, for the play's representation of desire and disease is informed by an awareness of the theater's status as site of contamination. If, as Sander Gilman suggests, "The fixed structures of art provide us with a sort of carnival during which we fantasize about our potential loss of control, perhaps even revel in the fear it generates within us, but we always believe that this fear exists separate from us,"[34] then Pandarus' transgression of the usual epilogic function (inviting the audience's consumption and approval) transgresses the conventional function of drama as well. Rather than offering a psychic strategy of separation, distance, projection, and hence imagined safety, Pandarus forces audience members to confront their own position within the representational nexus of the play, and thus their own possible hopes and fears: that in partaking of the "common" pleasure of dramatic spectatorship they will be implicated in the desire and disease, prostitution and corruption, circulating throughout and around the "place of the stage."[35] Under Pandarus' auspices, not only the play, but the audience as well, is re-figured as a potentially "syphilitic body." In short, his speech elicits an uneasy recognition of the very vulnerabilities we rely on art to manage and control, vulnerabilities even more palpably experienced within the socially porous walls of the early modern theater.

And yet, despite Pandarus' powerful final appeal to a fantasy of internalization, much of the play has already endorsed the strategy of projection; indeed, projection structures the two central "exchanges" in the play. For what is Troilus' response to Cressida in the Greek camp if not projection, in which he "reads" the "worst" in Cressida's actions, eliminating the possibility of ambiguity, ambivalence or even adroit manipulation in her vacillating responses to Diomedes? Occupying Thersites' position of voyeur, Troilus – "O Cressid! O false Cressid! False, false, false!" – comes to the same conclusion as Thersites: "A proof of strength she could not publish more,/ Unless she said 'My mind is now turn'd whore'" (V.ii.182, 116–17).

But such a conclusion was already in the process of being implemented in the play. After Cressida is traded for the prisoner Antenor, and is physically passed from one kissing man to the next (in a scene that reads very close to gang rape), Nestor praises her quick and bawdy wit. Ulysses, however, powerfully responds with this enraged outcry:

> Fie, fie upon her!
> There's language in her eye, her cheek, her lip,
> Nay, her foot speaks; her wanton spirits look out
> At every joint and motive of her body.
> O, these encounterers, so glib of tongue,
> That give a coasting welcome ere it comes,
> And wide unclasp the tables of their thoughts
> To every ticklish reader! Set them down
> For sluttish spoils of opportunity
> And daughters of the game.

> (IV.v.55–63)

As elsewhere in Shakespeare, female glibness of tongue is made to correspond to a veritable "body language," in which women's oral facility signifies sexual wantonness. Indeed, her very body "speaks" a language, with "wanton spirits" emerging from every orifice, every "joint and motive of her body." Like Gertrude, Ophelia, Desdemona, Hermione, and Falstaff, Cressida becomes representative of the "grotesque body": impure, open, loose, transgressive. Too open in speech, excessively inviting in body, Cressida becomes positioned – is projected – as a member of the "hold-door trade," a "slut," a "daughter of the game," incontinent inciter of her own rape. By this moment in the play we all know with what "sluttish spoils" prostitutes contaminate their clients – and just in case we miss it, Pandarus' departing reference to "some galled goose of Winchester" [syphilitic prostitute] reiterates the point (V.x.54).[36] Indeed, with this representation of the disease that, in its circulation throughout the erotic body mimes its circulation throughout sexual society, we encounter the most paranoid version of the "grotesque body" as "a subject of pleasure in processes of exchange . . . never closed off from either its social or ecosystemic context."[37] Here, though, neither the imposition of death nor ritual expulsion are upheld as possible resolutions of psychic distress; instead, the play lingers over the guilt it layers onto the female contaminant. As Cressida is blamed as agent of contamination, the circulating meanings of sexual exchange become located, even fixed, in her physical being. Her body is transfigured into an "encounterer," the projected site of exchange of the desire that *is* disease. Reduced from subject to object, a veritable "spoil" of war, Cressida-as-encounterer serves the psychic function for the male characters of localizing and thus holding at arm's length the paranoid fantasy of diseased erotic circulation. Once Cressida's erotic being is so fixed, all that remains to take place is Troilus' and Thersites' interpretations, excoriations, and individual attempts to expel it. That Troilus does so through a tortured disavowal and splitting of Cressida's "identity" – "This she? No, this is Diomed's Cressid. . . . This was not she. . . . This is, and is not Cressid" (V.ii.136–50) – speaks tellingly both of the inordinate powers of projection and the tragic costs of expulsion.

If the "exchanges" of Cressida's erotic body scapegoat her in a fashion familiar to those who study the social effects of epidemic disease, so too does the language of bawdy defend against the anxieties occasioned by venereal dis-ease. At the risk of privileging heterosexuality for the sake of a pun, what is bawdy if not "verbal intercourse"? But what distinguishes bawdy from other (economic, theological, romantic) tropes of sexuality – its signifying difference if you will – is its consistent re-materialization of the body. Evident aurally through the verbal pun bawdy/body, this materialization insists on body parts and functions as more than signs and symbols of something else, rather, as pleasurable and/or offensive in the body's own terms. Bawdy references in *Troilus and Cressida* do not merely *express* a contaminated sexuality; they also mediate the anxieties of syphilitic contagion. Bawdy functions here in much the same way as do cuckold jokes in other Shakespearean plays – expressing male hostility and fear, but also acting as compensation, revising male powerlessness. As Carol Cook argues:

> The telling of cuckold jokes . . . restores the male prerogative: it returns the woman to silence and absence, her absence authorizing the male raconteur to represent her in accordance with particular male fantasies, and produces pleasure through male camaraderie.[38]

Cuckold jokes, however, are unavailable in this play due to Menelaus' status as cuckold *originaire*: cuckoldry can no longer function as a joke when it is the sole cause of a lengthy and unpopular war.[39] Instead, "bawdy" jokes take their place as the primary means to manage social anxieties stemming from gender, erotic, and national conflict. That is, bawdy jokes about syphilis not only express the isomorphic relations between war, desire, and disease, but also *defend against* the perceived vulnerabilities of the warring body politic and the erotic body. If the "heroes" of the war – Achilles, Hector, Ajax – assert power and masculine selfhood through violent fantasies of another's loss of identity and power (as when Achilles says to Hector, "Tell me, you heavens, in which part of his body/ Shall I destroy him? Whether there, or there, or there?" IV.v.242–3), the non-participants of battle – Thersites and Pandarus – consistently use bawdy as a less dangerous mode of defense. Both bawdy jokes and militaristic posturing mediate the vulnerability occasioned by erotic and military "exchange."

With erotic and nationalist identities under strain, bawdy works in conjunction with militarism to reassert boundaries between self and other, Us and Them. It is hardly coincidental that this mode of separation is also a dominant social response to epidemic disease.[40] To our earlier formulation, "war equals sexuality, sexuality equals disease," we can circle back again to the equation, "response to disease equals war." Asserting such an enclosed circuit of desires, *Troilus and Cressida* defies any effort to imagine a sexuality that is not defensive or diseased – in short, a desire that is not already thoroughly anxious.

Except, perhaps, one. Insofar as male homoeroticism interrupts the war, it threatens to short-circuit the mutually sustaining relations of disease, desire, and violence. Indeed, the representations of male–male love here register a yearning less for homoerotic relations *per se* than for an erotic modality uncontaminated by the equation of desire and disease. As Achilles substitutes dallying with

Patroclus "Upon a lazy bed the livelong day" (I.iii.147) for martial engagement on the battlefield, erotic bonds between men threaten to disrupt the persistent homosocial equation between martial and erotic "arms." Though male homoeroticism exists contiguously with male homosocial militarism, it instigates neither projection nor internalization, remaining remarkably non-defensive, untainted by the logic of disease pervading other erotic relations.

This non-infectious mode of sexuality, however, is ultimately abandoned, as Patroclus, under male homosocial pressure, adopts the militaristic perspective, encouraging Achilles to take to the field:

> To this effect, Achilles, have I mov'd you.
> A woman impudent and mannish grown
> Is not more loath'd than an effeminate man
> In time of action. I stand condemn'd for this;
> They think my little stomach to the war
> And your great love to me restrains you thus.
> Sweet, rouse yourself, and the weak wanton Cupid
> Shall from your neck unloose his amorous fold,
> And, like a dewdrop from the lion's mane,
> Be shook to air.
>
> (III.iii.216–25)

Despite Patroclus' obvious tenderness here, male homoeroticism becomes refigured as military battle, as Achilles defines Hector's proposed engagement with Ajax as a "maiden battle" (IV.v.87) void of penetration and bloodshed, clearly preferring his own bloody fantasies of penetration and dismemberment which are finally roused to action by Patroclus' death. All difference collapses between Hector's homosocial invitation to embrace martial "arms" (I.iii.265–79) and the playful, intimate embraces occurring within Achilles' tent. Ultimately, representations of homoeroticism remain confined within, and the language of bawdy reasserts, the circularity of war, desire, and disease.

But to focus on homoerotic desire as such goes against the erotic ethos of the play itself. For Troilus and Cressida declines to differentiate types of desire. Both Achilles and Troilus are "effeminized" by their desires; both temporarily avoid the military action that in this play constitutes the masculine subject. The difference, of course, is that Troilus' preoccupation with Cressida matters little to anyone on the field, whereas Achilles' defection constitutes a threat to the

entire operation of the war. Yet desire presents not only an inter-
ruption of the war; it is finally shown to be the animating impulse
for it. The literal or figurative "death" of the beloved impels both
warriors back into battle: Achilles to kill Hector, that "boy-queller"
(V.v.45), and Troilus to fight the man who wears his love-token in
his helm.[41] The overarching sense of rage surrounding Patroclus'
death and Cressida's "betrayal" dissolves any possible distinction
between types of desire in the heat of violence; indeed, the play
displays an *in-difference* to the gender of erotic object.

It hardly seems fortuitous that this erotic in-difference takes place
within an obsessive resurrection of other distinctions. For the play's
recurrent anxieties about disease and desire overlay another fear,
circulating throughout, of nondifferentiation. Ulysses' rhetorical
set-piece regarding degree, for instance, pleads the necessity of
hierarchical distinction; without degree, all is chaos:

> Then every thing includes itself in power,
> Power into will, will into appetite;
> And appetite, an universal wolf,
> So doubly seconded with will and power,
> Must make perforce an universal prey,
> And last eat up himself.
>
> (I.iii.119–24)

Appetite, an Elizabethan commonplace for desire, is presented as
oral self-destruction, in an image that introduces the paranoia that
"infects" all bodily references in this play, and specifically prefigures
Thersites' use of the lechery/leprosy conflation: "lechery eats itself."
The categorical implosion of the dyads lechery/leprosy, lust/disease
apparent throughout the play is vividly alluded to in this passage
in the image of the voracious, passionate body *eating itself*. Taken
together, desire, lechery, leprosy, and syphilis are shown to enact
a relentless march toward the body's extinction. And disease,
like appetite, is the terror within, precisely because it does not
differentiate, does not know distinctions.

So too with war. Although the rhetoric of war is conventionally dependent on distinctions (self/other, general/foot soldier,
valiant/cowardly), the actuality of battle abolishes all difference
in indiscriminate carnage. Thus it is entirely in keeping with the
play's portrayal of disease and desire that Achilles ambush and
massacre Hector, for with that action all moral claims based on
the distinction between self and other vanish. The militarism that

in this play frames and impels desire is just as vigorous in its pursuit of death, which itself involves the loss of distinction, the reception of the body back into the boundlessness of an eternal void. The terror of this insight generates the defenses employed against it, the psychic mechanisms by which distinctions of gender, status, health, and finally, life are reinscribed.

In closing, it is crucial to realize that my reading of *Troilus and Cressida* is itself "contaminated" by the discursive history of syphilis. That is, it is almost impossible to bracket off or ignore the ideological baggage that accompanies, indeed has constituted, the meaning of sexually transmitted disease in early modern and contemporary cultures. The problem, I hope to have shown, is not merely one of biology, but of representation. Any distinction between the material and the psychological is blurred in the hermeneutics of disease. If desire can seem to leave a material mark on the body – an open sore, an ache in the bones, blindness – it is because the body makes palpable the intimacy of the relation between the biological and the cultural. Because of this intimacy, however, the meanings of desire and disease are not fixed; they are formulated through a process of discursive inscriptions, of ancillary meanings that are mobilized and put to use by dominant structures of power, knowledge, and exchange. The feelings of horror *we* experience at the final moment of Pandarus' invitation to indulge in diseased prostitution, as he bequeaths to us *his* diseases, is out of proportion to the "real" impact of syphilis on *us*, for whom that particular disease is no longer fatal. Our response is in part due to the constellation of anxieties which continues to overdetermine the intersection of erotic desire and disease.

Troilus and Cressida makes no attempt to reconfigure disease, its representation of syphilis remaining thoroughly claustrophobic, even nihilistic. And yet, the impact of contemporary discourses on AIDS suggests that it is imperative that we find ways to represent disease *differently* – neither as divine retribution, nor, in the liberal tradition of which *Troilus and Cressida* is a part, as military invasion. As the rhetoric of "protected" intercourse and "safe" sex reformulates the body as military fortress, defending against the "invasion" of "foreign" bodily fluids, we find ourselves once more in a situation – in a system of signification – in which "we" protect ourselves from "them." But who are "we," if not also "them"? What is projection, if not a futile attempt to defend against the diseased significations we have internalized as inhering in sexuality? Our bodies *are* vulnerable: disease is an unhappy function of our mortality. But that mortality is neither curse nor punishment; it is an inescapable fact, for which the rhetoric of blame is an impoverished and inappropriate mode of defense. Unfortunately, it remains to be seen if we can refigure the ideological nexus of desire and disease, to de-moralize and de-mobilize the defensive meanings of their still fatal "exchange."[42]

Part II

Erotic possibility

Chapter 4

Desire and the differences it makes

As the previous chapters make clear, Shakespeare studies is currently characterized by an intense self-consciousness, a hyper-awareness, of its modes of inquiry and analysis. As meta-commentary succeeds commentary it is therefore increasingly imperative for critics not only to situate their own activity, but to reflect on the perhaps unforeseeable implications of their critical positions. In this spirit of meta-commentary, I begin by way of Marguerite Waller's deconstruction of the gendered slippages of Stephen Greenblatt's interpretation in *Renaissance Self-Fashioning* of Sir Thomas Wyatt's sonnet, "Whoso list to hunt":

> Coinciding with the essentializing rhetoric of the passage, there seems to be an assumption that the owner of this absolutist twentieth-century perspective is both male and heterosexual. The pronoun "he," referring to the male reader implied by Wyatt's poem, is unselfconsciously elided with a "we," referring to Greenblatt and his readers, who are decidedly, not generically human, but stereotypically male. 'The poet twice addresses the reader as a potential hunter – 'Whoso list to hunt, Who list her hunt' – both inviting and dissuading *him*, making *him*, reenact the poet's own drama of involvement and disillusionment. *We* share the passage from fascination to bitterness. . . ." In other words, Greenblatt's text not only exploits the Wyatt poem to enhance its own authority, but, in the bargain, obliterates the position of the female (or nonheterosexual male) reader. The two gestures, in fact, go together. The liberal guilt which Greenblatt so graciously wishes to share with his reader ("*we* are forced to take responsibility as translators in our own right") does not undo the act of usurpation

and colonization being perpetrated either on Wyatt's text or on the reader who does not identify with the thrills and disillusionments of the male traffic in women. On the contrary, the expression of guilt is one more indication that the critic wants his own position to be regarded as "natural," as politically and epistemologically beyond question. (One feels guilty about that which one assumes one knows and controls.) To put the case conversely, Greenblatt's own rhetoric of critical mastery effectively delegitimates both the past in relation to the present and the female in relation to the male.[1]

I quote Waller at this length because my own subject in this chapter is also the denial of difference – but not gender difference. Rather, my topic is the erasure of erotic difference – the difference in/of sexuality which since the late nineteenth century has been coded as "homosexual" – which Waller's passage, dedicated to the exposure of Greenblatt's elisions, paradoxically enacts. Indeed, her passage both includes and then elides erotic difference in precisely the way Greenblatt progresses from reference to "we ourselves" to "the reader" to "potential hunter" to "him." As Waller deconstructs Greenblatt's rhetoric, her passage moves from a criticism of his assumption of universal maleness and heterosexuality (lines 2–4), to a subordination through parentheses of the "(nonheterosexual male) reader" in relation to the "female" reader (lines 14–15), to an erasure of that nonheterosexual male reader completely in the summation of "the female in relation to the male" (final line).

What is it that allows (requires?) the elision of erotic difference at the same time as one reasserts gender difference? Let us look at another passage, by Jean Howard, who is discussing Olivia in *Twelfth Night*:

At the beginning of the play she has decided to do without the world of men, and especially to do without Orsino. These are classic marks of unruliness. And in this play she is punished, comically but unmistakably, by being made to fall in love with the crossdressed Viola. The good woman, Viola, thus becomes the vehicle for humiliating the unruly woman in the eyes of the audience, much as Titania is humiliated in *A Midsummer Night's Dream* by her union with an ass.[2]

The syntactical parallelism of the final sentence sets up a semantic equation of two humiliations: for Olivia to fall in love with the cross-dressed Viola is equal to Titania falling in love with an ass. But *are* they equal humiliations within their respective plays? Howard contends that same-gender love between women becomes the marker of the unnatural in *Twelfth Night*, as the play displaces the anti-theatricalists' concern with the potential of male sodomy (occasioned by the boy actors' female costuming) onto women. Her concern is to show how the "unruly woman" becomes an object of comedy. However, Howard's own admission that Olivia is punished "comically but unmistakably" begs the question of the subject of this humor. To whom is desire between women funny? Though Howard sees the comic objectification of female homoeroticism love as unfortunate, she assumes (without contextualizing this assumption in an essay replete with historical reference) that love between women was readily available as both source of humor and humiliation for members of Shakespeare's audience.

To pose the question of the historical meaning of homoerotic desire and its erasure in our critical process is not to devalue the work of Howard and Waller, which has been remarkably enabling to feminist criticism of Shakespeare and the early modern period. In fact, I choose as examples the work of such prominent critics to demonstrate that even in the most sophisticated feminist analyses, homoeroticism is the subject of peculiar rhetorical slippages; such slippages, I believe, indicate untheorized assumptions circulating throughout our critical discourse.

Take, for instance, the work of Lisa Jardine which, in a radical analysis of cross-dressing, highlights the homoerotic exchanges entailed by the phenomenon of the boy actor. In *Still Harping on Daughters: Women and Drama in the Age of Shakespeare*, she argues that the erotic *double entendres* of the cross-dresser were culturally accessible to early modern audiences, inviting comprehension and appreciation of the attractions of male homoeroticism. The object of desire in Shakespeare's cross-dressed heroines is the "potentially rapeable boy," the young androgyne who, in his "submissiveness, coyness, dependency, passivity, exquisite whiteness and beauty" echoes feminine attractions.[3] Jardine's account obviates the possibility of a "feminist" Shakespeare precisely because the boy actor's role is so evidently a role, a representation of woman conceived, interpreted, and acted by males.

However, despite Jardine's contention that "Wherever Shakespeare's female characters in the comedies draw attention to their own androgyny . . . the resulting eroticism is to be associated with their *maleness* rather than their femaleness," she also argues that the *specific* erotic charge of the boy actor lies in his ability to mimic the attractions of "femininity."[4] She thus unwittingly dilutes the specificity of gender involved in *male* homoeroticism. To argue that the "erotic interest which hovers somewhere between the heterosexual and the homosexual" finally descends on the boy actor's "femininity" reconstitutes this interaction as implicitly *hetero*erotic.[5] Whereas pederasty *may* have been the dominant mode of homoeroticism among literate men for whom the Greeks were familiar models, and may have been the model for aristocratic "libertines" for whom love of adolescents was merely one of a retinue of risqué behaviors, we have little evidence that it structured the majority of early modern homoerotic encounters.[6] To take pederasty and "effeminacy" as the primary models of homoerotic desire, to posit all homoerotic desire as organized around poles of activity and passivity, and then to conflate male–male interactions with male–female encounters reduces the complexity of homoerotic desires, styles, and roles – in Shakespeare's time and in ours.[7]

What is happening (rhetorically, theoretically, politically) when the female reader can stand for "nonheterosexual males" (Waller), when women's same-sex love is equated with comic bestiality (Howard), or when male homoeroticism is modeled on heterosexuality (Jardine)? And what is at stake when gender difference is signified through the sign of heterosexual intercourse, as in the work of feminist Lacanian Jacqueline Rose;[8] or when critics use synonymously such terms as sexual difference and sexual identity, androgyny and bisexuality, femininity/masculinity and heterosexuality? The difficulty most readers will have in even *identifying* a problem is precisely the problem. I hasten to point out that the first term in each of the above pairings (i.e., sexual difference, androgyny, femininity/masculinity) denotes a *gender* relation and the second term (sexual identity, bisexuality, heterosexuality) an *erotic* one. In other words, gender and sexuality pose as synonymous in our critical discourse in a way that not only despecifies our analyses but denies and delegitimates erotic difference. Whose interests are served by this denial of difference?

In "Thinking Sex: Notes for a Radical Theory of the Politics of Sexuality," Gayle Rubin challenges

> the assumption that feminism is or should be the privileged site of a theory of sexuality. Feminism is the theory of gender oppression. To automatically assume that this makes it the theory of sexual oppression is to fail to distinguish between gender, on the one hand, and erotic desire, on the other.[9]

The preceding examples make it clear, I hope, that feminists need to theorize more accurately the specific relations between gender and sexuality, beginning by questioning the assumptions that this relationship is isomorphic and historically constant. For the purposes of dissecting this relationship, we must be willing to place sexuality at the center, rather than on the implied periphery, of our analyses, and only after that (1) detail the way *specific* erotic discourses and practices are informed by or associated with gender discourses and practices, and (2) analyze how race, ethnicity, and class differences inform the relationship between sexuality and gender at specific moments in time. To assume that gender *predicates* eroticism is to ignore the contradictions that have historically existed between these two inextricably related yet independent systems. While they are always connected, there is no simple fit between them. Gender ≠ sexuality.[10]

Feminists, materialist feminists, cultural materialists, and new historicists implicitly draw on a psychoanalytic construct whenever they pose the question of "desire." "Desire," like "power," has taken on a certain currency in contemporary critical discourse, in part because the popularization of Lacanian psychoanalysis has offered so much to two broadly defined readerships: to gender critics, Lacanians offer a reading of the simultaneous construction of gender and sexuality that problematizes even as it upholds patriarchal prerogatives; to historical critics, Lacanians offer a theory of the radical contingency of a speaking subject always constructed through social practices. The psychoanalytic construct "desire" combines these concerns into a tripartite structure of a radically discontinuous subjectivity, gender, and sexuality, in which the unruliness of the unconscious undercuts the subject's pretensions to self-identity.

According to the psychoanalytic narrative, subjectivity, gender, and sexuality are constituted contemporaneously. I want to argue that it is precisely the capacity of "desire" to connote this mutual complicity and constitutiveness that has rendered it such a powerful, provocative, and perversely hegemonic construct. Perversely hegemonic because, despite its disruptive Lacanian valences, "desire" often works as a totalization that conceals the dynamic divisions inherent in its construction: rather than holding the specificity of gender and sexuality in mutual tension, it conflates and then collapses them into the supposedly larger matrix of subjectivity.

For instance, discussions regarding the meaning of female presence and the possibility of female power in early modern texts often hinge on assumptions about "feminine desire." By relying on a Lacanian revision of the Freudian dictate that there is only one "libido" (a masculine one), in which the structural exigencies of phallocentrism not only delimit but deny the possibility of "feminine desire," some critics come perilously close to writing out of representation and history all female agency.[11] By focusing their analyses on "woman" only as she is positioned within a supposedly monolithic symbolic order, critics lose sight of the degree of agency constructed from the contradictions and fissures within the symbolic. For it is in the schism between "woman-as-representation" and the plurality of women that a negotiation for power within and against the phallocentric order takes place.[12]

However, merely to reassert the presence of female agency in the form of "feminine desire" is not an adequate response to the problem of women's subjectivity. First, any assertion of agency must address those constraints placed on women's lives by the conceptual and material demarcations of a phallocentric system. But secondly (and this is my main concern), reinserting "feminine desire" into discourse reinscribes women's eroticism as always already defined and reified by the gender category "feminine." The adjectival link between "feminine" and "desire" neutralizes the difference between an ascribed gendered subject-position and the erotic experiences and expressions of a female subject. In a move that obscures the constructedness of subjectivity, gender, and sexuality, the female subject is defined in terms of a desire that is implicitly passive, heterosexually positioned in relation to man. Generated as an appeal, "feminine desire" in fact operates as a trick, a double bind for women always already confined by their previous definition. *How* a woman's sexuality is positioned in accordance to gender ascriptions, and the possibility of *resistance* to that positionality are questions foreclosed by the appeal to "feminine desire."

This mutually referential circularity of gender and sexuality in our critical discourse not surprisingly can be traced to Freud. In his attempt to advance over late nineteenth-century sexologists by dividing sexuality into three independent variables – physical characteristics, mental characteristics, and object choice – Freud implicitly recognized the possibility of conflict between biological inheritance, gender role behaviour, and erotic identification.[13]

And yet, in spite of this theoretical move toward greater specification, in practice Freud continued to conflate gender and sexuality, and to link both to biological inheritance. Despite his well-known disclaimer that passivity is not the exclusive province of women, nor aggressiveness the sole prerogative of men, Freud reproduced precisely these gender determinisms to connote erotic positioning and style. This becomes most evident when, in his case histories, the signifiers for male homosexuality become "effeminacy" and "passivity," and for lesbianism, "masculinity" and "activity."[14] Consider the following statement:

> [I]t is just those girls who in the years before puberty showed a *boyish character and inclinations* who tend to become hysterical at puberty. In a whole series of cases the hysterical neurosis is nothing but an excessive over-accentuation of the typical wave of repression through which *the masculine type of sexuality is removed and the woman emerges.*[15]

In this remark we can see two characteristic moves. First, through a rhetorical sleight-of-hand, the phrase "masculine type of sexuality" collapses into one construct precisely those components Freud had taken such pains to distinguish. In its relationship to "boyish character and inclinations," the phrase "masculine type of sexuality" refers to what Freud called sexual attitude or character (gender role conformity); in its relationship to sexuality, the phrase refers to homoerotic object choice. In the second rhetorical conflation, "woman" in the final clause becomes the sign, not only of proper gender role behavior, but heterosexual object choice. Both gender role conformity and heterosexuality correspond to the essential woman. Likewise, the young boy who expresses a "feminine attitude" takes on a "passive role" toward a male object;[16] the desire to be touched on his genitals rather than be the agent of phallic penetration is a "passive aim." "[P]assive homosexuals," according to Freud, "play the part of the woman in sexual relations."[17]

The vocabulary employed by Freud demonstrates that, theoretical protestations to the contrary, his work is caught within a nineteenth-century paradigm of "inversion" which assumes that "normal" heterosexuality follows unproblematically from ascribed gender role, and that disruptions in gender role result in deviant object choice. Despite the gender of the persons involved, Freud's concept of homoeroticism (like his concept of heterosexuality) is based on a gender model of "masculine" activity and "feminine" passivity.

Whenever critics use "desire" to refer simultaneously to gender and eroticism, we implicitly reassert this dualistic, patriarchal, normalizing history inherent in "desire's" formulation. Even when no explicit reference to "desire" is made, critics often unwittingly follow Freud in referring *gender* conflict (whether between men and women, or within a woman) to bi*sexuality*. Consider, for example, the following statement by Karen Newman, in her otherwise brilliant analysis of ambivalence toward female power in *The Taming of the Shrew*: "We might even say that this conflict [between female speech and silence] shares the *bi-sexuality* Freud claims for the hysterical symptom, that the text itself is *sexually ambivalent*."[18] Newman is arguing that *The Taming of the Shrew* empowers Kate, even as it subordinates her, by putting the power of speech (even if it is an encomium to subordination) in her own mouth. Such an argument is largely persuasive – except when it is led, via Freud, to conflate gender and sexuality. Whatever *gender* ambivalence the text expresses, it is distinct from the text's consistently *non-ambiguous* definition of female erotic desire as the projection and fulfillment of male heterosexual fantasy. In *The Taming of the Shrew*, female desire is encoded as the desire-of-the-man.

While many gender and historical critics remain caught within the circularity of this conflation of gender and eroticism, gay and lesbian cultural analysts are asserting a counter-discourse of "desire." In this discourse, gender and eroticism not only are explicitly differentiated, but each is given greater specificity, and both are referred back to their cultural origins. As in psychoanalytic literature, gender is conceived as a matter of core gender identity (the persistent experience of oneself as male, female, or ambivalent: I am a man, I am a woman, I am both/neither), but the "core" here does not pre-exist representation; rather, it is constructed through representation, specifically through the acquisition of language and clothing which are gender encoded. In addition, gender is a matter of gender *role* (the degree to which one complies with the societal expectations of "appropriate" behavior) and gender *style* (the personal choices one makes daily to assert agency within the confines of gender). Generally believed to be in place by the age of three, core gender identity is the least flexible of these constructs. Although it is usually "consistent" with anatomical sex,[19] transsexuals demonstrate not only the occasional fallibility of this process but also the highly inflexible nature of core gender identity once it is constituted. Gender role, while also ascribed by culture, is open to greater improvisation as each child positions him/herself in relationship to activities culturally coded (and historically variable) as "masculine" or "feminine." Gender style is an even more personal matter, and can be complicit with or in contradiction to one's gender role behaviour. The difference between gender role behaviour and individual gender style can be understood by recognizing that a woman who identifies as "feminine" might choose to wear jeans, work boots, and a leather jacket without disrupting her own sense of gender role (whatever it might do to others' expectations). Most feminists, it could be argued, are feminists precisely because their core gender identity (woman) does not correspond to many conventional social expectations of the "feminine"; even so, there is a great deal of variety in our gender styles.

Eroticism, like gender, is also given greater differentiation in this counter-discourse. Most importantly, eroticism is defined as independent of gender identity, behavior, and style. As a recent article in *Outlook* put it: "Wearing high heels during the day does not mean you're a femme at night, passive in bed, or closeted on the job."[20] Of course, there are periods in history when wearing high heels is an erotic signifier – indeed, in the 1940s and 1950s North American "butch-femme" lesbian culture, high heels were erotic signifiers of the first degree (as they were, for that matter, in North American culture generally). But what they signified within that context – passivity, availability, self-confidence, sexual courage – is still a matter of debate.[21] The point is that there is no necessary connection between eroticism and gender role conformity – any connection is a matter of culturally contingent signifying practices.

Eroticism itself is increasingly being defined less as a fixed identity dependent on the gender of one's partner, and more as a dynamic mode based on the sum of one's erotic *practice*. The gender of object choice is only one variable among many, including erotic identification, fantasy, and preference for specific activities, all of which intermingle and conflict in various ways.[22] Erotic identification refers to one's sense of self as an erotic object or subject – the position one takes up at any given moment in any given erotic encounter (initiating, receiving, playful, passionate, bored, etc.). In contrast to psychoanalysis' designation of activity and passivity as rigid states of being, in this counter-discourse one's erotic identification can switch from one moment to the next, one partner to the next, one year to the next; most people do, however, have a general erotic script that provides the degree of safety mixed with excitement necessary for erotic arousal and orgasm.[23] Fantasy, obviously, has two levels, both conscious and unconscious, with conscious fantasy further distinguished by those one enacts and those one merely dreams. As Cindy Patton argues, "fantasy and actual practice are separate and different. . . . Fantasy can retain qualities of ambiguity, impossibility, and a connection with atemporal desire that no experience at any given moment can have."[24] Preferences for specific activities (scenes and situations, combinations of oral, genital, and anal stimulation) and types of partners (male, female, gender-identified "masculine" or "feminine," vulnerable, nurturing, aggressive, nonemotional, etc.) further differentiate and individuate each person's erotic mode.

From the perspective of this counter-discourse, psychoanalysis reduces sexuality to one variable – object choice (whether "latent" or manifest) – which is presumed to flow directly from gender identity. The contradiction at the heart of this problem, as well as the alternatives posed by this counter-discourse, can be better understood by imagining oneself in the following voyeuristic scenario: When viewing a love scene on a movie screen, you experience pleasure by watching an interplay of power and erotic desire. Your eye is drawn to particular body zones, and you are aroused not only by body type and position, but also by the "scene," the pace of interaction, the affective content. But whether you are aroused by watching a woman's body or a man's, two women together or two men, a woman with a man, or any other combination imaginable, the mere fact of your excitement does not explain what is happening on the dual levels of identification and erotic desire. That is, is your arousal dependent upon a process of identification with or desire for an eroticized object? To state it simplistically, do you *want* or do you *want to be* one of the images on the screen? Which one? Can you tell? Does your identification and/or desire shift during the interaction? And are your desire and identification dependent upon the *gender* or any one of many other constituents of the image: power, class, status, age, relative aggressiveness, vulnerability, energic level, clothing, skin color/texture, hair type/length, genital size/shape . . . ? Do specific acts (sucking, penetration, kissing) seem more relevant to your identification and/or desire than the gender of persons involved?

Rather than explain the manifold possibilities inherent in this phenomenon – desiring and identifying with the same gender; identifying with one gender and desiring the other; desiring both genders; desiring or identifying on some basis other than gender – psychoanalysis asserts that desire will follow gender identification. Men desire women because their gender role positions them as active; women desire men because their own "lack" must be filled. Men who desire men do so because they have taken up a "feminized" passive position in relation to other males; lesbians desire women in imitation of active male desire. All sexuality engages in a structurally heterosexual mode of operation based on the duality of passivity and activity: whatever your biological sex, if you identify as/with a man, then you will desire a woman, and vice versa. That this theory fails to address the presence of "masculine" gay men and "feminine" lesbians is only made more evident by post-Freudian efforts to differentiate between the "true invert" and the seduced, corrupted "pervert."[25]

For those who actually live the contradictions inadequately addressed by psychoanalysis, the conflation of gender and sexuality is specious at best. Contemporary lesbians and gay men at various moments have constructed their own erotic significations through the use of a deviant vocabulary: "butch, rough-fluff, and femme," "top/bottom," and sign systems of hanky codes and key signals. It may seem as though the gender polarities that structure these signifying systems remain within the psychoanalytic frame of reference. Not completely, however: while butch/rough-fluff/femme designations continue to conflate gender and eroticism, they recognize an implicit continuum rather than a dichotomy of identifications, and there are no rigid assumptions structuring who can be involved with whom (i.e., a butch can be with another butch, a rough-fluff, or a femme). And, the S/M rhetoric of top/bottom asserts each individual's erotic position as a matter of play, varying with each erotic "scene." Similarly, the position of hankies on the hip and keys on the belt can be altered at any time.

And yet, the difficulty of extracting a new erotic vocabulary out of the polarities of gender testifies both to the enduring consequences of a highly gender-inflected language, and to the imaginative limitations of us all; we can barely conceive of an eroticism even partially free of gender constraints. At most we seem to be able to enact a politics of what Jonathan Dollimore calls transgressive reinscription, wherein dominant categories and structures are appropriated, inverted, and perverted.[26] The virtue of such a politics is that it does not defer pleasure and social change to an indefinite and impossibly pure future. But whatever the political limitations of contemporary erotic practice, the tactics employed indicate the need to push erotic theory toward the recognition that, both within an intra-psychic framework and on a systematic, structural level, the "sex/gender system" is related to but incommensurate with sexuality. Gender, sexuality, and subjectivity are separate but intersecting discourses.

To attempt to historicize "desire," to tease out the mutually impli-cated but distinct relation between gender and eroticism, is the obvious task. Such a project involves specifying erotic discourses and practices; describing institutional delimitations on erotic prac-tice; detailing the resistance of subjects to the ideological and material constraints upon their erotic lives; and tracing the play of erotic discourses and practices within history. Both the congruences and the contradictions between dominant ideology and material practice must undergo thorough analysis. More problematically, insofar as the material and subjective experience of the erotic can also contradict – desire, after all, is experienced not only in the contact between bodies, and between bodies and institutions, but through the experience of subjective need, want, anxiety, and fulfillment – the subjective quality of desire's historical formulation must also be approached.

The contradictions with which I am most concerned – between gender and eroticism; between dominant discourses and subversive practices; between subjective, internal need, and material, institu-tional pressures – all are foregrounded in the early modern British experience of homoeroticism. By "experience" I mean to suggest the whole matrix of discourses and practices, the negotiations, interchanges, assertions, withholdings, and refusals that occurred in reference to erotic desire between members of the same gender.

Before I proceed, it is perhaps important to acknowledge that by positing the presence of homoerotic desire and anxiety in early modern society and texts, I move against the social constructivist stance that locates the advent of "homosexuality" in either the eighteenth or the nineteenth century.[27] I do not mean to dispute the evidence that homosexuality in the modern sense (as a distinct mode of identity) came into being under the auspices of sexological discourse. Nor do I mean to imply, as some "essentialists" do, that the "experience of homoeroticism" is unproblematically available to the historically inquiring eye – that it exists in some pure form, unmediated by language, political discourse, and the process of historical narrativization. I *do* mean to contest two assumptions that currently hinder historical analysis: that because of our inevitably skewed apprehension of it, early modern homoerotic experience can be treated as if it never existed; and that because neither homosexuality nor heterosexuality existed in the precise forms they do today, we cannot posit some form of historical connection between their postmodern and early modern forms.

I thus put into play the following hypothesis: like all forms of desire, homoerotic desire is implicit within all psyches; whether and how it is given cultural expression, whether and how it is manifested as anxiety, is a matter of culturally contingent signifying practices. What is culturally specific is not the fact or presence of desire toward persons of the same gender, but the meanings that are attached to its expression, and the attendant anxieties generated by its repression. In this, I reject the dominant constructivist trend that sees specific desires as being *produced* independently by discursive practices, and return to Freud's assertion of the polymorphous perversity and nondifferentiated nature of the infant's earliest desire. However, whereas Freud myopically focuses on the family as site of erotic development, I, like the social constructivists, emphasize the ideological character of the process of subjectification, by which the various modalities of desire are manipulated and disciplined: some are, in Foucault's terms, incited by discursive practices and institutions; some are, in the terms of psychoanalysis, displaced or repressed. That cultural forms that could be considered homoerotic have existed in virtually all societies argues for this erotic modality's inherent position as potentiality; that what differs from society to society is whether homoeroticism is ritualized or privatized, gender-encoded or free of gender associations, vilified, tolerated, or celebrated implies the constitutive import of complex and often contradictory discursive practices and social investments.[28]

The critical approaches that have been employed to address the textual representation of early modern homoeroticism have functioned in fairly conventional ways. For many years, the dominant critical discourse on homoeroticism in Shakespearean drama has been that of narcissism: Shakespeare's most basic identity configuration, the mirror image, has provided a fertile field for the psychoanalytic rehearsal of Freud's linkage of narcissism, paranoia, and homosexuality.[29] Whereas I agree that questions of self and other are usefully posed through the self-reflexivity of the mirror, and that narcissism, like jealousy and madness, plays an important role in the structure of dramatic conflict, I disagree that such "identity themes" are necessarily linked to one erotic mode. I therefore question not only this model's normalizing pretensions, but also its presupposition of the object of inquiry. That is, it takes as a given what remains more properly a question: *is* there a connection between narcissism and homoerotic desire beyond the rather obvious banality of gender similitude? The commonsense proposition that heterosexual arousal depends on gender difference, whereas homoerotic excitement depends on gender sameness obscures both the implication of gender in larger systems of power and the role of difference in erotic arousal. Erotic arousal is always imbricated with power differences – it functions by means of exchanges, withholdings, struggles, negotiations. Arousal can be generated through the play of all kinds of differentiations: clothes, looks, gestures, ornaments, body size and type. Because of the institutionalized character of heterosexuality, gender has appeared as the sole determinant of arousal, but I suspect that gender is only one among many power differentials involved: arousal may be as motivated by the differences *within* each gender as by gender difference itself.[30]

Currently, the critical trend is to move away from psychoanalytic paradigms in one of two directions. First, in the model of male homosociality developed by Eve Sedgwick, male homoerotic desire is situated in relation to male homosocial bonds and the patriarchal traffic in women.[31] This paradigm provides important access to the complex and historically varying relation between erotic and gender systems, as the structural congruity and differences between homo*social* and homo*sexual* desire engenders a thematics at once homophobic and misogynist. Although homosociality and homo-sexuality appear to exist on a continuum, the former is con-stituted by a disavowal, indeed, a violent repudiation, of the latter. Homosociality in fact underscores patriarchal heterosexu-ality. Precisely because of the focus on homosociality, however, in Sedgwick's work the specific *sexuality* of homoerotic *practice* is elided. Drawing the social back into the erotic illuminates the desire which sustains patriarchal configurations, but it does little to articulate the meanings of homoerotic sexuality. Structural congruity is not isomorphism. For the purpose of Sedgwick's analysis, the overshadowing of the erotic by the social seems to serve as a necessary means to foreground the intersection of *women's* oppression and homosociality; but, as a methodological problem it becomes more acute in the work of other feminist critics enamored of the homosocial paradigm who are less consistently careful than is Sedgwick to assert allegiance to an antihomophobic politics. The uncritical use of this model thus risks reproducing a homophobic discourse in the interest of advancing a particular feminist agenda. That the model also tends to deny the availability of female agency is a related, though separate problem.

Invigorated by Sedgwick's contribution, a pre-existing "gay and lesbian studies" criticism of early modern texts has increased in rigor and sophistication.[32] Whereas I view this evolving body of work as refreshingly progressive, and am especially pleased to see critics of various erotic identifications engaged in its formulation, this criticism unfortunately re-enacts some of the problems of progressivism in general: that is, it uncritically accepts the polar-izing structure of its problematic. Within Shakespearean criticism, this method seems to align itself along one of only two axes: either Shakespeare, as victim of dominant ideology, participated in the homophobia that is seen as defining early modern discourse, or he defied such homophobia in celebrating homoerotic love. (Or, correlatively, Shakespeare was or was not homosexual.) The oppositional structure of this paradigm not only reproduces a false binarism of desire/attraction versus anxiety/phobia, but also employs a reductive account of cultural power – namely, that cultures (and authors) either unequivocally deny or affirm *any* erotic mode.[33]

That neither denial nor affirmation provides an adequate theor-etical model to account for the complexity of Shakespearean rep-resentations of homoeroticism is suggested, firstly, by the lack of unitary discourse on homoeroticism in early modern England. Not only did legal, moral, religious, and literary discourses understand and evaluate homoeroticism differently, but within each discourse there existed contradictory positions. Officially condemned yet routinely ignored, a sinful potential within all subjects yet also a specific illegal physical act, homoeroticism (or more accurately, sodomy and buggery) was a matter of contradictory social invest-ments. Prosecutions were relatively rare (those that did occur often involved child molestation, rape, or some explicit political motivation), and punishments, despite the fact that sodomy was a capital crime after Henry VIII's statute of 1533, were usually moderate.[34]

In addition, Alan Bray argues persuasively that those institutions which condemned sodomy did so in such absolute, apocalyptic, and heretical terms, and within such a broad display of "unnatural" sins, that men who engaged in homoerotic activities routinely distanced such condemnations from the meanings they attached to their own behaviors.[35] As Jonathan Goldberg notes, sodomy "always was embedded in other discourses, those delineating antisocial behavior – sedition, demonism, atheism."[36] Thus, when James I wrote his treatise on kingship, *Basilikon Doron*, for example, he

> listed crimes that were treasonous and warranted death. Among them was sodomy. James, of course, was notorious for his overtly homosexual behaviour. Yet, his treatise does not simply dissimulate; rather, it shows that sodomy was so fully politicized that no king could possibly apply the term to himself.[37]

Although Goldberg seems to assume that James was, in modern terms, a homosexual, the fact remains that the king's publicly expressed affection for Buckingham (among other things, he fon-dled him and called him his wife) held no necessary implication of sodomy. A distance inserts itself between the discourse on sodomy and the subject of that discourse, *even as that subject discourses*. It is not only that through a kind of selective blindness the cognitive dissonance of those early moderns participating in homoerotic practices was kept at a minimum, but that sodomy itself was an unstable, internally contradictory category.

The contradiction posed here between discourse and practice cannot be neatly described as oppositional: homoerotic activity was not only condemned, but was afforded a social logic, a psychic space, within which it could be pursued. The implication of this ideological configuration is far-reaching; in Goldberg's words, sodomy "was disseminated throughout society, invisible so long as homosexual acts failed to connect with the much more visible signs of social disruption represented by unorthodox religious or social positions."[38] Sodomy was not, as in modern terms, sexually immoral in and of itself; whatever immorality accrued to it was by virtue of its power of *social* disruption.

If male homoeroticism was officially invisible unless associated with other social transgressions, female homoeroticism was even more so. Indeed, how *women* understood their own homoerotic desires is still very much under-investigated and under-theorized. Two strategies suggest themselves as ways of exploring the female homoerotics of Shakespearean drama: a "revisioning" of close female friendship in the sense proposed by Adrienne Rich, and enacted by such scholars as Carroll Smith-Rosenberg and Lillian Faderman;[39] and a detailed examination of the erotic predicaments of the cross-dressed heroines of the comedies. We might want to look, for instance, at the relationships between Rosalind and Celia in *As You Like It*, Helena and Hermia in *A Midsummer Night's Dream*, and Marina and Philoten in *Pericles*, and ask why we assume that the images of "a double cherry" and of "Juno's swans . . . coupled and inseparable" are qualitatively different, somehow less erotic, than the "twin'd lambs" of Polixenes and Leontes in *The Winter's Tale*.[40] To pose the question in this way is to highlight the fact that, whatever the actual erotic practice of women historically, in terms of critical discourse female homoeroticism must be thought into existence.

For now, however, I must limit myself to the second strategy. Most critics would agree that the device of cross-dressing involves the suggestion of homoeroticism. A problem arises, however, in delineating precisely what kind of homoeroticism is represented. The materialist critic often turns to the theatrical practice of using boy actors to play female parts; from that material practice, it can be argued (as I did in my discussion of Lisa Jardine's work) that the homoeroticism embodied by the cross-dressed heroine is implicitly male: If Olivia is attracted to Viola/Cesario, or Phebe to Rosalind/Ganymede, the presence of boy actors suggests that the homoerotic exchange occurs between the transvestized boy actor playing Olivia or Phebe and the boy actor who (once dramatically transvestized as Viola or Rosalind) is now back in masculine dress.

But before we too quickly ratify the maleness inherent in this action, is it not also possible that these exchanges express female desire? If we focus on the text rather than theatrical practice, the desires circulating through the Phebe/Rosalind/Ganymede relation, or the Olivia/Viola/Cesario interaction, represent woman's desire for woman. Indeed, this is the reading Jean Howard implicitly proposes, with Olivia bearing the brunt of an anti-homoerotic humor. I will argue that the female (and male) homoeroticism of *As You Like It* and *Twelfth Night* is a mutual exchange (though not without anxieties and complications) which the contemporary practice of employing *female* actors for these parts can heighten.

But objections immediately present themselves to this "feminist formalism." If Phebe is attracted to the "feminine" in Rosalind/ Ganymede, could this be merely an indication of her preferred erotic style (that is, having a small, lithe lover), and having no reference to object choice (a female)? In other words, is it possible to separate early modern erotic *style* from gender inflections? Is such a separation merely the imposition of late twentieth-century preoccupations upon an earlier era? Or, does the foregoing analysis of Freud suggest that the conflation of gender and sexuality is a distinctly *modern* formulation?

In the absence of historical analysis of female homoeroticism, such questions are impossible to answer. Indeed, women's general illiteracy, which impeded first-hand recording of their experience, combined with the relative absence of legal and ecclesiastical documents pertaining to women's erotic investments in one another confounds the very possibility of historical analysis. If the materialist feminist's method is to return to the site of inscription, how does one read the difficulty of such a return?[41] The dearth of historical materials supports a number of possibly conflicting interpretations: assuming that women *did* engage in homoerotic behaviors, as cross-cultural anthropological evidence would suggest they did, it is possible that the nature of their erotic contacts did not invite sexual interpretations (by themselves? by others?); that such behavior was unremarkable insofar as it did not threaten the basis of the social contract – the open lineage family; that women's relative confinement in the household not only privatized their sexual contact but prevented the formation of those wider social networks which provided the embryonic basis of male homoerotic subcultures; and that the internal distancing evident in male homoeroticism was even more pronounced in that of female.

What evidence we do have suggests that in early modern England women were not summoned before courts on accusations of "sodomy"; according to Louis Crompton, England's "buggery" statute "was not interpreted as criminalizing relations between women."[42] Randolph Trumbach observes that the pre-eminent judicial scholar, Sir Edward Coke "took for granted that a woman's action came under the sodomy statute primarily 'if she commit buggery with a beast.'"[43] Crompton provides evidence, however, that in other Western European countries (France, Spain, Italy, Germany, and Switzerland) sexual acts between women "were regarded as legally equivalent to acts of male sodomy and were, like them, punishable by the death penalty."[44] The French sodomy statute, for instance, specifically criminalized female penetration of other women. According to James Saslow, however, across Western Europe punishment was rarely inflicted for female–female sexual acts: "The total number of known prosecutions ranges from four in sixteenth-century France to two in Germany and one each in Spain, Italy, Geneva, and the Netherlands."[45] Whatever the significance of this widespread reluctance to prosecute, it seems clear that in terms of criminal *law*, England was uniquely unconcerned with female homoeroticism. It may be that the ideology of Catholic countries was less tolerant, more apt to link homoeroticism with heresy, than that of Protestant ones. Saslow speculates that, in general,

> male authorities viewed lesbianism [*sic*] itself as more grave the more it laid claim to active male prerogatives: In Spain, two women were merely whipped and sent to the galleys for sex "without an instrument," but the penalty for penetration with a dildo was burning, suffered by two fifteenth-century nuns.[46]

The minimal concern about female homoeroticism displayed by the English did not derive from an assumption that women were asexual. As the plethora of cases involving pre-marital sexuality, adultery, and bastardy make clear, the reticence surrounding homoerotic activity contrasts sharply with the *lack* of impunity in cases of heterosexual transgression. Here the drama's concerns with the regulation of female heterosexual activity seem to parallel that of the culture for, as Katharine Eisaman Maus demonstrates, "anxiety about female sexual fidelity ran high in English Renaissance culture"; she reports that the majority of defamation suits were prompted by the opprobrious terms whore, whoremaster, and cuckold.[47]

Curiously, the term "sodomitess" was used synonymously with "whore" as a generic insult, and yet, unlike "whore," it was not employed as accusation in the courts. The question of why the "sodomitess" lacked legal culpability when so many other insults (scold, shrew, adulteress, whore) carried the onus of defamation leads only to more questions. Were specific erotic behaviors associated with the legally and socially execrated "whore," while others were reserved for the socially denigrated but legally unculpable "sodomitess"? Or was female sodomy defined as a matter of erotic *excess*, of quantity rather than kind? Whereas we have come to believe that early modern ideology regarding women's sexuality was informed by the patriarchal need to control women's reproductive capacities, we do not yet know the extent to which erotic behavior between women either challenged or existed coextensively with that political mandate.

Not only were the regulatory mechanisms toward heterosexual and homoerotic transgressions asymmetrical, so too was the erotic system inconsistent with the gender system – as evidenced by the fact that when women cross-dressed, they did *not* experience impunity. Although there was no English law against cross-dressing (as there was in France), from at least 1580 on, women wearing "masculine" attire were regularly castigated from pulpits and by pamphlets, and by 1620 were perceived to be such a threat that James I spoke out against the practice.[48] The gender and class infraction of female cross-dressing *was* linked to prostitution through labeling cross-dressers as "whores" and "trulls," but it does not seem to have occasioned accusations of homoerotic deviancy automatically – not, at least, for women.[49]

That the anti-theatricalists regularly, even obsessively, returned to the allegedly sodomitical transgressions of the *male* cross-dresser, including those of the boy actor, underscores the asymmetry most palpably expressed later on in the eighteenth century: women who not only cross-dressed but *passed* as men were prosecuted for *fraud*, while their male counterparts were called to court for sodomy (a rather telling instance of woman's metaphysical positioning – to uphold, indeed embody, the truth).[50] And, notoriously, in the nineteenth century Queen Victoria refused to sign an anti-sodomy bill until all references to women were deleted – she professed complete disbelief in the possibility of women engaging in such acts.[51]

The official invisibility of early modern female homoeroticism, however, tells us little about its *popular* cultural significations. What does seem clear is that in England, women's sexuality did not derive wholly from gender identity or role ascriptions. That is, deviations in gender role did not automatically implicate women as "unnatural" in their sexual tastes; deviations in erotic behavior were not necessarily coded as gender transgressions. The conflation of gender and eroticism that we so often bring to our critical activity does not adequately address early modern women's homoeroticism.

Whatever its significations, they were not identical to those of male homoeroticism, which had both a greater social and discursive presence and, one would suspect, a greater range of practice. In contrast to the silence surrounding female homoeroticism, many early modern English words denote male homoerotic activity: ganymede, catamite, ingle, androgyne. As terms of disparagement, they conflated youthful androgyny, "effeminacy," and transvestism in one package of gender and erotic transgression.[52] Yet there is also some evidence to suggest that the discourse of sodomy did not always map easily onto the discourse of, for instance, the ganymede – that the categories in certain contexts might have been distinguished and disarticulated (to us) to an extraordinary degree.

In short, the meanings of homoerotic desire during the early modern period seem to have been remarkably unfixed, with contradictory meanings existing across a complex and fractured field of signification. The discourses of homoeroticism were neither monological nor monovocal. Most importantly, homoerotic activity – for men or women – was not a primary means of identification of the self. Homoeroticism had little to do with any of the social roles, statuses, and hierarchies in which an early modern subject might be located and thereby define him or herself. Early moderns simply did not essentialize homoeroticism in quite the way we do.[53]

My use of two seemingly opposed yet not directly antonymic terms – homo/eroticism and hetero/sexuality – is a response to the early modern social configuration. In the early modern period, neither heterosexuality nor homosexuality (or sexuality itself for that matter) existed in our modern senses of the terms. Yet, despite the absence of both concepts from the early modern consciousness, it is still possible to speak of crucial differences in the social organization of those activities which we now term "homo" or "hetero." Although neither an originating cause nor an organizing principle, heterosexual object choice was involved in the social formation both subjectively and institutionally in the following ways: as a subjective state of desire, if not for an object proper, then for the results that union with that object would hopefully ensure (family, name, property, rank, lineage – all that is connoted by the early modern term "house"); as a well-defined and well-investigated erotic act (fornication) organized around the presence or absence of female chastity; and as a dominant ideology which found its teleology in the material institution of marriage. Insofar as elite marriages were primarily dedicated to breeding, the perpetuation of lineage, and the consolidation and dispersal of property, and to the extent that these social mandates were threatened by the expression of unregulated female sexuality, it could be said that in certain contexts, heterosexual *desire* was in excess of marriage, even at odds with it. If this were true, hetero*sexuality* would be that which the upper classes displaced onto the laboring classes, as landed gentry and aristocrats indulged in a patriarchal fantasy of marriage that secured lineage and property without sexual intercourse.[54] Despite this possible difference in the erotics of class, however, my use of the linguistic root "sexuality" is meant to imply heterosexuality's institutional and political mandate, in which identity was situated in relation to one's sexual congress as a socially ascribed subject-position – as husband, mistress, wife, widow or widower, for instance. To that extent, heterosexuality performed a crucial function of subjectification *vis-à-vis* the dominant social order.

In contrast, homosexuality – as subject position, ideology, or institution – did not exist. What did exist discursively, in the form of sodomy and buggery, were a number of dispersed acts, organized around penetration: anal intercourse between males or between males and females, intercourse with children, fellatio, and bestiality – none of which in England referred to specific acts between women.

Following the implicit lead of the documentary discourses of law, religion, and morality, many critics thus focus on early modern homoeroticism as an *act*, defining it in terms of sodomitical practice. To do so, however, is to conflate homoeroticism with other forms of so called "sexual confusion," to ignore the gender asymmetry of sodomy's definition, and to obviate the subjective motivation for and experience of homoerotic activity. Legal, ecclesiastical, and moral discourses positioned homoeroticism as other, and within that logic, refused the power of speech to those who would speak from the position of their own intentionality. I want to argue that to the extent that material practice did not exhaust homoeroticism's meaning – either for those who experienced it or those who represented it in literature – what is in excess remains in the amorphous register of erotic *desire*.[55] More accurately, homoeroticism was a position taken in *relation* to desire – a position, however, that was neither socially mandated nor capable of conferring identity or role.

And yet, even as I formulate homoeroticism as a position taken in relation to desire, I am in danger of reifying what is really a relational process – desire or eroticism – and granting it a certain structural autonomy. Such a method risks attributing agency to desire by raising it to the status of ontology or attributing to it a teleology. It represents, at best, an interim strategy, a way to keep the exigencies of materiality and subjectivity poised in mutual tension, while at the same time insisting on the material and subjective asymmetry between hetero/sexuality and homo/eroticism.

In the next chapter I attempt to resist fixing erotic identity onto specific characters, and instead argue that the texts themselves display a homoerotic circulation of desire; homoerotic energy is elicited, exchanged, and displaced as it confronts the pleasures and anxieties of its meanings in early modern culture. As it traverses "masculine" and "feminine" sites, this desire challenges the binary language of identity that upholds the modern erotic economy. At the same time, however, homoerotic desire must be located within a matrix of gender and status relations, since its signification, like that of heterosexuality, differs along hierarchical lines. Thus, it is not so much homoeroticism "itself" that is analyzed, as its relation to other modes of power. The issue becomes less a matter of "proving" the existence of homoerotic desire than of refusing to credit such a request in the first place. Once the hierarchy between homoerotic and heterosexual is dissolved within the critical enterprise, homoerotic significations are everywhere – both in their expansive, inclusive modes, and in their anxious and repressed forms. That this is true seems to me to be less a matter of the critic's own projective desire (although there is certainly an element of that in all of our reading) than of the polymorphous potential of desire itself, which Shakespeare so assiduously evokes and controls.

*

Several implications evolve from the problems and methodology I have outlined here. First, by arguing that eroticism *is* cultural practice – material, ideological, and subjective – I encourage literary and cultural critics to recognize and distinguish the workings of eroticism in the texts and cultures they analyze. If even the most sophisticated feminist materialist analyses misrecognize gender as a signifier in such a way that eroticism is conveniently forgotten, clearly both gender and historical critics need to rethink their assumptions about the meaning and significance of erotic practice.

Secondly, implicit throughout my book is the belief that the problems posed by erotic desire demand feminist analysis from two angles simultaneously: historical materialist analysis of ideological and material practices, and psychoanalysis of subjective states of desire. Indeed, the case of early modern homoeroticism(s) demonstrates the extent to which the opposition between the material (institutions and practices) and the psychic (desires and fantasies) is a false one. Despite psychoanalysis' belatedness, its construction within the specific problematics of modernity, and its unfortunate history as a normalizing institution, its recognition that eroticism involves several modes of desire is crucial to the possibility of a non-normalizing analytic. To investigate homoeroticism only from the standpoint of ascertainable material practice, our understanding of which is limited, for the early modern period, to the dominant discourses of legal and religious records, is to ignore the subjective erotic dramas of countless early modern people. We cannot know the content of those subjective dramas, but we can reconstruct partial (that is, both incomplete and necessarily biased) approximations of their meaning from the contemporary rhetorical strategies employed to describe them. To my mind, this is where a historical, discourse-based model faces its greatest challenge: to delineate not only those statements that circulate throughout the social fabric, but also to "re-vision" and put into play those historical meanings that have been repressed, lost, or unspoken.

The viability of the kind of critical *rapprochement* I advocate – feminist-historical-materialist-psycho-analysis – depends on the continuing deconstruction of psychoanalysis' will to mastery. The first move in such a project is the internal displacement of those totalizations that obscure historical and social processes. One such totalization, I hope to have demonstrated, is "desire" itself.

The work I've begun here is only a small first step in the

much larger project of deconstructing "sex-desire" in the words of Foucault, in the interests of "bodies and pleasures."[56] Insofar as gay men and lesbians are still subject to institutionalized oppression (including the recent revision of the archaic "sodomy" law to specifically criminalize homosexual acts in the state in which I live, and the revoking of the right to freedom of speech in matters homoerotic in Great Britain), asserting the specificity of homoeroticism is politically progressive.

It is not, however, radically deconstructive, if only because it continues to pay implicit obeisance to the prestige of object choice as the primary criterion of sexuality. A more radical project would not only move beyond the regime of object choice, but also beyond the representational strategy that supports it: the hegemony of the phallus. Both the phallus and object choice depend on a binary system that reifies eroticism by privileging one erotic position over all others. Even in Lacanian psychoanalysis, in which the phallus represents a "lack-in-being," the recourse to phallus-as-signifier-of-desire defines the problematic of presence/absence as ontologically originating in the male body. Rather than demystifying male sexuality as it exposes subjectivity as a (w)hole, it reproduces male genitalia as transcendental signifier (not of presence but of absence), in an inversion that leaves the privilege of the term undisturbed. Male sexuality remains both the referent and repetition of the problem of subjectivity "itself."[57] And the static relations between power and desire remain uncontested, with power always the "substitute of choice" for what we always already, and always will, essentially lack.

The deconstruction of erotic binarism would involve putting into play more heterogeneous and heteronomous representations, by recognizing what Jonathan Dollimore has called the "creative perversity of desire itself."[58] People of all erotic persuasions – and I stress that this is not solely the task of erotic minorities – can renegotiate the terms by which desire is lived and understood, setting into critical motion the various contingencies that structure arousal and foster erotic satisfaction. Beginning to conceptualize desire as the sum of discontinuous and incongruent discourses, practices, identifications, fantasies, preferences for specific activities, as well as object choice(s), we could do worse than adopt as a critical strategy the kind of rhetorical displacement evident on the following political T-shirt:

so-do-my
neighbors
parents
friends

Deconstructing "desire" opens up a field of inquiry, a way of thinking about bodies, pleasures, and history that allows us to ask previously unapproachable questions. Indeed, questions that hitherto seemed ahistorical may be viewed with a new historicity. For instance, what precise intersections of discourses, both early modern and postmodern, on power, gender, bodies, and pleasures produce the possibility of reading *Twelfth Night*'s Antonio as akin to the macho "Castro clone" encased in leather in San Francisco? Or, why is it possible to interpret Sebastian as the "bisexual" who can go either way? And why does Viola and Rosalind's adoption of "doublet and hose" seem to speak to our own taste for androgynous and practical fashions?

But where is Olivia?

Perhaps sitting at her computer, wearing high heels.

Chapter 5

The homoerotics of Shakespearean comedy

The phenomenon of boy actors playing women's parts in Shakespearean comedy has engendered analyses primarily along three axes. The boy actor: (1) is merely a theatrical convention in the lineage of medieval drama; (2) is a political convention specifically necessitated by the determination to keep women, excepting Elizabeth I, off any public stage or platform; or (3) is an embodiment of the meta-dramatic theme of identity itself: always a charade, a masquerade, other. Certainly it is too much of a caricature to label the first formulation as formalist, the second as feminist, and the third as new historicist. And yet it might be provisionally useful to do so, if only to place these positions in the context of debates about: (1) the relative political import and impact of aesthetic events; (2) the determining power of patriarchal ideology within a general political economy; and (3) the extent to which politics and gender impinge on the problematics of subjectivity. It is as an intervention in these debates that I situate the following chapter.

I want to argue first that the practice of employing boys to act the parts of women was not merely a dramatic convention, nor was it solely a patriarchal strategy. As Stephen Orgel points out, boy actors were "a uniquely English solution"; when, in 1599, women were banned from the Spanish stage, "the spectacle of transvestite boys was found to be even more disturbing than that of theatrical women, and the edict was rescinded four years later."[1] However much the practice did keep women from too publicly displaying themselves, it continued not merely because of its negative power of constraint, but because it made possible complex desires and fantasies, and mediated cultural anxieties. Those desires and anxieties were not only gendered but erotic in their origination and implication. Secondly, costuming boys as women, who might then impersonate men (and then sometimes women as well), was especially well suited for a drama devoted to exploring the construction and dissolution of identity; however, the relevant concept of identity was not that of a generic, nondifferentiated "selfhood," but of a complex subjectivity always already imbricated by gender and erotic pressures.

I propose that the boy actor works, in specific Shakespearean comedies, as the basis upon which homoeroticism can be safely explored – working for both actors and audiences as an expression of non-hegemonic desire within the confines of conventional, comedic restraints. The phenomenon of the boy actor is not the by-product or the side-effect of a drama "really" about identity or illustrative of misogyny, but rather is the basis upon which a specific deployment of erotic desire and anxiety can be played out. In this chapter I mean to demonstrate my earlier assertion that certain Shakespearean texts display a homoerotic circulation of desire, that homoerotic energy is elicited, exchanged, negotiated, and displaced as it confronts the pleasures and anxieties of its meanings in early modern culture. Shakespearean drama not only responded to the ideological matrix, explored in Chapter 4, by which homoerotic desire was understood; it also contributed, in its own ambivalent way, to the early modern signification of homoeroticism. Neither a transparent mirror, mimetically reflecting social reality, nor a literary-historical aberration explainable by the author's sexual preference, the homoerotics of Shakespearean comedy are most accurately perceived as a cultural intervention in a heterosexually overdetermined field. They thus provide us with a useful theoretical analytic, not only of early modern sexualities, but of contemporary erotic concerns.

The circulation of homoerotic desire in *As You Like It* and *Twelfth Night* is what I mean to invoke when I employ the term transvestism over disguise or cross-dressing to describe the consequences of Rosalind's and Viola's adoption of (what was then perceived to be) masculine attire. Although psychoanalytically, transvestism implies the erotic excitement achieved by wearing the clothes of a different gender, and thus is anachronistically and illegitimately applied to the activities of these characters, it is nonetheless because of the specifically erotic valence of the term that I use it. The transvestism in these plays has a more generalized erotic effect, dispersed throughout the entire fabric

of the text, rather than located and fixed within one character's desire.

Part of my support for such assertions comes from the anti-
theatricalists themselves, who increasingly focused their condemnations of the theater on the figure of the boy actor. In a mimetic
theory of sexuality, the anti-theatricalists not only charged that the
boy actor dressed as a woman aroused the erotic interest of men in
the audience, but that spectators were encouraged to play out their
fantasies in off-stage, behind-the-scenes scenes. The specifically
erotic images with which Stephen Gosson, John Rainoldes, Phillip
Stubbes, and William Prynne denounced theatrical practices demonstrates that they perceived actors in their costumes to cross not
only status and gender boundaries, but erotic boundaries as well.[2]

However much we might discredit the anti-theatricalists as
"fanatics" or crude mimeticists, their intuitions about erotic arousal
should not be presumed to be incidental to theatrical production.
Bodies, in their culture as in ours, were invested with erotic
meanings – bodies making a spectacle of themselves on stage
even more so. And clothing, as both the anti-theatricalists and
the upholders of sumptuary laws made clear, was an important
indicator of one's sexual stance, denoting erotic availability or lack
thereof. The anti-theatricalist claim that the theater was a site of
erotic, specifically homoerotic, arousal is not in itself pathological;
as Stephen Greenblatt notes, "Shakespearean comedy constantly
appeals to the body and in particular to sexuality as the heart
of its theatrical magic."[3] What *is* pathological, however, is the
anti-theatricalist paranoia about what this circulation of eroticism
implies for male subjectivity. At any rate, it is not a paranoia shared
with other early modern texts that represent homoeroticism as a
legitimate mode of desire; for instance, Spenser's *The Shepherd's
Calendar* and Marlowe's *Hero and Leander*.[4]

Psychoanalytic and early feminist readings of the transvestism of
As You Like It and *Twelfth Night* stress the liberating effect caused
by the temporary inversion of hierarchical gender arrangements,
"through release to clarification," to use C. L. Barber's influential
phrase.[5] Whereas some early feminist readings also posited gender
role inversion as an impulse toward androgyny, later feminist and
new historicist critics argued that any subversion of gender is
contained by the comic form which mandates marriage in the
final act. Recent debates on the relative subversive or containing
power of gender in Shakespeare's plays focus on the extent to which

women (through transvestite disguise or appropriation of speech) challenge and disrupt gender difference, or are securely repositioned as objects of exchange in a patriarchal economy dependent on "the traffic in women."[6]

Clearly, insofar as gender hierarchies seem to be both temporarily transgressed *and* formally reinstated, the question of subversion versus containment can only be resolved by crediting *either* the expense of dramatic energy *or* comedic closure. Yet, to do either is also to reproduce the artificial distinction between content and form – a capitulation to the logic of binarism. One way beyond such fruitless polarization is to historicize the moment in which subversion is thought to occur, to situate *abstract* transgression within a concrete network of overdetermined social pressures and effects.[7] Another way, evident in Chapters 1 through 3, is to stress less the fact of foreclosure than the *way* such containment is attained: the mechanisms and displacements set to work by the anxiety elicited through subversive action. In the following analysis of erotic transgression, I will attempt to do both.

To the extent that the various critics who have recently written about the phenomena of boy actors and female transvestism have recognized the homoeroticism residing in theatrical transvestism, they have initiated the possibility of a homoerotic analytic.[8] For the most part, however, they have focused their attention on *gender* rather than sexuality – even though, as I discussed in Chapter 4, their language confuses the issue by using synonymously such terms as sexual difference and sexual identity, androgyny and bisexuality, femininity (or masculinity) and heterosexuality. After mentioning the erotic complications raised by the boy actor, they more often than not decline to interrogate how homoeroticism works in specific plays, how homoerotic desire is differentiated between plays, and whether homoeroticism is distinguished along gender lines.

Even in those analyses specifically devoted to uncovering the material reality of homoerotic practice, gender remains the dominant lens of analysis, as in Lisa Jardine's suggestion that male homoeroticism animates all of the cross-dressing scenes. The conclusion extrapolated from Jardine's analysis is that in "playing the woman's part" the boy actor renders unexceptionable and unthreatening female autonomy and erotic power for a predominantly male audience. If young boys are erotically compelling because of their "femininity," it is in part because they represent all of the attractions and none of the threats of female heterosexuality. More recently, Stephen Orgel concurs with this line of reasoning:

> The dangers of women in erotic situations, whatever they may be, can be disarmed by having the women play men, just as in the theatre the dangers of women on the stage (whatever *they* may be) can be disarmed by having men play the women.[9]

Whatever the objective truth of these conclusions, they ultimately say more about the gender anxieties of early modern patriarchal culture than about the specificity of homoeroticism. Chapter 4 demonstrates that although gender and eroticism are deeply connected, they are not isomorphic. Here, reliance on a gender model causes Orgel and Jardine to refer the motivation of male homoeroticism to a single cause: the fantasized dangers posed by women. Despite their antihomophobic intentions, Orgel and Jardine continue to place homoeroticism within a category requiring ontological explanation and justification, in which traditional psychoanalytic interpretations are surprisingly reinstalled.

It may well be that gender anxiety is a determining factor in the specific ways homoerotic *practice* is manifested and encoded with social meaning within early modern patriarchal culture. I question, however, whether gender anxiety is *the* salient factor in the construction of homoerotic *desire*. Gender anxiety is no more, and no less, constitutive of homoerotic desire than it is of heterosexual desire. A plenitude of desires are available as unconscious erotic modes within every psyche. But whether a particular mode of desire is given expression or repressed – that is, whether it is manifested as desire or anxiety – is a matter of ideological and institutional elicitations, enticements, and disciplines. To take this argument one step further, whether representations of gendered bodies elicit repulsion or attraction, fear or fascination, is in some ways irrelevant; as I stated in my Introduction, anxiety and desire are two sides of the same erotic coin. As Sedgwick suggests, desire itself is less "a particular affective state or emotion" than "the affective or social force, the glue, even when its manifestation is hostility or hatred."[10] Despite the particular affect involved, the psychic investment is, in each case, comparable. Arbitrary divisions of desire into heterosexual and homoerotic are more indicative of socio-political prerogatives than of inherent psychic or biological imperatives.

Whereas formalist critics often ignore the impact of the boy actor on the text's signification, historical critics such as Jardine and Orgel conversely emphasize the extent to which early modern theatrical practice enabled what is increasingly being called a "transvestite theater." In this, they follow the lead of the anti-theatricalists in conflating the material reality of the boy actor with the play's action. Indeed, the concept of a "transvestite theater" *per se* seems to confuse mimetically not only the reality of the play with the world of the theater, but also the phenomena of transvestism and male homoeroticism. In my view, transvestism does not correlate in a simple fashion with any particular erotic mode: theoretically, it could engender heterosexual as well as homoerotic desires. Rather, I would like to suggest that homoerotic activity within Shakespeare's plays is predicated on, but not identical to, the presence of boy actors playing female parts. The material conditions of the early modern theater offered a de facto homoerotic basis upon which to build structures of desire, which were then, through theatrical representation, made available not only to male but to female audience members. This dual-gender availability suggests a problem with another increasingly popular term, "sodomitical theatrics"; when used to describe the entire constellation of desires criss-crossing such plays as *As You Like It* and *Twelfth Night*, it fails to distinguish between the erotic practices of both genders; as much as it brings to the fore homoerotic desires among men, it neglects the female desires constructed by the playtexts and imagistically available to female play-goers.

The following comparative analysis of *As You Like It* and *Twelfth Night* attempts to demonstrate the differential ways homoeroticism is treated: how it is experienced as pleasure and when it elicits anxiety for both male and female characters. These plays are sites of struggle for the signification of homoeroticism: they demonstrate that within the early modern erotic economy the homoerotic relation to desire could be represented as both celebratory and strained. At the same time, the representations of homoeroticism in these comedies are as much cultural fantasies as is the representation of the maternal body in the *Henriad* – both representations are "fantasmic" interventions in "real" cultural practices, and as such signal the dialectical relation between the psychic and the social.

The homoeroticism of *As You Like It* is playful in its ability to transcend binary oppositions, to break into a dual mode, a simultaneity, of desire. Insofar as Rosalind/Ganymede is a multiply sexual object (simultaneously heterosexual and homoerotic), Orlando's effusion of desire toward her/him prevents the stable reinstitution of heterosexuality, upon which the marriage plot depends. By interrupting the arbitrary binarism of the heterosexual contract, male homoeroticism, even as it affirms particular masculine bonds, transgresses the erotic imperative of the Law of the Father. The proceedings of Hymen that conclude the play, once read in terms of the "mock" marriage which precedes them, enact only an ambivalent closure. The reinstitution of gender role (and Rosalind's political subordination under her husband's rule) is incommensurate with a rigidification of sexuality.

The homoeroticism of *Twelfth Night*, on the other hand, is anxious and strained. This text explores a diversity of desire, proceeding with erotic plurality as far as it can; then, in the face of anxiety generated by this exploration, it fixes the homoerotic interest onto a marginalized figure. The homoerotic energies of Viola, Olivia, and Orsino are displaced onto Antonio, whose relation to Sebastian is finally sacrificed for the maintenance of institutionalized heterosexuality and generational continuity. [11] In other words, *Twelfth Night* closes down the possibility of homoerotic play initiated by the material presence of the transvestized boy actors. The fear expressed, however, is not of homoeroticism *per se*; homoerotic pleasure is explored and sustained *until* it collapses into fear of erotic exclusivity and its corollary: non-reproductive sexuality. The result is a more rigid dedication to the ideology of binarism, wherein gender and status inequalities are all the more forcefully reinscribed.

> Much virtue in If
>
> Touchstone, *As You Like It*

In "'The Place of a Brother' in *As You Like It*: Social Process and Comic Form," Louis Adrian Montrose began the pathbreaking work of placing women's subordination in Shakespearean drama within the context of male homosocial bonds. [12] In a historicization and politicization of C.L. Barber's analysis of Rosalind in *Shakespeare's Festive Comedy*, Montrose argued that

> Rosalind's exhilarating mastery of herself and others has been a compensatory "holiday humor," a temporary, inversionary rite of misrule, whose context is a transfer of authority, property, and title from the Duke to his prospective male heir. [13]

More recently, Jean Howard continues within the Barber–Montrose lineage:

The representation of Rosalind's holiday humor has the primary effect, I think, of confirming the gender system and perfecting rather than dismantling it by making a space for mutuality within relations of dominance.[14]

However, she complicates the analysis of Rosalind's subordination through reference to the French feminist analytic of female "masquerade:"

the figure of Rosalind dressed as a boy engages in playful masquerade as, in playing Rosalind for Orlando, she acts out the parts scripted for women by her culture. Doing so does not release Rosalind from patriarchy but reveals the constructed nature of patriarchy's representations of the feminine and shows a woman manipulating those representations in her own interest, theatricalizing for her own purposes what is assumed to be innate, teaching her future mate how to get beyond certain ideologies of gender to more enabling ones.[15]

The distance traversed in the progression from Barber to Montrose to Howard indicates a corresponding movement from an essentialist view of gender, to an emphasis on social structure as determining gender, to an assertion of the limited possibilities of subversive manipulation within dominant cultural codes. The subjective if constrained agency conferred by Howard upon Rosalind as a woman can be extended as well to Rosalind as erotic subject. In excess of the dominant ideology of monogamous heterosexuality, to which Rosalind is symbolically wed at the end of the play, exist desires unsanctioned by institutional favor. By means of her male improvisation, Rosalind leads the play into a mode of desire neither heterosexual nor homoerotic, but both heterosexual *and* homoerotic. As much as she displays her desire for Orlando, she also enjoys her position as male object of Phebe's desire and, more importantly, of Orlando's. S/he thus instigates a deconstruction of the binary system by which desire in subsequent centuries came to be organized, regulated, and disciplined.

That homoerotic significations will play a part in *As You Like It* is first intimated by Rosalind's adoption of the name Ganymede when she imagines donning doublet and hose. Of all the male names available to her, she chooses that of the young lover of Zeus, familiar to educated Britons through Greek and Latin literature and European painting, and to less privileged persons as a colloquial term used to describe the male object of male love. As James Saslow, who traces the artistic representation of Ganymede in Western culture from the fifteenth to the seventeenth centuries, argues, "the very word *ganymede* was used from medieval times well into the seventeenth century to mean an object of homosexual desire."[16] Saslow's argument is seconded by Orgel: "the name Ganymede [could not] be used in the Renaissance without this connotation."[17]

That Rosalind-cum-Ganymede becomes the object of another woman's desire is obvious. Consciously, of course, Phebe believes Ganymede to be a man, and is thus merely following the dominant heterosexual course. And yet, what attracts Phebe to Ganymede are precisely those qualities that could be termed "feminine." Notice the progression of the following speech:

> It is a pretty youth – not very pretty. . . .
> He'll make a proper man. The best thing in him
> Is his complexion. . . .
> He is not very tall; yet for his years he's tall.
> His leg is but so so; and yet 'tis well.
> There was a pretty redness in his lip,
> A little riper and more lusty red
> Than that mix'd in his cheek; 'twas just the difference
> Betwixt the constant red and mingled damask.
>
> (III. v. 113–23)

During the first half of her recollection, as she measures Ganymede against the standard of common male attributes – height, leg – Phebe fights her attraction, syntactically oscillating between affirmation and denial: he is; he is not. In the last four lines, as she "feminizes" Ganymede's lip and cheek, she capitulates to her desire altogether.

Many critics acknowledge the underlying homoeroticism of Phebe's attraction; however, they tend to undermine its thematic importance by relegating it to the status of a temporary psychosexual stage. C.L. Barber, for instance, remarks: "She has, in effect, a girlish crush on the femininity which shows through Rosalind's disguise; the aberrant affection is happily got over when Rosalind reveals her identity and makes it manifest that Phebe has been loving a woman."[18] When Barber says that Phebe's "aberrant" affection is "happily got over" he reveals the extent to which homophobic anxiety structures the developmental logic of his response. But if a "girlish crush" is outgrown or overcome, what are we to make of Rosalind's desire to "prove a busy actor" in the "pageant truly play'd" of Phebe and Silvius? (III.iv.50–8). Although her ostensible motivation is her belief that "the sight of lovers feedeth those in love" (56), s/he soon interjects in order to correct the literal-mindedness that feeds Phebe's "proud disdain" (III.iv.52). And yet the pleasure Rosalind/Ganymede takes in this task seems in excess of her putative function. Significantly, it is s/he who first mentions the possibility of Phebe's attraction, interpreting and then glorying in Phebe's changed demeanor:

> Why, what means this? Why do you look on me?
> I see no more in you than in the ordinary
> Of nature's sale-work. 'Od's my little life
> I think she means to tangle my eyes too!
>
> (III.v.41–4)

Is there not a sense in which Rosalind/Ganymede *elicits* Phebe's desire, constructing it even as she refuses it? Indeed, in these lines the conflict between discourses of gender and of sexuality are intensely manifested: at the level of gender, Rosalind restates compulsory heterosexuality; at the level of sexuality, Ganymede elicits a desire for that which falls outside (or on the cusp) of the binarism of gender. At any rate, s/he is represented as delighting in her role of the rejecting male:

> Down on your knees,
> And thank heaven, fasting, for a good man's love;
> For I must tell you friendly in your ear,
> Sell when you can, you are not for all markets.
>
> (III.v.57–60)

And why does s/he put Silvius through the exquisite torment of hearing Phebe's love letter to Ganymede read aloud, if not to aggrandize her own victorious position as male rival? (IV.iii.14–64). Indeed, as a male, her sense of power is so complete that s/he presumes to tell Silvius to tell Phebe, "that if she love *me*, I charge her to love *thee*" (IV.iii.71–2, my emphasis).

Homoerotic desire in *As You Like It* thus circulates from Phebe's desire for the "feminine" in Rosalind/Ganymede to Rosalind/Ganymede's desire to be the "masculine" object of Phebe's desire. Even more suggestive of the text's investment in homoerotic pleasure is Orlando's willingness to engage in love-play with a young shepherd. Throughout his "courtship" of Ganymede (who is now impersonating Rosalind), Orlando accepts and treats Ganymede as his beloved. To do so requires less his willing suspension of disbelief than the ability to hold in suspension a dual sexuality that feels no compulsion to make arbitrary distinctions between kinds of objects. That Rosalind-cum-Ganymede takes the lead in their courtship has been noted by countless critics; that there is a certain homoerotic irony in that fact has yet to be noted. As a "ganymede," Rosalind would be expected to play the part of a younger, more receptive partner in an erotic exchange. S/he thus not only inverts gender roles; s/he disrupts alleged homoerotic roles as well.

What began as a game culminates in the "mock" marriage, when Orlando takes for his wife the boy he believes to be fictionalizing as Rosalind. It is Celia, not Orlando, who hesitates in playing her part in the ceremony – "I cannot say the words," she responds to Orlando's request that she play the priest (IV.i.121) – in part because those words possess a ritualistic power to *enact* what is spoken. Insofar as ritual was still popularly believed to be imbued with sacred or magical power, the fact that Orlando does not hesitate, but eagerly responds in the precise form of the Anglican marriage ceremony – "I take thee, Rosalind, for wife" (IV.i.129) – suggests the degree to which the play legitimizes the multiple desires it represents. The point is not that Orlando and Ganymede formalize a homosexual marriage, but rather that as the distance between Rosalind and Ganymede collapses, distinctions between homoerotic and heterosexual collapse as well. As the woman and the shepherd boy merge, Orlando's words resound with the conviction that, for the moment, he (as much as Rosalind and the audience) is engaged in the ceremony as if it were real. As both a performative speech act and a theatricalization of desire, the marriage is both true and fictional at once. The subversiveness of this dramatic gesture lies in the dual motion of first, appropriating the meaning of matrimony for deviant desires; and second, exposing the heterosexual imperative of matrimony as a reduction of the plurality of desire into the singularity of monogamy. The "mock" marriage is not a desecration but a deconstruction – a displacement and subversion of the terms by which desire is encoded – of the ritual by which two are made one.

When Hymen in Act V symbolically reintroduces the logic of heterosexual marriage, the text's devotion to simultaneity would appear to be negated. The terms in which Hymen performs the quartet of marriages make the ideological function of the ritual clear: "Peace, ho! I bar confusion./ 'Tis I must make conclusion/ Of these most strange events" (V.iv.124–6). "Hymen's bands" (V.iv.128) are called forth to "make conclusion" not only of erotic "confusion" but of the play. And yet the play does not end with Hymen's bars and bands, but with a renewed attack on the pretensions of erotic certitude. In a repetition of her previous gender and erotic mobility, Rosalind-cum-boy actor, still wearing female attire, leaps the frame of the play in order to address the audience in a distinctly erotic manner: "If I were a woman I would kiss as many of you as had beards that pleas'd me, complexions that lik'd me, and breaths that I defied not" (Epilogue 16–19). As Orgel, Howard, Phyllis Rackin, and Catherine Belsey all intimate, the effect of this statement is to highlight the constructedness of gender and the flexibility of erotic attraction at precisely the point when the formal impulse of comedy would be to essentialize and fix both gender and eroticism.

Throughout the play, what makes erotic contingency possible is a simple conjunction: "if." Indeed, Touchstone's discourse on the virtues of "if" can serve as an index of the play's entire erotic strategy: "If you said so, then I said so" (V.iv.99–100). The dependence on the conditional structures the possibility of erotic exploration without necessitating a commitment to it. Orlando can woo and even wed Ganymede as "*if* thou wert indeed my Rosalind" and as *if* the marriage were real (IV.i.189–90, my emphasis). Through the magic of "if," the boy actor playing Rosalind can offer and elicit erotic attraction to and from each gender in the audience. "If" not only creates multiple erotic possibilities and positions, it also conditionally resolves the dramatic confusion that the play cannot sustain. As Rosalind says to Silvius, Phebe, and Orlando, respectively: "I would love you, if I could"; "I will marry you, if ever I marry a woman, and I'll be married tomorrow"; and, "I will satisfy you, if ever I satisfied man, and you shall be married tomorrow" (V.ii.108–12). Even Hymen's mandate is qualified: "Here's eight that must take hands/ To join in Hymen's bands/ *If* truth hold true contents" (V.iv.127–9, my emphasis).

My own reliance on "if" should make it clear that I am not arguing that Rosalind or Orlando or Phebe "is" "a" "homosexual." Rather, at various moments in the play, these characters temporarily inhabit a homoerotic position of desire. To insist on a mode of desire as a position taken up also differs from formulating these characters as "bisexual": as Phyllis Rackin reminds us, bisexuality implicitly

defines the desiring subject as divided in order to maintain the ideologically motivated categories of homo- and hetero- as inviolate.[19]
The entire logic of *As You Like It* works against such categorization,
against fixing upon and reifying any one mode of desire.

Simultaneity and flexibility, however, are not without their costs.
Insofar as the text circulates homoerotic desire, it displaces the
anxieties so generated in the following tableau described by Oliver,
Orlando's brother:

> A wretched ragged man, o'ergrown with hair,
> Lay sleeping on his back. About his neck
> A green and gilded snake had wreath'd itself,
> Who with her head nimble in threats approach'd
> The opening of his mouth. . . .
> A lioness, with udders all drawn dry,
> Lay couching, head on ground, with catlike watch,
> When that the sleeping man should stir. . . .
>   (IV.iii.107–17)

The dual dangers to which the sleeping Oliver is susceptible
are, on the face of it, female: the lioness an aged maternal
figure ("with udders all drawn dry"), the female snake seductively
encircling Oliver's neck. Let us first give this passage a conventional
psychoanalytic reading: the virile and virtuous Orlando banishes
the snake and battles with the lion while his evil "emasculated"
brother, unconscious of his position as damsel in distress, sleeps
on – their sibling rivalry displaced onto and mediated by gender
conflict. Yet at the same time as the snake encircles her prey,
she approaches and almost penetrates the vulnerable opening of
Oliver's mouth. Rather than posit the snake, in this aspect, as a
representation of the "phallic mother," I want to argue that in the
snake's figure are concentrated the anxieties generated by the text's
simultaneous commitment to homoeroticism and heterosexuality.
If Oliver is endangered by the snake's "feminine" sexual powers,
he is equally threatened by her phallic ones. He becomes both the
feminized object of male aggression and the *ef*feminized object of
female desire. The snake thus represents the erotic other of the
text, the reservoir of the fears elicited by homoerotic exchanges
– fears, I want to insist, that are not inherent in the experience of
homoerotic desire, but that are produced by those ideologies that
position homoeroticism as unnatural, criminal, and heretical.

Indeed the relations represented in this tableau suggest that no desire, male or female, heterosexual or homoerotic, is free of anxiety. As Touchstone says in a lighter vein, "as all is mortal in nature, so is all nature in love mortal in folly" (II.iv.52–3). But what is most interesting is that in this play sexual danger is encoded as feminizing to the object persistently figured as male. Consistently, the text seems less interested in the threat of a particular mode of desire (hetero/homo) than in the dangers desire *as such* poses to men. It is, in this sense, thoroughly patriarchal, positing man as the center of, and vulnerable to, desire. That the text marginalizes this expression of vulnerability by not dramatizing it on stage but reporting it only in retrospect suggests the extent to which the anxiety is repressed in the interests of achieving comic, heterosexual closure, however partially or problematically.

My highlighting of the affirmative possibilities of multiple pleasures is not meant to imply that *As You Like It* represents a paradisiacal erotic economy, a utopian return to a polymorphously perverse body unmediated by cultural restraints. As the penultimate gesture toward the institution of marriage clearly indicates, endless erotic mobility is difficult to sustain. But just as clearly, *As You Like It* registers its lack of commitment to the binary logic that dominates the organization of desire. If *As You Like It* suggests the "folly" of desire, part of that folly is the discipline to which it is subject.

> My desire/ More sharp than filed steel
>
> Antonio, *Twelfth Night*

The sexual economy of *Twelfth Night* is saturated with multiple erotic investments: Viola/Cesario's dual desire for Olivia and Orsino; Orsino's ambivalent interest in Viola/Cesario; Sebastian's responses to Olivia and Antonio; and finally, Antonio's exclusive erotic wish for Sebastian. Although Viola's initial impulse for adopting male disguise is to serve the duke as a eunuch (I.ii.56), her status as sexually neutral dissipates as she quickly becomes both erotic object and subject. Critics often mention Viola's passivity, her inclination to commit "What else may hap to time" (I.ii.60), but they fail to recognize that as Cesario she woos Olivia with a fervor that exceeds her "text" (I.v.227). S/he asks, with no apparent mandate, to see Olivia's face; and upon viewing the "picture" (I.v.228), responds, "if you were the devil, you are fair" (I.v.246).

Critics also point to Viola/Cesario's anxiety over the predicament caused by the disguise:

I am the man. If it be so, as 'tis,
Poor lady, she were better love a dream.
Disguise, I see, thou art a wickedness
Wherein the pregnant enemy does much. . . .
How will this fadge? My master loves her dearly;
And I, poor monster, fond as much on him;
And she, mistaken, seems to dote on me.
What will become of this? As I am man,
My state is desperate for my master's love;
As I am woman – now alas the day! –
What thriftless sighs shall poor Olivia breathe!
O time, thou must untangle this, not I;
It is too hard a knot for me t'untie.

(II.ii.25–41)

The image by which Viola/Cesario expresses her plight is far more resonant than many critics have noted. The implied double negative of a *knot* that *cannot* be untied is precisely the figuration of her complex erotic investments: s/he "fonds" on her master, while simultaneously finding erotic intrigue and excitement as the object of Olivia's desire. The flip side of her anxiety about Olivia's desire is her own desire to be the *object* of Olivia's desire. This desire s/he can *(k)not* untie because of its status as negation. Why this desire is negated in this play I will take up in a moment. For now, what is important is that the play sets up Viola/Cesario's dual erotic investment, not so much to resolve it as to sustain its dramatic possibilities and to elicit the similarly polymorphous desires of the audience, whose spectator pleasure would be at least in part derived from a transgressive glimpse of multiple erotic possibilities.

To substantiate the play's investment in erotic duality, one can compare the language used in Viola/Cesario's two avowals of love: the first as Orsino's wooer of Olivia, and the second as s/he attempts to communicate love to Orsino. In both avowals, Viola/Cesario theatricalizes desire, using a similar language of conditionals toward both erotic objects. Compare the syntactical and semantic structure of Viola/Cesario's comment to Olivia, "If I did love you in my master's flame,/ With such a suff'ring, such a deadly life,/ In your denial I would find no sense;/ I would not understand it" (I.v.259–62) to her comment to Orsino: "My father had a daughter lov'd a man,/ As it might be, perhaps, were I a woman,/ I should your lordship" (II.iv.107–9). What predisposes us to credit the second comment as truth but the first as false, a suspect performance, is, I suggest, largely our assumption of universal heterosexuality. Both speeches are equally theatricalizations of desire. As such, both work to undermine the dichotomy between truth and falsehood, fiction and reality, heterosexuality and homoeroticism.

This is not to suggest that Viola/Cesario's position in relation to homoerotic desire is celebrated in the text: unlike Rosalind, her erotic predicament threatens her with destruction – or at least so s/he believes – at the hands of Sir Andrew, who is manipulated by Sir Toby to challenge his rival to a duel. The weapon of choice is not incidental, as the whole point of the threatened battle is for Viola/Cesario to demonstrate the "little thing" that "would make me tell them how much I lack of a man" (III.iv.302–3). As Toby says: "Therefore, on, or strip your sword stark naked; for meddle you must, that's certain, or forswear to wear iron about you" (III.iv.252–54). At this (phallic) point, Viola/Cesario's "lack" is upheld as the signifier of gender difference. And yet, to the extent that masculinity is embodied in the sword, it depends upon a particular kind of performance rather than any biological equipment. This theatrical moment simultaneously reinscribes a binary code of gender into the action, *and* suggests the extent to which gender is prosthetic.[20] It seems telling that at precisely this point of pressure on the meaning of gender, the play of erotic difference is abandoned. Or, more accurately, deflected, for who should enter to defend Viola/Cesario but Antonio, the figure who is positioned most firmly in a homoerotic relation to desire.

The entire first scene between Antonio and Sebastián is focused on Sebastian's denial of the sailor's help, and Antonio's irrepressible desire not only to protect but accompany the man with whom, we later learn, he has spent "three months . . ./ No int'rim, not a minute's vacancy./ Both day and night" (V.i.90–2). Antonio singlemindedly pursues Sebastian through the (to him) dangerous streets of Illyria: "But come what may, I do adore thee so/ That danger shall seem sport, and I will go" (II.i.44–5). It is not fortuitous that this scene (II.i) intervenes between Viola/Cesario's wooing of Olivia, when s/he exceeds her "text" (I.v), and her contemplation of the danger inherent in this action: "It is too hard a knot for me t' untie" (II.ii). For Antonio's words allude to the perils in early modern culture of an exclusively homoerotic passion: in order to remain in the presence of one's beloved, "danger" must be figuratively, if not literally, transformed into "sport." That the danger is not limited to the threat of Orsino's men (the force of law) is revealed in Antonio's plea to Sebastian, "If you will not murder me for my love, let me be your servant" (II.i.33–4). The love Antonio extends is somehow capable of inciting the beloved to murder.

An even greater danger is intimated in this scene, which will ultimately have severe repercussions on the fate of Antonio's desire. Sebastian explains to Antonio that his father "left behind him myself and a sister, both born in an hour. If the heavens had been pleas'd, would we had so ended! But you, sir, alter'd that, for some hour before you took me from the breach of the sea was my sister drown'd" (II.i.17–22). Sebastian's life is saved when he is pulled from the "breach of the sea," an image of the surf that invokes the re-birthing we expect from Shakespearean shipwrecks. But this rebirth is coincident with the supposed death of Sebastian's sister; she is "drown'd already . . . with salt water" and drowned again in Sebastian's tearful "remembrance" (II.i.29–30). In other words, Sebastian's rebirth into Antonio's love is implicated in the destruction of the only woman Sebastian has loved: Viola.

As mentioned, Viola/Cesario *is* threatened with destruction. Crucially, it is Antonio who saves her/him, thinking that he is defending his beloved. His entrance at this moment enacts the central displacement of the text: when the ramifications of a simultaneous homoeroticism and heterosexuality become too anxiety-ridden, the homoerotic energy of Viola/Cesario is displaced onto Antonio – the one figure, as Laurie Osborne notes, whose passion for another does not arise from deception or require a woman for its expression.[21]

Just before the swordfight Antonio finds Sebastian, and greets him with these words:

> I could not stay behind you. My desire,
> More sharp than filed steel, did spur me forth;
> And not all love to see you, though so much
> As might have drawn one to a longer voyage,
> But jealousy what might befall your travel,
> Being skilless in these parts. . . . My willing love,
> The rather by these arguments of fear,
> Set forth in your pursuit.
>
> (III.iii.4–12)

Why do editors gloss "jealousy" as anxiety, when both words were available to Shakespeare, and both scan equally well?[22] Antonio is clearly both anxious about the dangers that might "befall" his beloved, and jealous of the attractions that might entice him. And not without reason: Sebastian falls rather easily to the "relish" of Olivia's charms (IV.i.59).

Antonio's discourse partakes of what I will call a "rhetoric of penetration." Male desire in Shakespearean drama is almost always figured in phallic images – which may seem tautological until one remembers the commonly accepted notion that Shakespeare's fops are not only "effeminate" but "homosexual." On the contrary, *Twelfth Night* represents male homoerotic desire as phallic in the most active sense: erect, hard, penetrating. Antonio describes his desire in terms of sharp, filed steel which spurs him on to pursuit, "spur" working simultaneously to "prick" him (as object) and urge him on (as subject). To the extent that heterosexual desire in Shakespearean drama is often associated with detumescence (the triumph of Venus over Mars, the pervasive puns on dying), and homoerotic desire is figured as permanently erect, it is the desire of man for man that is coded as the more "masculine."[23]

Many critics have noted in addition that in the early modern period excessive heterosexual lust seems to engender in men fears of "effeminacy." Romeo, for instance, complains that desire for Juliet "hath made me effeminate,/ And in my temper soft'ned valor's steel!" Similarly, the Romans maintain that Antony's lust for Cleopatra has so compromised his gender identity that he "is not more manlike/ Than Cleopatra, nor the queen of Ptolemy/ More womanly than he." In contrast, extreme virility, manifested in Spartan self-denial and military exploits, is not only depicted as consistent with erotic desire for other men; it also is expressed in it, as when Aufidius says to Coriolanus, "Let me twine/ Mine arms about that body, whereagainst/ My grained ash an hundred times hath broke," and goes on to compare the joy he feels at seeing Coriolanus as being greater than that which he felt "when I first my wedded mistress saw/ Bestride my threshold."[24]

Fops, on the other hand, while commonly perceived as having a "passive" interest in male homoerotic encounters, are almost always involved in pursuing (if unsuccessfully) a heterosexual alliance.[25] Sir Andrew, for instance, hopes to marry Olivia, if only for her status and money. True, he is manipulated by Sir

Toby, and he may therefore be seen to partake of a homoerotic triangular relation, whereby he woos his ostensible object (Olivia) in order to concretize ties with his real object (Toby).[26] However, Sir Andrew seems more accurately represented as void of erotic desire, merely attempting to fulfill the social requirements of heterosexuality. Indeed, he seems a vessel into which others" desires are poured, especially Sir Toby's triangular manipulation for wealth, ease, and power through the exchange of the body of his niece. Rather than being homosexual, fops are figured as always already effeminated by their heterosexual relation to desire.

Orsino, whose languid action and hyper-courtly language situate him as foppish, appears to be more in love with love than with any particular object. As Jean Howard points out, Orsino

> initially poses a threat to the Renaissance sex-gender system by languidly abnegating his active role as masculine wooer and drowning in narcissistic self-love. . . . His narcissism and potential effeminacy are displaced, respectively, onto Malvolio and Andrew Aguecheek, who suffer fairly severe humiliations for their follies.[27]

Orsino is narcissistic and "effeminate," but I would argue that neither his narcissism nor his "effeminacy" is indicative of desire for males *per se*. Orsino's "effeminacy," a gender characteristic, accompanies both his heterosexual desire for Olivia and his homoerotic desire for Cesario. What is most interesting, however, is the extent to which Orsino's desire is anxious, or in our modern parlance, homo*phobic*. In contrast to Orsino's homosocial ease with Cesario – their intimacy is established in three days (I.iv.3) – the possibility of a homo*erotic* basis to his affection for his servant creates tension: he defers accepting Viola as his betrothed until she has adopted her "maiden weeds" (V.i.252). Indeed, he refuses to really "see" her as a woman, continuing to refer to her as Cesario, "For so you shall be, while you are a man;/ But when in other habits you are seen,/ Orsino's mistress and his fancy's queen" (V.i.383–5). To the extent that his anxiety *is* desire, Orsino figures as the repressed homoerotic analogue to Antonio.

Throughout his canon, Shakespeare associates "effeminacy" in men with the fawning superciliousness of the perfumed courtier, and with the "womanish" tears of men no longer in control. Both

Hotspur and Hamlet, for example, rail against the "effeminacy" of courtiers; Laertes and Lear describe their tears as "womanish." Hamlet is as disgusted by Osric and Guildenstern as he is by Ophelia and Gertrude; it is this fear of "effeminacy" that stimulates the homophobic disgust in his charge, "'Sblood, do you think I am easier to be play'd on than a pipe?"[28]

There is little in the canon to suggest that Shakespeare linked "effeminacy" to homoeroticism, unless we look to the "feminine" qualities of Cesario that ambivalently attract Orsino to his page. Historically, the charge of "effeminacy" seems to have been limited to such "boys" as Cesario, or to those adult men who were "uxoriously" obsessed with women. The unfailing correspondence of adult homoeroticism and "effeminacy" is a later cultural development, and is imported into Shakespeare's texts by critics responding to a different cultural milieu.[29] In *Twelfth Night*, both Antonio and Sebastian pointedly use their phallic swords, and are implicitly contrasted to Sir Andrew, whom even Viola/Cesario one-ups, despite the "little thing that would make [her] tell them how much [she] lack[s] as a man." "Appropriate" male desire is phallic, whether homoerotic or heterosexual; without that phallic force, men in Shakespearean drama are usually rendered either asexual or nominally heterosexual.

Despite the attractions of homoeroticism, the pleasure *Twelfth Night* takes in it is not sustained. Not only are Viola/Cesario and Sebastian betrothed respectively to Orsino and Olivia, but Antonio is marginalized – in part because he publicly speaks his desire, in part because his desire is exclusive of other bonds. Like *The Merchant of Venice*'s Antonio, this Antonio gives his beloved his "purse"; shortly thereafter he is seized by the duke's men. As he struggles with the officers, Antonio states to "Sebastian":

> This comes with seeking you.
> But there's no remedy; I shall answer it.
> What will you do, now my necessity
> Makes me to ask you for my purse? It grieves me
> Much more for what I cannot do for you
> Than what befalls myself.

(III.iv.333–8)

After Viola/Cesario offers money but denies not only their acquaintance, but knowledge of Antonio's "purse," the officers attempt to take Antonio away; but he resists:

> Let me speak a little. This youth that you see here
> I snatch'd one half out of the jaws of death,
> Reliev'd him with such sanctity of love,
> And to his image, which methought did promise
> Most venerable worth, did I devotion.
>
> (III.iv.360–4)

"What's that to us?" reply the officers, and Antonio is compelled to curse:

> But O how vile an idol proves this god!
> Thou hast, Sebastian, done good feature shame.
> In nature there's no blemish but the mind;
> None can be call'd deform'd but the unkind.
>
> (III.iv.366–9)

To which the officers conclude: "The man grows mad. Away with him!" (III.iv.372)

Antonio is labeled mad by the law not only because of the linguistic and class impropriety of his speech, but because his vocalization of desire is caught uncomfortably between the only two discourses available to him: platonic friendship and sodomy. There are literally no early modern terms by which Antonio's desire can be understood.

Antonio's imprisonment, we conventionally expect, will be revoked when Viola/Cesario's problems are resolved. With the entrance of Sebastian not only do brother and sister rediscover each other, but "nature to her bias," according to most critics, draws Olivia to Sebastian and Orsino to Viola (V.i.257). This appeal to "nature" can be seen to dissolve the previous dramatic energy expended in portraying socially illegitimate alliances, the conventional betrothals displacing the fantasy embodied by Viola/Cesario of holding in tension simultaneous objects of desire. Many feminist and psychoanalytic critics read this conclusion as a celebration of psychic androgyny in which Viola/Cesario is fantastically split, "An apple cleft in two" into Viola and Sebastian (V.i.221). However pertinent such a reading may be to the gender politics of the play (and I think that it bypasses rather than resolves the question of gender identity posed by transvestism), it ignores the erotic politics. Antonio's final query, "Which is Sebastian?" is answered by the "identification" of Sebastian and Viola and the quick, symmetrical pairings. Or is it? Is the Sebastian whose words to Antonio are: "Antonio, O my dear Antonio!/ How have the hours rack'd and torture'd me,/ Since I have lost thee!" (V.i.215–17) the same Sebastian who has just sanctified his love to Olivia? Despite his miraculous betrothal, Sebastian's own desire seems more complicated than the assumption of "natural" hetero-sexuality would suggest. In fact, Sebastian's desire, like Viola/Cesario's, seems to obliterate the distinction between homoerotic and heterosexual – at least until the institution of marriage comes into (the) play. As a reassertion of the essential heterosexu-ality of desire, Sebastian's allusion to "nature's bias" seems a bit suspect.

Joseph Pequigney offers an alternative interpretation of "nature to her bias" which not only reopens the question of the meaning of "bias," but inverts its relation to "nature." He notes that "bias" derives from

> the game of bowls played with a bowl or ball designed to run obliquely, and "bias" denotes either the form of the bowl that causes it to swerve or, as in the metaphor, the curved course it takes. Nature then chose an oblique or curved rather than a straight way of operating . . . This homoerotic swerving or lesbian [sic] deviation from the heterosexual straight and narrow is not unnatural, but, to the contrary, a modus operandi of Nature.[30]

Despite its closure, then, *Twelfth Night's* conclusion seems only ambivalently invested in the "natural" heterosexuality it imposes.

Comparison of the treatment of homoeroticism in *As You Like It* and *Twelfth Night* suggests that when homoeroticism is not a mutual investment it becomes problematic. This may seem distressingly self-evident, but to say it underscores the point that the anxiety exposed in Shakespearean drama is not so much about a particular mode of desire, as about the psychic exposure entailed by a lack of mutuality. Heterosexual desire is equally troubling when unrequited. Despite *Twelfth Night's* nod to heterosexual imperatives in the ambiguous allusion to "nature to her bias," and despite both texts" ultimate movement toward heterosexu-ality, homoeroticism is constructed throughout as merely one more mode of desire. As Antonio puts it, in the closest thing we have to an antihomophobic statement in an early modern text: "In nature there's no blemish but the mind;/ None can be call'd deform'd but the unkind" (*Twelfth Night*, III.iv.368–9). Both modes of desire are responsive to social and institutional pressures; both are variously attributed to "noble" and "irrational" impulses. In other words, Shakespearean drama measures homoerotic and heterosexual impulses on the same scale of moral and philosophical value.

Secondly, the relative ease or dis-ease with homoerotic desire seems to depend on the extent to which such desire is recuperable within a simultaneous homoeroticism and heterosexuality that will ensure generational reproduction. Specifically, in these plays the dramatized fantasy of eliding women in erotic exchanges seems to initiate anxiety. When homoerotic exchanges threaten to replace heterosexual bonds, when eroticism is collapsed into anxiety about reproduction, then homoeroticism is exorcized at the same time as the female gender is resecured into the patriarchal order.

The specific anxiety about reproduction I hypothesize as a *structuring* principle for the movement of these comedies is not explicitly voiced in either play. It is, however, a dominant theme in the sonnets, beginning with the first line of the first poem to the young man: "From fairest creatures we desire increase/ That thereby beauty's rose might never die."[31] As the poet exhorts his beloved to "Look in thy glass, and tell the face thou viewest/ Now is the time that face should form another" – that if he should "Die single . . . thine image dies with thee" (Sonnet 3) – the failure to reproduce is figured in narcissistic, even masturbatory, terms: "For having traffic with thyself alone/ Thou of thyself thy sweet self dost deceive" (Sonnet 4). The sonnets' psychic strategy is founded on a paradox: the narcissism of taking the self as masturbatory object can only be countered and mastered by the narcissism of reproducing oneself in one's heirs.

That the failure to reproduce signified by this masturbatory fantasy is a veritable death knell is evidenced by Sonnet 3: "who is he so fond will be the tomb/ Of his self-love, to stop posterity?" Indeed, if one notes that the final couplet of six out of the first seven sonnets explicitly offers death as the sole alternative to reproduction, the anxiety animating the exhortation to reproduce becomes quite clear. The sheer repetition of the sentiment (twelve sonnets out of the first sixteen) attests to the presence of a repetition compulsion, indicating unresolved psychic distress.[32]

Such distress obviously structures the reproductive madness of Sonnet 6:

> Then let not winter's ragged hand deface
> In thee thy summer, ere thou be distill'd.
> Make sweet some vial; treasure thou some place
> With beauty's treasure, ere it be self-kill'd.
> That use is not forbidden usury
> Which happies those that pay the willing loan;
> That's for thyself to breed another thee,
> Or ten times happier, be it ten for one;
> Ten times thyself were happier than thou art,
> If ten of thine ten times refigur'd thee.

That ten is ten times better than one is self-evidently true only if the one is not the one who carries, labors, and delivers those ten offspring. The misogynistic pun on vial, referring both to the vessel of the womb and its supposedly vile character indicates a structuring ambivalence. The logic of the sequence implies that homoerotic love can only be justified through a heterosexual reproductivity that is always already degraded by its contact with female genitalia – the underlying fantasy being the wish for reproduction magically untainted by the female body.

"Make thee another self, *for love of me*" (Sonnet 10, my emphasis). Surely it is not fortuitous that the homoerotic investment of the sonnets elicits such a strong investment in reproduction. This investment is finally mediated, and the anxiety regarding women's necessary role in reproduction is displaced, as the poet appropriates for himself reproductive powers. From Sonnet 15, in which the poet claims to "engraft" his beloved "new," through the subsequent four poems, heterosexual reproduction slowly but surely gives way to the aesthetic immortality "engrafted" on the beloved by the poet's skill. The power to create life is transformed into the exclusively male power of the poet's invocation to an exclusively male audience: "So long as men can breathe or eyes can see,/ So long lives this and this gives life to thee" (Sonnet 18).

The historical reasons for the reproductive anxiety explicitly rendered in the sonnets, and implied by the structure of the comedies, are obviously complex. In order to unpack them, it may be useful to reinsert gender provisionally as a relevant analytic category, to examine the relation of homoerotic desire to the gender system. Eve Sedgwick argues that male homoeroticism was not perceived as threatening in early modern culture because it was not defined in opposition or as an impediment to hetero-sexuality; Trumbach and Saslow emphasize that the general pattern of male homoeroticism was "bisexual." *Exclusive* male homoeroti-cism, however, homoeroticism that did not admit the need for women, would disrupt important early modern economic and social imperatives: inheritance of name, entitlement, and property. Each of these imperatives, crucial to the social hierarchies of early modern England, was predominantly conferred through heterosexual marriage. I am suggesting, then, that the salient concern may be less the threat posed by homoerotic desire *per se* than that posed by non-monogamy and non-reproduction.

In addition, despite patriarchal control of female sexuality through the ideology of chastity and laws regulating marriage and illegitimacy, there seems to have been a high cultural investment in female erotic pleasure – not because women's pleasure was perceived as healthy or intrinsically desirable, but because it was thought necessary for successful conception to occur. According to Thomas Laqueur, early modern medical texts (including those of midwives) judged both male and female erotic pleasure as essential to generation.[33] Viewed as structurally inverted men, women were thought to ejaculate "seed" at the height of their sexual pleasure; conception supposedly began at the meeting of male and female seed. Because they were perceived as naturally cooler than men, women were thought to achieve orgasm only after the proper "heating" of their genitalia. In light of this social investment, it seems possible that an exclusive male homoeroticism could be seen as leaving female reproductive organs out, as it were, in the cold.

Insofar as *As You Like It* gestures outward toward an eroticism characterized by a diffuse and fluid simultaneity, it does so because the text never feels compelled to fix, to identify, or to name the desires it expresses. In contrast, *Twelfth Night* closes down erotic possibility precisely to the degree it complies with the social imperative to name desire, to fix it within definitive boundaries, and to identify it with specific characters. The "unmooring of desire, the generalizing of the libidinal" that Greenblatt sees as "the special pleasure of Shakespearean fiction" is, when one gets down to it, more comfortably evidenced in *As You Like It* than in *Twelfth Night*.[34] In the tensions exposed between the two plays, it may be that we start to move from what we are beginning to discern as Renaissance homoeroticism to what we know as modern homosexuality, from an inventive potentiality inherent in each subject to the social identity of a discrete order of being.[35]

It is of more than passing interest that insofar as each play enacts a "textual body," only *Twelfth Night* depends on a phallic representation of male homoeroticism. Much recent feminist and film criticism has implicated a phallic mode of representation within the visual economy of the "gaze," wherein value is ascribed according to what one sees (or fails to see): hence, the psychoanalytic verities of female "castration" and "penis envy." In those modes of representation governed by phallocentric prerogatives, argue many feminist film theorists, only two positions seem possible: the subject and the object of the gaze.[36] Although many theorists are now complicating this binary picture, arguing that women, in particular, negotiate as subjects and not merely as objects of the gaze, it might be helpful to distinguish the erotic economies of *Twelfth Night* and *As You Like It* along the following lines: *Twelfth Night* is predominantly phallic and visual; not only is Antonio's desire figured in phallic metaphors, but Orsino's desire waits upon the ocular proof of Viola/Cesario's "femininity." The final value is one of boundary setting, of marginalizing others along lines of exclusion. The erotics of *As You Like It*, on the other hand, are diffuse, non-localized, and inclusive, extending to the audience an invitation to "come play" – as does Rosalind-cum-boy-actor in the Epilogue.[37] Bypassing a purely scopic economy, *As You Like It* possesses provocative affinities with the tactile, contiguous, plural erotics envisioned by Luce Irigaray as more descriptive of female experience. We don't return to such a polymorphous textual body until the cross-gendered erotic play of *Antony and Cleopatra*.

This introduction of a diffuse, fluid erotics, and my analysis of the reproductive anxieties engendered by male homoeroticism, provoke the broader question of the relation of male homoeroticism to feminist politics. Contrary to the beliefs of those feminists who conflate male homosociality with homoeroticism, male homoeroticism has no unitary relationship to the structures and ideologies of male dominance. Patriarchal power is homosocial; but it also has been, at various times including the present, homophobic. As Sedgwick has demonstrated, "while male homosexuality does not correlate in a transhistorical way with political attitudes toward women, homophobia directed at men by men almost always travels with a retinue of gynephobia and antifeminism."[38] Male homoeroticism can be manipulated to reinforce and justify misogyny, or it can offer itself up as the means to deconstruct the binary structures upon which the subordination of women depends.

The logic of the sonnet sequence is, I believe, thoroughly misogynistic, and its homoerotics seem utterly entwined with that misogyny: a debased female reproduction is excised, and its creative powers appropriated, by the male lover-poet who thereby celebrates and immortalizes his male beloved. Conversely, the circulation of male homoerotic desire in *As You Like It* and *Twelfth Night* does not seem to depend upon an aversion to women or an ideology of male dominance as its *raison d'être*. The homoeroticism of *As You Like It* is not particularly continuous with the homosociality of the Duke's court (the homoerotic exchanges occur primarily between those excluded from it), nor are Antonio's, Viola/Cesario's, Orsino's, or Olivia's homoerotic interests particularly supportive of the patriarchal impulses of *Twelfth Night*. Indeed, whether the homoeroticism is embodied as male or female does not seem to have much impact on its subversive potential. Viola/Cesario's desire for a dual mode of eroticism is more threatening within the play than is Orlando's similar desire, but it is less dangerous than the exclusivity posed by Antonio.

In fact, the male and female homoeroticism of both plays interrupts the ideology of a "natural" love based on complementary yet oppositional genders. In so doing, the deviations from the dominant discourse of desire circulating throughout these texts transgress the Law of the Father, the injunction that sexuality will follow gender in lining up according to a "natural" binary code. By refusing such arbitrary divisions of desire, homoeroticism in *As You Like It* and *Twelfth Night* disrupts the cultural code that keeps both men and women in line, subverting patriarchy from within.

This is not to suggest that Shakespeare's plays do not demonstrate countless commitments to misogyny. Why homoeroticism would be so thoroughly supportive of the misogyny of the sonnets, and so seemingly independent of misogyny in these plays is an important question raised by my analysis. To what extent does genre influence the expression of erotic desire and anxiety? To begin to answer that question, and to substantiate those claims I have made, the treatment of homoeroticism in Shakespeare's predecessors, contemporaries, and followers must be analyzed. Obvious sites of inquiry would be a comparison of Shakespearean homoeroticism with that of Marlowe, and a study of the use of transvestism in Lyly, Sidney, Spenser, Jonson, Middleton, and Dekker.[39] What is crucial at this point is that the relation between gender and eroticism be carefully teased out, that eroticism be posed as a problematic in its own right – both intimately connected to and rigorously differentiated from gender.

The danger of pursuing this kind of inquiry at this moment is in ignoring gender differentials altogether, in an energetic pursuit of "sexuality." But if we remember that the analyses of both gender and eroticism are only part of a larger project of theorizing about and from the multiple subject positions we all live, and if we reflect on the complexity of our own erotic practices, perhaps we can trace the play of our differences without reifying either them or ourselves. Erotic choice is, as Robert Stoller remarks, "a matter of opinions, taste, aesthetics;" it is also a matter of political theater, in which we all, even now, play a part.[40]

Afterword

Much contemporary criticism of Shakespearean drama has hinged on the question: does the drama subvert or contain the dominant ideologies of early modern England? Along with several other critics, I have felt that the terms in which this question is posed reify text and culture to static and coherent wholes, with the univocality of textual and cultural meanings not only assumed, but frozen in time.[1] In an effort to bypass this polarizing debate, I have emphasized throughout *Desire and Anxiety* less the *fact* of ideological containment than the *work* involved in, and the anxieties suggested by, such an aesthetic-political project. In the nine texts I have examined, the primary method shown to accomplish the containment of female characters is the formal constraint of genre: the comedic closure of heterosexual marriage, the exclusion of women from the historical process, and the tragic (in the dual sense of genre and sentiment) infusion of male heterosexual anxiety in the construction of the "masculine" self. However, even though the textual containment of female characters seems a foregone, because generic, conclusion, I have attempted to show that such textual certainty is destabilized by its own necessary representation of female transgression. Within formal, generic restraints, the work of containing the female gender and of constructing woman-as-representation is *staged*, enacted both in the text and in the theater as dramatic conflict – with female characters, and male characters and bodies figured as female, struggling for the power that both inheres in and defies representation. The marriages of Viola and Rosalind that purportedly conclude their plays represent the patriarchal closure of heterosexual marriage, but only after the plots embody desires that exceed institutional heterosexuality. The staging of Falstaff's exclusion (reproduced in microcosm in

Katharine's linguistic and erotic subjugation) enacts the exclusion of women from the historical genre, yet provides the means for its own meta-critique. Not surprisingly, the tragedies and *Troilus and Cressida* (in my reading, more a tragedy than a comedy) least express a deconstructive impulse, as the imposition of stasis on Ophelia, Desdemona, and Hermione, and the figuration of Cressida as site of venereal disease, literally and figuratively "body forth" the physical and psychic containment of female bodies. Yet in the representation of the forcibly closed or disease-ridden female body the drama unwittingly if necessarily exhibits its own system of repression, its paranoia. The project of containment is inherently unstable, subverted by the process of dramatizing the ideological work of the play.

Crucially, whatever containment of female subjectivity is textually achieved depends upon the repression of female *erotic* power. In this signifying system, the maintenance of gender asymmetry is *predicated* on the containment of female sexuality. And yet, the comparison of the simultaneously dual desires of Orlando and Viola in Chapter 5 suggests that erotic deviance and transgression are not the exclusive province of males: erotic desire may sometimes productively *exceed* gender constraints. The sex/gender/sexuality system as represented by Shakespeare was not continuous, unified, cohesive, or closed, but fractured, unstable, contradictory, open to negotiation and resistance. To the extent that a coherent erotic system can be said to exist at all, it seems less rigidly structured in terms of erotic desire than gender role: gender repression depends on erotic repression, but sexual play is not solely a masculine prerogative.

What makes the ideological work of this drama even more unstable are the desires of readers and spectators. Whatever the textual address of these plays, it does not subsume or totally determine audience response.[2] Individual desires and anxieties, fantasies and fears complicate the experience of spectatorship, and, while we cannot know the subjective experience of sixteenth-century audiences, it seems probable that their desires were encoded along gender and status lines. This does not mean that their desires were gender or class determined – for instance, that all male merchants would have desired in the same way – it merely means that male and female desires would have signified according to gendered definitions of masculinity and femininity that were also inflected with status distinctions. In addition, the context of spectatorship

– whether it takes place within a rowdy, sexually licentious public playhouse located in the "liberties" of London, or within a hierarchically controlled private theater situated in the city proper – most likely affected the audience's experience and expression of desire. The ideological work of these plays, in other words, would have been fractured, in every performance, across lines of gender, sexuality, status, and locale.

In highlighting the contradictions in Shakespearean representations and audience responses, I mean to gesture toward similar contradictions within our modern sex/gender/sexuality system. The ways Shakespearean subjects negotiate for erotic agency within a social, political, and aesthetic field of constraints implies through comparison some of the possibilities and limitations of our own erotic negotiations. Specifically, to the extent that Shakespearean drama endorses containment and repression within an overall paranoiac economy, it highlights the anxieties which, when left unacknowledged and unattended, lead to psychic and social destruction. However, to the extent that the drama embodies erotic plurality, heteronomy, and possibility, it provides an affirmative model for refiguring contemporary erotic modes: toward desires, practices, and identities neither homosexual nor heterosexual, but provisional and flexible and, above all, resistant to normalization and militaristic significations. That Shakespearean drama yields up such configurations of desire is undoubtedly a function of my own desires and anxieties, my own projections and wish-fulfillments, my own experiences in the movie-theater and the classroom. But it is equally an indication of the extent to which Shakespearean drama offers itself up to the reader, to make of its play of desires, in the words of *Twelfth Night*, "what you will." If our erotic realities are not "as we like them," the slippages, transformations, and transgressions of Shakespearean drama encourage us to make of them what *we* will. Such an invitation to empowerment is at once, however, genuine *and disingenuous*, as Shakespearean drama demonstrates the extent to which erotic "choice" is afforded, deferred, and denied. But those are the necessary conditions within which we play, speak, and write, and it is with a consciousness of much the same sensibility that I offer *Desire and Anxiety* up to its own circulation.

Notes

INTRODUCTION

1 My reading of *Romeo and Juliet* is indebted to that of Coppélia Kahn in *Man's Estate: Masculine Identity in Shakespeare* (Berkeley: University of California Press, 1981).

2 See Catherine Belsey, *The Subject of Tragedy: Identity and Difference in Renaissance Drama* (London: Methuen, 1985).

3 Stephen Greenblatt, *Shakespearean Negotiations: The Circulation of Social Energy in Renaissance England* (Oxford: Clarendon Press, 1988).

4 ibid., pp. 2 and 4.

5 David Halperin, "Sex Before Sexuality: Pederasty, Politics, and Power in Classical Athens," *Hidden From History: Reclaiming the Gay and Lesbian Past*, ed. Martin Duberman, Martha Vicinus, and George Chauncey, Jr. (New York: New American Library, 1989), p. 52.

6 René Girard, *Deceit, Desire, and the Novel: Self and Other in Literary Structure*, trans. Yvonne Freccero (Baltimore: Johns Hopkins University Press, 1965).

7 Sigmund Freud, "Anxiety," *Introductory Lectures on Psychoanalysis*, ed. James Strachey (London: W. W. Norton, 1966), pp. 392–411.

8 See Jonathan Dollimore, "The Cultural Politics of Perversion: Augustine, Shakespeare, Freud, Foucault," *Genders* 8 (Summer 1990), pp. 3–16.

9 Sigmund Freud, *Civilization and its Discontents* (1930), trans. and ed. James Strachey (New York: W. W. Norton, 1961).

10 Michel Foucault, *The History of Sexuality* Vol. 1 (New York: Random House, 1978), p. 103.

11 Jeffrey Weeks, *Sexuality and its Discontents* (London: Routledge and Kegan Paul, 1985), p. 44.

12 In this, I find Madelon Sprengnether to be the most eloquent spokesperson: "For me Freud's greatness lies in the process rather than the product of his interpretations: in his description of the transference phenomenon, for instance, and of the compulsion to repeat, as well as his reliance on free association and his bedrock belief in the hidden agency of the unconscious. The developmental theory that Freud regarded as essential to his thought introduces a certain warp

into an otherwise neutral array of hermeneutic strategies – a warp that reproduces some aspects of Freud's own culture", *The Spectral Mother: Freud, Feminism, and Psychoanalysis* (Ithaca: Cornell University Press, 1990), p. x.

13 Robert J. Stoller, M.D. *Observing the Erotic Imagination* (New Haven: Yale University Press, 1985), p. viii.

14 ibid., p. viii.

15 Stephen Greenblatt, "Psychoanalysis and Renaissance Culture," *Literary Theory/Renaissance Texts*, ed. Patricia Parker and David Quint (Baltimore: Johns Hopkins University Press, 1986), pp. 215–16.

16 Greenblatt, "Fiction and Friction," in *Shakespearean Negotiations*, pp. 75–6.

17 See especially Louis Adrian Montrose, "The Elizabethan Subject and the Spenserian Text," *Literary Theory/Renaissance Texts*, ed. Patricia Parker and David Quint (Baltimore: Johns Hopkins University Press, 1986), pp. 303–40.

18 Natalie Zemon Davis, "Boundaries and the Sense of Self in Sixteenth-Century France," *Reconstructing Individualism: Autonomy, Individuality, and the Self in Western Thought*, ed. Thomas C. Heller, *et al.* (Stanford: Stanford University Press, 1986), p. 63.

19 Teresa de Lauretis, *Alice Doesn't: Feminism, Semiotics, Cinema* (Bloomington: Indiana University Press, 1984), p. 99.

20 Michel de Certeau, *The Practice of Everyday Life*, trans. Steven Rendall (Berkeley: University of California Press, 1984).

21 Greenblatt, "Fiction and Friction," *Reconstructing Individualism*, ed. Heller, p. 52. Greenblatt himself seems to have recognized as much: in the revised version in *Shakespearean Negotiations*, "ultimate sexual reality" is changed to "different sexual reality" (p. 93).

22 De Certeau defines "strategy" as "the calculus of force-relations which becomes possible when a subject of will and power . . . can be isolated from an 'environment'. A strategy assumes a place that can be circumscribed as *proper* (propre) and thus serve as the basis for generating relations with an exterior distinct from it." A "tactic," on the other hand, is "a calculus which cannot count on a 'proper' (a spatial or institutional localization) . . . A tactic insinuates itself into the other's place, fragmentarily, without taking it over in its entirety, without being able to keep it at a distance." (*Practice of Everyday Life*, p. xix.)

23 ibid., p. xiii.

24 I am indebted to Catherine Belsey for suggesting this clarification.

25 Gayle Rubin, "Thinking Sex: Notes for a Radical Theory of the Politics of Sexuality," *Pleasure and Danger: Exploring Female Sexuality*, ed. Carole Vance (London: Routledge and Kegan Paul, 1984), p. 267.

1 JEWELS, STATUES, AND CORPSES

1 Ruth Kelso, *Doctrine for the Lady of the Renaissance* (Urbana: University of Illinois Press, 1956), p. 24.

2 Carol Cook, "'The Sign and Semblance of Her Honor'": Reading Gender Difference in *Much Ado About Nothing*,' *PMLA* 101:2 (1986), p. 187.

3 I say this despite evidence that male children wore "female" dress until the age of seven. My point is not that historical differences in the construction of gender do not exist, but that early modern "masculinity" entailed a separation from the body of the female – like that narrated by Freud – even if that separation was less unequivocal and more protracted over time.

4 See Tania Modleski, *The Women Who Knew Too Much: Hitchcock and Feminist Theory* (London: Methuen, 1988), p. 99.

5 Abbe Blum, "'Strike all that look upon with mar[b]le': Monumentalizing Women in Shakespeare's Plays," *The Renaissance Englishwoman in Print: Counterbalancing the Canon*. ed. Anne M. Haselkorn and Betty S. Travitsky (Amherst: University of Massachusetts Press, 1990), 99–118.

6 Peter Stallybrass suggests a similar taxonomy of erotic/political signification in his examination of the connection between "the [female's] enclosed body, the closed mouth, and the locked house" in "Patriarchal Territories: The Body Enclosed," *Rewriting the Renaissance*, ed. Margaret Ferguson, Maureen Quilligan, Nancy Vickers (Chicago: University of Chicago Press, 1986), pp. 123–42.

7 Stephen Greenblatt, "Fiction and Friction," *Shakespearean Negotiations: The Circulation of Social Energy in Renaissance England* (Oxford: Clarendon Press, 1988), pp. 66–93.

8 Joel Fineman, "Fratricide and Cuckoldry: Shakespeare's Doubles," *Representing Shakespeare: New Psychoanalytic Essays*, ed. Murray M. Schwartz and Coppélia Kahn (Baltimore: Johns Hopkins University Press, 1980), p. 73.

9 See in particular Madelon Gohlke, "'I wooed thee with my sword': Shakespeare's Tragic Paradigms," Schwartz and Kahn, *Representing Shakespeare*, pp. 170–87.

10 I.ii.135–7, *The Complete Works of Shakespeare*, 3rd edn, ed. David Bevington (Glenview: Scott, Foreman & Co., 1980); all other textual references hereafter cited parenthetically refer to this edition.

11 See Ernest Jones, *Hamlet and oedipus* (Garden City: Doubleday, 1954). I find the most persuasive evidence of oedipal conflict in the ambiguous syntax of these lines: "How stand I then,/ That have a father kill'd, a mother stain'd" (IV.iv.56–7).

12 Although I read both "lust" and "radiant angel" as referring to Gertrude, "radiant angel" is equally compelling as King Hamlet's self-characterization.

13 The image of a locked female sexuality seems obviously connected to the medieval chastity belt.

14 The grave here is symbolically and geographically analogous to the marriage bed in *Othello*. A comparison of both the grave and marriage bed to the tomb of *Romeo and Juliet* extends the implications of each. The tomb is characterized by the Friar as the earth's womb, to which all humankind must return (II.iii.9–12). The implication of all three

plays is that women, because of their procreative capacities, are to be blamed for male mortality. Apparently, women grant less the gift of life than the curse of death: men are condemned to live only to die.

15 The *Oxford English Dictionary* defines "consummation" as "The completion of marriage by sexual intercourse" for as early as 1530. Other early meanings include (1) "The action of completing, accomplishing, fulfilling, finishing, or ending," (2) "Completion, conclusion, as an event or condition; end; *death*," (3) "The action of perfecting; the condition of full and perfect development, *perfection*, acme," and (4) "A condition in which desires, aims, and tendencies are fulfilled; crowning or fitting end; *goal*" (my emphasis).

16 Stallybrass, "Patriarchal Territories," p. 139.

17 Edward A. Snow, "Sexual Anxiety and the Male Order of Things in *Othello*," *English Literary Renaissance* 10 (1980), p. 407. The status of their consummation is a matter of debate. In II.iii.11–13, Othello implies that they have yet to make love – "The purchase made, the fruits are to ensue; that profit's yet to come 'tween me and you" – but it seems clear that by III.iii.consummation has occurred.

18 Stephen Greenblatt, "The Improvisation of Power," *Renaissance Self-Fashioning* (Chicago: University of Chicago Press, 1980), pp. 222–54.

19 For an analysis of how Othello's "monstrosity" intersects with cultural identifications of femininity as monstrous, see Karen Newman, "'And wash the Ethiop white': Femininity and the Monstrous in *Othello*," *Shakespeare Reproduced: the Text in History and Ideology*, ed. Jean E. Howard and Marion F. O'Connor (New York: Methuen, 1987), pp. 143–62.

20 I.i.89–92, 111–14, 116–18, 127; I.ii.71–2; I.iii.64, 100, 292–3.

21 Martin Orkin, "Othello and the 'plain face' of Racism," *Shakespeare Quarterly* 38:2 (Summer 1987), pp. 166–88.

22 Snow and Greenblatt both mention Desdemona's sexual frankness; see Snow, "Sexual Anxiety," p. 406. However, the weight of Greenblatt's analysis comes perilously close to blaming the victim: Desdemona's "frank acceptance of pleasure and submission to her spouse's pleasure, is . . . as much as Iago's slander the cause of Desdemona's death, for it awakens the deep current of sexual anxiety in Othello, anxiety that with Iago's help expresses itself in quite orthodox fashion as the perception of adultery'; *Renaissance Self-Fashioning*, p. 250.

23 For an excellent analysis of this passage, see Greenblatt, *Renaissance Self-Fashioning*, pp. 240–3.

24 The bond between Hermione and Leontes is restored in much the way as is the bond between Hero and Claudio: the woman is hidden away, presumed to be dead, and then re-offered in a ritual marriage ceremony; in both plays, the attempted rejuvenation of an emotional bond fails. See Cook, "'The Sign and Semblance of Her Honor.'"

25 Most psychoanalytic interpretations of *The Winter's Tale* agree that it enacts a reparative vision. See Murray M. Schwartz, "Leontes' Jealousy in *The Winter's Tale*," *American Imago* 30:3 (Fall 1973), pp. 250–73 and "*The Winter's Tale*: Loss and Transformation," *American Imago* 32 (1975), pp. 145–99; Richard Wheeler, "'Since first

we were dissevered': Trust and Autonomy in Shakespearean Tragedy and Romance," and Murray M. Schwartz, "Shakespeare through Contemporary Psychoanalysis," Schwartz and Kahn, *Representing Shakespeare*, pp. 150–69, 21–32; Janet Adelman, "Male Bonding in Shakespeare's Comedies," *Shakespeare's Rough Magic*, ed. Coppélia Kahn and Peter Erickson (Newark: University of Delaware Press, 1985), pp. 73–103; and W. Thomas MacCary, *Friends and Lovers: The Phenomenology of Desire in Shakespearean Comedy* (New York: Columbia University Press, 1985). An interesting exception is Kay Stockholder's chapter on *The Winter's Tale* in *Dream Works: Lovers and Families in Shakespeare's Plays* (Toronto: University of Toronto Press, 1987).

26 That hands are cathected with erotic energy is evident as the angry Polixenes interrupts Florizel and Perdita just as they clasp hands.

27 Schwartz, "Leontes" Jealousy in *The Winter's Tale*," p. 267.

28 The threat to the male body continues as Polixenes repeats and inverts this image in his warning to Perdita: "If ever henceforth thou/These rural latches to his entrance open,/Or hoop his body more with thy embraces,/I will devise a death as cruel for thee/As thou are tender to't" (IV.iv.438–42).

29 For Leontes" admission of guilt, see V.i.16–18.

30 Jonathan Dollimore, "Shakespeare, Cultural Materialism, Feminism and Marxist Humanism," *New Literary History* 21:3 (Spring 1990), p. 487.

31 Cook, "'The Sign and Semblance of Her Honor,'" p.186.

32 See, for instance, Juliet Dusinberre, *Shakespeare and the Nature of Women* (New York: Barnes and Noble, 1975); Marilyn French, *Shakespeare's Division of Experience* (New York: Ballantine Books, 1981); Irene G. Dash, *Wooing, Wedding, and Power: Women in Shakespeare's Plays* (New York: Columbia University Press, 1981); and Marianne L. Novy, *Love's Argument: Gender Relations in Shakespeare* (Chapel Hill: University of North Carolina Press, 1984). In what I believe is the most interesting of these works, Novy analyzes the conflict between mutuality and patriarchy, emotion and control, emphasizing the ambiguity of the plays" representations which invites conflicting readings.

33 See, for instance, Coppélia Kahn, *Man's Estate: Masculine Identity in Shakespeare* (Berkeley, University of California Press, 1981); Carol Thomas Neely, *Broken Nuptials in Shakespeare's Plays* (New Haven: Yale University Press, 1985); and Marilyn L. Williamson, *The Patriarchy of Shakespeare's Comedies* (Detroit: Wayne State University Press, 1986).

34 Cook, "'The Sign and Semblance,'" p. 190. Cook's approach has some affinities with that of Linda Bamber, *Comic Women, Tragic Men: A Study of Gender and Genre in Shakespeare* (Stanford: Stanford University Press, 1982).

35 Kathleen McLuskie, "The Patriarchal Bard: Feminist Criticism and Shakespeare: *King Lear* and *Measure for Measure*," *Political Shakespeare: New Essays in Cultural Materialism*, ed. Jonathan Dollimore and Alan Sinfield (Ithaca: Cornell University Press, 1985), pp. 88–108.

36 See Nancy Chodorow, *The Reproduction of Mothering: Psychoanalysis*

and the Sociology of Gender (Berkeley: University of California Press, 1978) and Dorothy Dinnerstein, *The Mermaid and the Minotaur: Sexual Arrangements and Human Malaise* (New York: Harper and Row, 1976).

37 See Coppélia Kahn's excellent analysis of the feud in *Man's Estate*.

38 I owe this insight to Abbe Blum.

2 PRINCE HAL'S FALSTAFF

1 Mikhail Bakhtin, *Rabelais and His World*, trans. Helene Iswolsky (Bloomington: Indiana University Press, 1984).

2 Madelon Sprengnether, *The Spectral Mother: Freud, Feminism, and Psychoanalysis* (Ithaca: Cornell University Press, 1990), p. xi.

3 According to Thomas Laqueur, *Making Sex: Body and Gender from the Greeks to Freud* (Cambridge: Harvard University Press, 1990), the contemporary medical literature conceived of males and females as structurally inverted: both genders originate as female, with the greater presence of "heat" in the male forcing outward that which lies hidden in the interior folds of the female – hence, male genitalia. The male fantasy of reversion is explored by Greenblatt in "Fiction and Friction," *Shakespearean Negotiations: The Circulation of Social Energy in Renaissance England* (Oxford: Clarendon Press, 1988).

4 Phyllis Rackin, "Historical Difference/Sexual Difference," forthcoming, in *Privileging Gender in Early Modern England*, ed. Jean R. Brink (Kirksville: 16th Century Journal Publishers, 1992).

5 See Lawrence Stone, *The Family, Sex and Marriage in England 1500–1800* (New York: Harper and Row, 1977). Infants of the upper and to some extent the middle classes were farmed out to working-class households for the first twelve to eighteen months of life.

6 I am indebted to Peter Stallybrass for this particular turn of phrase.

7 Stephen Orgel, "Nobody's Perfect: Or Why Did the English Stage Take Boys for Women?" *South Atlantic Quarterly* 88 (1989), pp. 7–29.

8 Important exceptions to this trend are Phyllis Rackin, "Anti-Historians: Women's Roles in Shakespeare's Histories," *Theatre Journal* 37 (1985), pp. 329–44, and "Patriarchal History and Female Subversion" in *Stages of History: Shakespeare's English Chronicles* (Ithaca: Cornell University Press, 1990), pp. 146–200, as well as Linda Bamber, *Comic Women, Tragic Men: A Study of Gender and Genre in Shakespeare* (Stanford: Stanford University Press, 1982), pp. 135–68. Marilyn French, *Shakespeare's Division of Experience* (New York: Ballantine Books, 1981) and Irene G. Dash, *Wooing, Wedding, and Power: Women in Shakespeare's Plays* (New York: Columbia University Press 1981) examine the Henry VI tetralogy, but not the *Henriad*. Coppélia Kahn, *Man's Estate: Masculine Identity in Shakespeare* (Berkeley: University of California Press, 1981), Peter Erickson, *Patriarchal Structures in Shakespeare's Drama* (Berkeley: University of California Press, 1985), and David Sundelson, *Shakespeare's Restorations of the Father* (New Brunswick: Rutgers University Press, 1983) all include chapters on

the development of male subjectivity through the reproduction of male bonds in the histories, but they do not focus specifically on the role of women. Although Marilyn Williamson's *The Patriarchy of Shakespeare's Comedies* (Detroit: Wayne State University Press, 1986) includes a chapter on the romances, it excludes the histories. Marianne L. Novy, *Love's Argument: Gender Relations in Shakespeare* (Chapel Hill: University of North Carolina Press, 1984) Carol Thomas Neely, *Broken Nuptials in Shakespeare's Plays* (New Haven: Yale University Press, 1985), Kay Stockholder, *Dream Works: Lovers and Families in Shakespeare's Plays* (Toronto: University of Toronto Press, 1987), Thomas W. MacCary, *Friends and Lovers: The Phenomenology of Desire in Shakespearean Comedy* (New York: Columbia University Press, 1985), and the essays in *Representing Shakespeare: New Psychoanalytic Essays*, ed. Murray M. Schwartz and Coppélia Kahn (Baltimore: Johns Hopkins University Press, 1980) all focus on plays other than the histories.

9 Carol Thomas Neely, "Constructing the Subject: Feminist Practice and the New Renaissance Discourses," *ELR* 18:1 (Winter 1988), pp. 5–18.

10 For the "rehearsal" of culture, see Steven Mullaney, *The Place of the Stage: License, Play, and Power in Renaissance England* (Chicago: Chicago University Press, 1988).

11 Jacques Lacan, "The Signification of the Phallus," *Ecrits: A Selection*, trans. Alan Sheridan (New York: W. W. Norton, 1977), pp. 281–91, and *Feminine Sexuality: Jacques Lacan and the école freudienne*, ed. Juliet Mitchell and Jacqueline Rose, trans. Jacqueline Rose (New York: Norton, 1982).

12 Shirley Nelson Garner, Claire Kahane, and Madelon Sprengnether, *The (M)Other Tongue: Essays in Feminist Psychoanalytic Interpretation* (Ithaca: Cornell University Press, 1985), p. 21.

13 Jane Gallop, *The Daughter's Seduction* (Ithaca: Cornell University Press, 1982), p. 97.

14 Such a subjugation of gender categories under the rubrics of "identity" and "power" seems to occur in the recent Shakespearean criticism of Jonathan Goldberg, "Shakespearean Inscriptions: the Voicing of Power," and Joel Fineman, "The Turn of the Shrew," both in *Shakespeare & the Question of Theory*, ed. Patricia Parker and Geoffrey Hartman (New York: Methuen, 1985), pp. 116–37 and 138–59, as well as in Stephen Greenblatt's "Fiction and Friction," *Shakespearean Negotiations*, pp. 66–93. For a critique of this subjugation, see Neely, "Constructing the Subject," Lynda E. Boose, "The Family in Shakespeare Studies; or – Studies in the Family of Shakespeareans; or – The Politics of Politics," *Renaissance Quarterly* 40 (Winter 1987), pp. 707–42; Peter Erickson, "Rewriting the Renaissance, Rewriting Ourselves," *Shakespeare Quarterly* 38:3 (1987), pp. 327–37; Marguerite Waller, "Academic Tootsie: The Denial of Difference and the Difference it Makes," *Diacritics* 17:1 (1987), pp. 2–20; and Judith Newton, "History as Usual? Feminism and the 'New Historicism,'" *Cultural Critique* (1988), pp. 87–121.

15 Ernst Kris, "Prince Hal's Conflict," *Psychoanalytic Explorations in Art* (New York: International University Press, 1952), pp. 273–88.

16 Schwartz, discussion at the University of Massachusetts, Amherst, 1986.

17 Erickson, *Patriarchal Structures in Shakespeare's Drama*, p. 46.

18 *The Comedy of Errors* (III.ii.81–154) and *Romeo and Juliet* (II.v.29–52).

19 At least four other critics have noted Falstaff's "femininity." In "The Prince's Dog," W. H. Auden notes that a fat man "looks like a cross between a very young child and a pregnant mother . . . fatness in the male is the physical expression of a psychological wish to withdraw from sexual competition and, by combining mother and child in his own person, to become emotionally self-sufficient," *The Dyer's Hand and Other Essays* (New York: Random House, 1962), pp. 195–6. In *Man's Estate*, Kahn credits Falstaff with a "curiously feminine sensual abundance" and goes on to remark that "a fat man can look like a pregnant woman, and Falstaff's fatness is fecund; it spawns symbols." However, Kahn sees in Falstaff mainly an "avoidance of sexual maturity," a "wish to bypass women" (pp. 72–3). Kahn refers to a talk by Sherman Hawkins, "Falstaff as Mom," given at the 1977 MLA Annual Meeting, but Hawkins" article has not, as far as I know, appeared in print. More recently, Patricia Parker includes Falstaff as one of her "literary fat ladies" in her book *Literary Fat Ladies: Rhetoric, Gender, Property* (London: Methuen, 1987). In a brilliantly "dilated" argument about the link between gender and the denial of textual closure, she sees Falstaff's corpulence as embodying Prince Hal's delay in "reformation" (pp. 20–2).

20 *Henry IV, part 1*, II.ii.110, II.iv.540, II.iv.109, II.ii.5, II.ii.30, II.iv.138, II.iv.224–5, III.iii.158, III.iii.177.

21 *Henry IV, part 1*, II.iv.521, II.iv.226, II.ii.197–8. According to J. Dover Wilson, in Renaissance usage the word "tallow" referred to "liquid fat, as well as dripping or suet or animal fat rendered down . . . [H]uman sweat, partly owing perhaps to the similarity of the word to 'suet', was likewise thought of as fat, melted by the heat of the body," *The Fortunes of Falstaff* (New York: Macmillan, 1944), p. 28.

22 Peter Stallybrass and Allon White, *The Politics and Poetics of Transgression* (Ithaca: Cornell University Press, 1986), pp. 9 and 22. In "Patriarchal Territories: The Body Enclosed," Stallybrass suggests that the dominant Renaissance ideology constructed "woman's body" as "*naturally* grotesque" (*Rewriting the Renaissance*, ed. Margaret Ferguson *et al.*, Chicago: University of Chicago Press, 1986), p. 126; he ends his essay with a "validation of the female grotesque" (p. 142). In "Female Grotesques: Carnival and Theory," *Feminist Studies/Critical Studies*, ed. Teresa de Lauretis (Bloomington: Indiana University Press, 1986), pp. 213–29, Mary Russo delineates the difficulties involved in such a validation. And, in an essay that complements mine, Gail Kern Paster deciphers blood as a trope of gender in a reformulation of the Bakhtinian "grotesque"; see "'In the spirit of men there is no blood": Blood as Trope of Gender in *Julius Caesar*," *Shakespeare Quarterly* 40:3 (1989), pp. 284–98.

23 Falstaff is also referred to as "blown Jack" (*H.IV. pt 1*, IV.ii.48), "brawn" [fatted swine] (*H.IV.* pt 1, II.iv.109; (*H.IV. pt 2*, I.i.19), "martlemas" [fatted ox killed at Martinmas] (*H.IV. pt 2*, II.ii.96), "old boar" (*H.IV. pt 2*, II.ii.138) and "Bartholomew boar-pig" [roast succulent pig] (*H.IV. pt 2*, II.iv.228-9).

24 Sigmund Freud, "Femininity," *New Introductory Lectures on Psychoanalysis*, ed. James Strachey (New York: W.W. Norton, 1965), p. 104.

25 In "Language, Linguistics and the Study of Literature," *Tracking the Signifier: Theoretical Essays: Film, Linguistics, Literature* (Minnesota University Press, 1985), pp. 113-30, Colin MacCabe informs us that "The verb *to womb*, meaning *to enclose an empty space*, gave rise to a series of nominal derivations which included both the sexually unspecific *stomach* as well as the meaning of *uterus* that is current today. It is crucial to a reading of the role of Falstaff to recognise that both meanings were available at the end of the sixteenth century, and we should not be surprised at Falstaff's consequent sexual ambiguity, particularly in the context of a claim about the disruption of the normal order of language. . . . [S]uch a figure should undermine even the possibility of representing sexual difference. Falstaff's body constitutes a polymorphously perverse threat to the possibility of representation. It even claims to undo the arbitrary and social nature of the sign and to speak its own name independently of any social order of language" (116-17). Ivy Schweitzer also suggested to me that Falstaff's linguistic style exhibits the "semiotic" as described by Julia Kristeva.

26 Two references which specifically link mothers with the excretions of tears are *H.IV. pt 1*, II.iv.391-4 and *H.V*, IV.iv.29-32. For an analysis of early modern body fluids, see Gail Kern Paster, "Leaky Vessels: The Incontinent Women of City Comedy," *Renaissance Drama* 18 (1987), pp. 43-65.

27 Falstaff's genealogical forebears in stage devils, vice figures, and iniquity further position him as "grotesque."

28 I am indebted to Stephen Greenblatt for bringing my attention to "churching" in "Martial Law and the Land of Cockaigne," *Shakespearean Negotiations*, pp. 129-63.

29 See C. L. Barber, "The Family in Shakespeare's Development: Tragedy and Sacredness," *Representing Shakespeare*, ed. Schwartz and Kahn, pp. 188-202.

30 Sigmund Freud, *Dora: An Analysis of a Case of Hysteria*, ed. Philip Rieff (New York: Collier Books, 1963), p. 47, and "The Most Prevalent Form of Degradation in Erotic Life," *Sexuality and the Psychology of Love*, ed. Philip Rieff (New York: Collier Books, 1963), p. 69. See also Simone de Beauvoir, *The Second Sex* (New York: Vintage Books, 1952).

31 I have learned much from Janet Adelman's analyses of fantasies of the maternal in Shakespearean drama; see especially "'Born of Woman': Fantasies of Maternal Power in *Macbeth*," *Cannibals, Witches, and Divorce: Estranging the Renaissance*, ed. Marjorie Garber (Baltimore: Johns Hopkins University Press, 1987), pp. 90-121, and "'This Is and Is Not Cressid': The Characterization of Cressida," in Garner

et al., The (M)Other Tongue, pp. 119–41. In addition to (Gohlke) Sprengnether, Dinnerstein, and Chodorow, I am indebted to the work of Adrienne Rich, *Of Woman Born: Motherhood as Experience and Institution* (New York: Norton, 1976), and Susan Bordo, "The Cartesian Masculinization of Thought," *Signs* 11:3 (1986), pp. 439–56.

32 C. L. Barber, *Shakespeare's Festive Comedy: A Study of Dramatic Form and its Relation to Social Custom* (New York: Princeton University Press, 1963), p. 219.

33 *The Riverside Shakespeare*, ed. G. Blakemore Evans (Boston: Houghton Mifflin, 1974).

34 Compare these and the following images of maternal destruction to those concerning Richard III in *Henry VI, part 3* (III.iii.168–81), and Macduff, Malcolm, and Macbeth in *Macbeth*. See Adelman, "'Born of Woman,'" pp. 92–3, 100, and 107.

35 See Joel Fineman, "Fratricide and Cuckoldry: Shakespeare's Doubles" in *Representing Shakespeare*, ed. Schwartz and Kahn, pp. 70–109.

36 The *Oxford English Dictionary* [*OED*] defines "tilt" (1511) as "A combat or encounter (for exercise or sport) between two armed men on horseback, with lances or similar weapons, the aim of each being to throw his opponent from the saddle." David Bevington glosses "mammets" as "dolls, or else, breasts."

37 Nancy Chodorow, *The Reproduction of Mothering: Psychoanalysis and the Sociology of Gender* (Berkeley: University of California Press, 1978) p. 113.

38 The *OED* defines "prick" as "the penis" (1592). Its earlier definitions are "A pointed weapon or implement. Applied to a dagger or pointed sword" (1552); and "to select (persons) . . . to appoint, choose, or pick *out*" (1557).

39 Erickson, *Patriarchal Structures*, p. 60.

40 I am indebted to Linda Boose for insisting on viewing Katharine as a subject in her own right. However, I am aware that one can both laugh *with* Katharine and *at* her at the same time, depending on inflection and how the scene is played. Thus, as Peter Erickson pointed out to me, Shakespeare seems to have it both ways through the juxtaposition of Henry's Harfleur speech (III.iii) and Katharine's tutorial (III.iv): he detaches himself from Henry without going over unequivocally to Katharine's side.

41 Helen Ostovich, "'Teach you our princess English?' Equivocal Translation of the French in *Henry V*," unpublished manuscript, pp. 8–9.

42 For an analysis of the homosocial exchange of women in Shakespearean drama, see Karen Newman, "Portia's Ring: Unruly Women and Structures of Exchange in *The Merchant of Venice*," *Shakespeare Quarterly* 38:1 (1987), pp. 19–33.

43 Women's bodies figure territory in other Shakespearean plays; notably, Falstaff's counterpart in *The Comedy of Errors*, Nell, is imagined as a monstrous globe. "She is spherical, like a globe. I could find out countries in her," Dromio says, proceeding to enumerate the Western European nations embodied in her abundant flesh and foul breath (III.ii.114–15). Comic though this treatment is (supposed to be), it was

given a more serious precedent in the Ditchley portrait of Queen Elizabeth as conquering ruler standing firm atop a map of England. See Roy Strong, *Portraits of Queen Elizabeth* (Oxford: Clarendon Press, 1963), pp. 75–76 and plate XV.

44 Stallybrass and White, *Politics and Poetics*, pp. 21–2.

45 See *Romeo and Juliet* (II.iii.9–14), and Freud, "The Theme of the Three Caskets" (1913), *The Standard Edition of the Complete Psychological Works of Sigmund Freud*, ed. James Strachey, (London: Hogarth Press, 1958) Vol. 12, pp. 291–301.

46 Although *Othello*'s Bianca and *The Comedy of Errors*' "courtesan" are ostensibly courtesans, they are treated as common whores by the other characters. For an analysis of the figure of the courtesan, see Ann Rosalind Jones, "City Women and Their Audiences: Louise Labe and Veronica Franco," in *Rewriting the Renaissance*, pp. 299–316. For prostitution in Italy, see Guido Ruggiero, *The Boundaries of Eros: Sex Crime and Sexuality in Renaissance Venice* (New York: Oxford University Press, 1985).

47 Julia Kristeva, "Stabat Mater," *The Kristeva Reader*, ed. Toril Moi (New York: Columbia University Press, 1986), pp. 160–86, esp. p. 163.

48 Jane Gallop's review of *The (M)Other Tongue*, "Reading the Mother Tongue: Psychoanalytic Feminist Criticism," *Critical Inquiry* (Winter 1987), pp. 314–29 and Claire Kahane, "Questioning the Maternal Voice," *Genders* 3 (Fall 1988), pp. 82–91 both take up feminists' tendency to idealize the mother.

49 See Coppélia Kahn, "The Absent Mother in *King Lear*," and Stephen Orgel, "Prospero's Wife," in *Rewriting the Renaissance*, pp. 33–64.

50 Garner *et al.*, *The (M)Other Tongue*, p. 25. See also *In Dora's Case*, ed. Charles Bernheimer and Claire Kahane (New York: Columbia University Press, 1985). In a MLA presentation (San Francisco, 1987) Margaret Homans provocatively suggested that the repudiation of the maternal body is replicated in the repressions of critical theory itself.

51 Sprengnether, *The Spectral Mother*, p. 194.

52 For the critics' view of Henry V as Britain's hero, see, for instance, Maynard Mack's Introduction to the *Signet Classic* edition of *Henry IV, part 1*, where Henry is called "an ideal image of the potentialities of the English character." *The History of Henry IV, part one*, ed. Maynard Mack (New York: New American Library, 1965). J. Dover Wilson in *Fortunes of Falstaff* says Henry "represents the ideal king, whether leader or governor, in Elizabethan eyes," (p. 62). Moody E. Prior calls Henry a "near-perfect epic hero" in *The Drama of Power: Studies in Shakespeare's History Plays* (Evanston: Northwestern University Press, 1973), p. 272.

53 Chodorow, "Gender, Relation, and Difference in Psychoanalytic Perspective," *The Future of Difference*, ed. Hester Eisenstein and Alice Jardine (New Brunswick: Rutgers University Press, 1985), p. 8.

54 Sprengnether, *The Spectral Mother*, pp. 234–6.

55 Ellie Ragland-Sullivan, *Jacques Lacan and the Philosophy of Psychoanalysis* (Urbana: University of Illinois Press, 1986), p. 271.

56 A recent production of *The Merry Wives of Windsor* inverted this

structure by using a female actor to play Falstaff. See a review of Pat Carroll's performance in "An Artful Falstaff Who Transcends Sex," *The New York Times*, Thursday, 7 June 1990. See also the subsequent letters of 29 June 1990, which mention female forerunners who played Falstaff, however unsuccessfully, in the eighteenth and nineteenth centuries, including one actress, Ludia Webb, who played Falstaff in *Henry IV, part 1* on 21 July 1786.

57 For a discussion of the cultural response to the problem of Elizabeth's succession, see Leonard Tennenhouse, *Power on Display: The Politics of Shakespeare's Genres* (New York: Methuen, 1986), pp. 85–6.

58 Prologue to V. line 30. I am indebted to Peter Erickson for this insight.

59 Montrose, "The Elizabethan Subject and the Spenserian Text," *Literary Theory/Renaissance Texts*, ed. Patricia Parker and David Quint (Baltimore: Johns Hopkins University Press, 1986), p. 309.

60 ibid., p. 310.

61 See also Montrose, "'Eliza, Queene of Shepheardes' and the Pastoral of Power," *ELR* 10:2 (1980), pp. 153–82.

62 Leah S. Marcus, "Erasing the Stigma of Daughterhood: Mary I, Elizabeth I, and Henry VIII," p. 402, *Daughters and Fathers*, ed. Lynda E. Boose and Betty S. Flowers (Baltimore: Johns Hopkins University Press, 1989), pp. 400–17. See also her "Shakespeare's Comic Heroines, Elizabeth I, and the Political Uses of Androgyny," *Women in the Middle Ages and the Renaissance: Literary and Historical Perspectives*, ed. Mary Beth Rose (Syracuse: Syracuse University Press, 1986), pp. 135–53.

3 INVADING BODIES/BAWDY EXCHANGES

1 In addition to the works cited below, particularly insightful analyses of the representation of AIDS are Paula A. Treichler, "AIDS, Homophobia, and Biomedical Discourse: An Epidemic of Signification," *October* 43 (Winter 1987), pp. 31–70; Lee Edelman, "The Plague of Discourse: Politics, Literary Theory, and AIDS," *South Atlantic Quarterly* 88:1 (Winter 1989), pp. 301–17; Cindy Patton, *Sex and Germs: The Politics of AIDS* (Boston: South End Press, 1985); Allan Brandt, "AIDS and Metaphor: Toward the Social Meaning of Epidemic Disease," *Social Research* 55:3 (Autumn, 1988), pp. 413–32; and Elizabeth Fee and Daniel M. Fox (eds), *AIDS: The Burdens of History* (Berkeley: University of California Press, 1988).

2 According to Dorothy Nelkin and Sander Gilman, "Placing Blame for Devastating Disease," *Social Research* 55:3 (Autumn 1988), pp. 361–78, every early modern European nation "defined syphilis as a disease of other nations" (p. 365). This view is corroborated by Anna Foa in "The New and the Old: The Spread of Syphilis (1494–1530)," *Sex and Gender in Historical Perspective*, ed. Edward Muir and Guido Ruggiero, trans. Margaret A. Gallucci *et al.* (Baltimore: Johns Hopkins University Press, 1990), pp. 26–45.

3 Sander L. Gilman, "AIDS and Syphilis: The Iconography of Disease,"

October 43 (Winter 1987), p. 87; Susan Sontag, *AIDS and its Metaphors* (New York: Farrar, Straus and Giroux, 1988), pp. 47–8. Many medical historians question whether syphilis was a novel disease when it broke out in epidemic proportions. In *History and Geography of the Most Important Diseases* (New York: Hafner, 1965), pp. 117–27, Erwin H. Ackerknecht presents evidence that syphilis had long been present among the laboring classes, and was new only to the learned surgeons who limited their clinical practice to the elite. He mentions prescriptions for antisyphilitic drugs that were prescribed by barber surgeons in 1457 in Germany, 1470 in Italy, and 1475 in England. For a summary of early modern medical theories about the origin of syphilis, and their current status within the medical profession, see Danielle Jacquart and Claude Thomasset, *Sexuality and Medicine in the Middle Ages* (Princeton: Princeton University Press, 1988), pp. 177–83; William H. McNeill, *Plagues and Peoples* (New York: Anchor Press, 1976), pp. 218–20; and Thomas Parran, *Shadow on the Land: Syphilis* (New York: Reynal and Hitchcock, 1937). According to Nelkin and Gilman, to the early modern European, "syphilis *had* to come from the New World: it was the final sign of the cataclysmic changes of that period. . . . As it became necessary to distinguish the goals of European colonialism from those of the indigenous population, Indians became not only diseased, they were defined as the source of disease," ("Placing Blame," p. 364). In this light, Eric Partridge's gloss on "malady of France" is particularly instructive for its characterization of origins: "Syphilis seems to have come to England from France; to France from Italy; to Italian ports . . . from the Levant; and perhaps the disease-breeding filth of the Levant received its accretion from the pullulating populousness of the farther East," *Shakespeare's Bawdy: A Literary and Psychological Essay and a Comprehensive Glossary* (New York: E.P. Dutton, 1969), p. 144. I particularly call attention to the tone of disgust animating "disease breeding filth" and "pullulating populousness.'

4   See Foa, "The New and the Old," for the way the Indian functioned as the other in Italian discourses of disease.

5   See, for instance, the work of Mary Douglas, Peter Stallybrass and Gail Kern Paster.

6   Arthur Rossiter first noticed this aural pun in *Angel with Horns and Other Shakespearean Lectures*, ed. Graham Storey (London: Longmans, Green, 1961), p. 133.

7   I.i.103, II.iii.19. Bevington glosses "placket" as "a slit in a petticoat; hence (indecently) a woman."

8   Paris, for instance, says of Helen, "But I would have the soil of her fair rape/Wip'd off, in honorable keeping her" (II.ii.148–9).

9   Bevington glosses "merry Greek" as slang for a frivolous person, loose in morals. As such, it stands as a signifier of sexually licentious behavior.

10 René Girard, "The Politics of Desire in *Troilus and Cressida*," *Shakespeare and the Question of Theory*, ed. Patricia Parker and Geoffrey Hartman (New York: Methuen, 1985), pp. 188–209.

11 Linda Charnes, "'So Unsecret to Ourselves': Notorious Identity and the Material Subject in Shakespeare's *Troilus and Cressida*," *Shakespeare Quarterly* 40:4 (Winter 1989), pp. 413–40. Charnes' complex argument posits the following circuit of desire: "possession of Helen generates desire for war, desire for war generates desire for Helen, desire for Helen generates mimetic desire, mimetic desire generates competitive identification between Greek and Trojan men, competitive identification generates homoerotic aggression, homoerotic aggression generates desire for more war, and finally, desire for more war reproduces desire for Helen" (p. 437). In "Emulous Factions and the Collapse of Chivalry: *Troilus and Cressida*," *Representations* 29 (Winter, 1990), pp. 145–79, Eric S. Mallin employs a homosocial grid to argue that a "submerged axis" of male homosexuality, narcissism, and misogyny animates the play. Assuming a "natural" correlation between homosexuality and antifeminism leads Mallin to employ a normalizing psychoanalytic model of male narcissism in the interest of a feminist critique. Both Charnes and Mallin tend to conflate male homoeroticism and homosociality, seeing the first as the logical extension of the second. For instance, Charnes" term "homoerotic aggression," which I take to mean male–male rape and eroticized battle, comes to represent all homoerotic desires in the play, including the relationship of Achilles and Patroclus. My view is somewhat different, as I am concerned to show the possible divergences of male homosocial and homoerotic desire.

12 The equation between desire and disease is evident in others of Shakespeare's plays, notably *Hamlet, Twelfth Night, Measure for Measure*, and in a lighter vein, *As You Like It*.

13 Mallin, "Emulous Factions," interestingly places this "neurosis of invasion" in the Elizabethan context of Britain's political fortunes and the Queen's personal symbology.

14 For an excellent analysis of how Cressida is positioned as whore, see Janet Adelman, "'This Is and Is Not Cressid': The Characterization of Cressida," in Garner *et al.* (eds), *The (M)Other Tongue: Essays in Feminist Psychoanalytic Interpretation* (Ithaca: Cornell University Press, 1985), pp. 119–41.

15 Other types of exchange, especially mercantile commerce, are also important to the signification of desire in the play.

16 According to Sontag, *AIDS and its Metaphors*, syphilis and leprosy were the first two diseases to be described as repulsive.

17 Debate exists as to whether early modern syphilis and its modern counterpart are the same disease. Both lack of resistance on the part of the European population and the exceptional virulence of the early strain combined to produce the following symptoms: high fever, delirium, violent headaches, bone pains, sores, bone ulcers, and death. However, part of this virulence may have been due to other accompanying diseases and malnutrition. At least some of the epidemics of syphilis correspond to periods of famine.

18 Steven Mullaney, *The Place of the Stage: License, Play, and Power in Renaissance England* (Chicago: Chicago University Press, 1988), p. 37.

19 Ibid., p. 32.

20 Girard, "Politics of Desire," p. 208.

21 According to Partridge in *Shakespeare's Bawdy*, "sunburnt" meant infected with venereal disease, and "soddon business" and "stew'd phrases" refer to brothels and the sweating treatment for syphilis.

22 Girard, "Politics of Desire," p. 202. Mallin, in "Emulous Factions," follows Girard in viewing the plague metaphorically, but he places the illness of emulation and factionalism within the historical context of the Elizabethan court.

23 Bruce Boehrer, "Early Modern Syphilis," *Journal of the History of Sexuality* 1:2 (Autumn, 1990), 197–214.

24 ibid., pp. 200, 209.

25 Women's sores were usually on the hidden lip of the cervix. See Charles Dennie, *A History of Syphilis* (Springfield: Thomas, 1962), and Jacquart and Thomasset, *Sexuality and Medicine*, pp. 181, 189–90.

26 Boehrer, "Early Modern Syphilis," p. 213. For later "inventions" of syphilis as moral category, see Allan M. Brandt, *No Magic Bullet: A Social History of Venereal Disease in the United States since 1880* (Oxford: Oxford University Press, 1985).

27 Geoffrey Eatough (trans.), *Fracastoro's "Syphilis"* (Liverpool: Francis Cairns, 1984).

28 I am told that in a recent Royal Shakespeare Company production at Stratford, Thersites wears surgical gloves – an obvious insertion of AIDS discourse into the play.

29 This sense of lechery as "burning" within the body is repeated in Thersites" aside, "Fry, lechery, fry!" (V.ii.58–9).

30 For the confusion between leprosy and syphilis, see Jacquart and Thomasset, *Sexuality and Medicine*, pp. 177–93, and Foa, "The New and the Old," pp. 37–42. In addition to the fact that the rise of syphilitic infection temporarily coincided with the abolition of the Order of Lazarus and the scattering of 19,000 leper houses, the aural similarity between leper and lecher should be acknowledged as contributing to this conflation. Foa also argues that Jews were used as a mediating term between leprosy and syphilis. The language by which syphilis was described confused it not only with leprosy, but also with the bubonic plague and typhus. For a powerful rendition of this conflation, see Robert Henryson's medieval poem, "Testament of Cresseid," which transforms Cressida into an itinerant leper, an image that makes explicit the need to imagine the infected as carrying off the disease, *Testament of Cressed*, ed. Denton Fox (London: Nelson, 1968).

31 Bleeding, purging, sweating, and applications of mercury were the standard therapeutic treatments for syphilis. Baths were valued for their palliative effect on aching bones.

32 For the coincidence of syphilis and prostitution in other plays, see in *Henry V* the references to powdering tubs and tub-fasts, and the particularly interesting invocation of Cressida as leprous whore: "to the spital go,/ And from the powd'ring tub of infamy/ Fetch forth the lazar kite of Cressid's kind,/ Doll Tearsheet she by name" (II.i.75–8); indeed, it is reported that Doll Tearsheet dies of "a malady of France"

(V.i.81). In *Timon of Athens*, Timon says to Timandra: "Be a whore still. They love thee not that use thee;/ Give them diseases, leaving with thee their lust./ Make use of thy salt hours. Season the slaves/ For tubs and baths; bring down rose-cheek'd youth/ To the tub-fast and the diet" (IV.iii.84–8).

33 Sander L. Gilman alludes to precisely this dynamic in *Disease and Representation: Images of Illness from Madness to AIDS* (Ithaca: Cornell University Press, 1988): "It is the fear of collapse, the sense of dissolution, which contaminates the Western image of all diseases . . . But the fear we have of our own collapse does not remain internalized. Rather, we project this fear onto the world in order to localize it and, indeed, to domesticate it. For once we locate it, the fear of our own dissolution is removed. Then it is not we who totter on the brink of collapse, but rather the Other. And it is an-Other who has already shown his or her vulnerability by having collapsed" (p. 1).

34 ibid., p. 2.

35 For an excellent analysis of the theater as site of such contamination, see Mullaney, *The Place of the Stage*. For an examination of the theater as site of sexuality, see Colin MacCabe, "Abusing Self and Others: Puritan Accounts of the Shakespearean Stage," *Critical Quarterly* 30:3 (1988), pp. 3–17.

36 According to Ann Haselkorn, the Bishop of Winchester had jurisdiction over financial gains from prostitution, and women inmates of Bankside Street, Southwark, located near the Bishop's palace, were known as "Winchester geese," *Prostitution in Elizabethan and Jacobean Comedy* (Troy: Whitson, 1983). See also E. J. Burford, *Bawds and Lodgings: A History of the London Bankside Brothels c. 100–1675* (London: Peter Owen, 1976). Foa "The New and the Old," also alludes to the alleged role of prostitutes in the dissemination of syphilis in depictions from sixteenth-century Italian fabulae.

37 Peter Stallybrass and Allon White, *The Politics and Poetics of Transgression* (Ithaca: Cornell University Press, 1986), p. 22.

38 Carol Cook, "'The Sign and Semblance of Her Honor': Reading Gender Difference in *Much Ado About Nothing*," *PMLA* 101:2 (1986), p. 189.

39 Thersites, of course, does joke about Menelaus, calling him "the primitive statue and oblique memorial of cuckolds," but his humor is moderated by his repugnance: "Ask me not what I would be, were I not Thersites; for I care not to be the louse of a lazar, so I were not Menelaus" (V.i.54–5, 63–5).

40 See in particular David F. Musto, "Quarantine and the Problem of AIDS," and Guenter B. Risse, "Epidemics and History: Ecological Perspectives and Social Responses," in Fee and Fox, *AIDS: The Burdens of History*, pp. 33–85.

41 Troilus' sleeve, like Othello's handkerchief, operates as an emblem of the circulation of desire.

42 Unlike Sontag (*AIDS and its Metaphors*), I do not believe that disease can be totally de-metaphorized; indeed, I believe that such a desire is born of precisely the self-protectiveness I try to question. However,

I do believe that we must metaphorize sexually transmitted diseases differently. Leo Bersani makes some provocative comments on the conflation of desire and disease in "Is the Rectum a Grave?" *October* 43 (Winter 1987), pp. 197–222.

4 DESIRE AND THE DIFFERENCES IT MAKES

1 Marguerite Waller, "Academic Tootsie: The Denial of Difference and the Difference it Makes," *Diacritics* 17:1 (1987), pp. 4–5.
2 Jean E. Howard, "Crossdressing, the Theatre, and Gender Struggle in Early Modern England," *Shakespeare Quarterly* 39:4 (1988), p. 432.
3 Lisa Jardine, "'As boys and women are for the most part cattle of this colour': Female Roles and Elizabethan Eroticism," *Still Harping on Daughters: Women and Drama in the Age of Shakespeare* (Brighton: Harvester Press, 1983), p. 8.
4 ibid., p. 20.
5 ibid., p. 11.
6 James M. Saslow, "Homosexuality in the Renaissance: Behavior, Identity, and Artistic Expression," and Randolph Trumbach "The Birth of the Queen: Sodomy and the Emergence of Gender Equality in Modern Culture 1660–1750," *Hidden From History: Reclaiming the Gay and Lesbian Past*, ed. Martin Duberman, Martha Vicinus, and George Chauncey Jr (New York: New American Library, 1989), pp. 90–105 and 129–140. They assume that pederasty was the dominant model, but their analyses are based on depictions of seventeenth-century aristocratic males. Saslow suggests that the intergenerational pattern was probably class linked; he reports that working-class men were more likely to have sexual contact with men the same age.
7 Activity and passivity, of course, have long been a subject of debate in gay and lesbian theory. In early modern Italy, as in classical Greece, the vocabulary differentiated between the actions of penetrating and being penetrated: *soddomitare* meant "to sodomize," *farsi soddomitare* meant "to let oneself be sodomized." In England, however, "sodomite" *seems* to have been used to describe both the "active" and "passive" partners of illicit sex. Part of my concern here is to question the viability of such binary discriptions of sexual encounters.
8 See Jacqueline Rose's analysis of Leonardo da Vinci in *Sexuality in the Field of Vision* (London: Verso, 1986), p. 226.
9 Gayle Rubin, "Thinking Sex: Notes for a Radical Theory of the Politics of Sexuality," *Pleasure and Danger: Exploring Female Sexuality*, ed. Carole Vance (London: Routledge and Kegan Paul, 1984), p. 307. See also Pat Caplan, *The Cultural Construction of Sexuality* (London: Tavistock, 1987), pp. 1–30, and Jeffrey Weeks, *Sexuality and its Discontents: Meanings, Myths and Modern Sexualities* (London: Routledge and Kegan Paul, 1985). Eve Kosofsky Sedgwick has taken up precisely this question in "Across Gender, Across Sexuality: Willa Cather and Others," *South Atlantic Quarterly* 88:1 (1989), pp. 53–72.

10 In "Shakespeare, Cultural Materialism, Feminism, and Marxist Humanism," *New Literary History* 21:3 (Spring 1990), pp. 471–93, Jonathan Dollimore perceptively uses "(hetero) sexual difference" simultaneously to enact a division and maintain a connection between the erotic and gender systems. For polemical purposes, however, I find it important at this stage to eschew "sexual difference" altogether: it, as differentiated from "gender difference," implicitly refers social processes to biological origins.

11 In an important passage, Freud writes, "There is only one libido, which serves both the masculine and the feminine sexual functions. To it itself we cannot assign any sex; if, following the conventional equation of activity and masculinity, we are inclined to describe it as masculine, we must not forget that it also covers trends with a passive aim. Nevertheless the juxtaposition 'feminine libido' is without any justification," "Femininity," *New Introductory Lectures on Psychoanalysis*, ed. James Strachey (New York: W. W. Norton, 1965), p. 116. See also Joel Fineman, "The Turn of the Shrew," *Shakespeare and the Question of Theory*, ed. Patricia Parker and Geoffrey Hartman (New York: Methuen, 1985), pp. 138–60; and Carol Cook, "'The Sign and Semblance of Her Honor': Reading Gender Difference in *Much Ado About Nothing*," *PMLA* 101, p. 190.

12 See Teresa de Lauretis, *Technologies of Gender: Essays on Theory, Film, and Fiction* (Bloomington: Indiana University Press, 1987), and "Feminist Studies/Critical Studies: Issues, Terms, and Contexts," in *Feminist Studies/Critical Studies* ed. de Lauretis (Bloomington: Indiana University Press, 1986), pp. 1–19.

13 Sigmund Freud, "The Psychogenesis of a Case of Homosexuality in a Woman" (1920), *The Standard Edition of the Complete Psychological Works of Sigmund Freud*, ed. J. Strachey, Vol. 18, p. 170.

14 Freud, "Psychogenesis," p. 154, and "Leonardo da Vinci and a Memory of his Childhood" (1910), *Standard Edition* Vol. 11, pp. 59–137.

15 Freud, "General Remarks on Hysterical Attacks" (1909), *Dora: An Analysis of a Case of Hysteria*, ed. Philip Rieff (New York: Macmillan, 1963), p. 157, my emphasis.

16 Freud, "From the History of an Infantile Neurosis" (1918), *Three Case Histories*, ed. Philip Rieff (New York: Macmillan, 1963), p. 305.

17 Freud, "Leonardo da Vinci," p. 86.

18 Karen Newman, "Renaissance Family Politics and Shakespeare's *The Taming of the Shrew*," *ELR* 16:1 (1986), p. 99, my emphasis.

19 Nancy Chodorow, *The Reproduction of Mothering: Psychoanalysis and the Sociology of Gender* (Berkeley: University of California Press, 1978), p. 150. See also Julia Epstein, "Either/Or – Neither/Both: Sexual Ambiguity and the Ideology of Gender," *Genders* (Spring 1990), pp. 99–142 for an excellent analysis of the ideological character of "biological" gender categories.

20 Arlene Stein, "All Dressed Up, But No Place to Go? Style Wars and the New Lesbianism," *Outlook: National Lesbian and Gay Quarterly* 1:4 (1989), p. 38.

21 See Joan Nestle, "Butch-Fem Relationships: Sexual Courage in the

1950s," *Heresies: A Feminist Publication on Art and Politics* 3:4 (1981), pp. 21–4.

22 For an initiating but problematic attempt at this new erotic theory, see Esther Newton and Shirley Walton, "The Misunderstanding: Toward a More Precise Sexual Vocabulary," *Pleasure and Danger: Exploring Female Sexuality*, ed. Carol Vance (London: Routledge and Kegan Paul, 1984), pp. 242–50. I find particularly perceptive the following formulation: "In any given sexual exchange, the top is the person who conducts and orchestrates the episode, the one who 'runs the fuck.' The bottom is the one who responds, acts out, makes visible or interprets the sexual initiatives and language of the top. How this exchange takes place is not a given. The top might not move much, only issuing verbal or subtle kinetic instructions. The bottom might be very expressive and physically active, rather than the inert being conjured up by the word 'passive'" (p. 246).

23 Robert Stoller, *Observing the Erotic Imagination* (New Haven: Yale University Press, 1985).

24 Cindy Patton, *Sex and Germs: The Politics of AIDS* (Boston: South End Press, 1985), p. 105.

25 See Henry L. Minton, "Femininity in Men and Masculinity in Women: American Psychiatry and Psychology Portray Homosexuality in the 1930s," *Journal of Homosexuality* 13:1 (Fall 1986), pp. 1–21, and Kenneth Lewes, *The Psychoanalytic Theory of Male Homosexuality* (New York: Simon and Schuster, 1988). Actually, a more complicated notion of the pervert is offered by Freud: the pervert, in refusing to repress, takes the "happy" path away from psychosis and neurosis. Such a notion of perversion, which cannot be mapped on to the "passive," obviously exceeds the dichotomy I have been exploring here.

26 See Jonathan Dollimore, "Subjectivity, Sexuality, and Transgression: The Jacobean Connection," *Renaissance Drama* 17 (1986), pp. 53–81.

27 Actually, within social constructivist theory, there exists considerable disagreement as to the date of emergence of the "modern homosexual." Saslow cautiously suggests that "the Renaissance planted the first seeds of a new identity and social status for homosexuality," "Homosexuality in the Renaissance," p. 105. See also his *Ganymede in the Renaissance: Homosexuality in Art and Society* (New Haven: Yale University Press, 1986) and "'A Veil of Ice between My Heart and Fire': Michelangelo's Sexual Identity and Early Modern Constructs of Homosexuality," *Genders* 2 (1988), pp. 77–90. Randolph Trumbach, in "Birth of the Queen" and "London's Sodomites: Homosexual Behavior and Western Culture in the Eighteenth Century," *Journal of Social History* 11:1 (Fall 1977), pp. 1–33 and Alan Bray, *Homosexuality in Renaissance England* (London: Gay Men's Press, 1982) date modern homosexuality from the appearance of London's "molly houses" and the exclusive adult male sodomite in the early eighteenth century. Michel Foucault, *The History of Sexuality* Vol. 1 (New York: Random House, 1978), Jeffrey Weeks, *Sexuality and its Discontents*, Lillian Faderman, *Surpassing the Love of Men: Romantic Friendship and Love Between Women from the Renaissance to the Present* (New York: William

Morrow, 1981), and George Chauncey, Jr, "From Sexual Inversion to Homosexuality: Medicine and the Changing Conceptualization of Female Deviance," *Salmagundi* 58/59 (Fall 1982/Winter 1983), pp. 114–46 argue that not until the sexologists" medicalization of sexual deviance at the end of the nineteenth century did a homosexual identity emerge. All constructivists agree that urbanization (and the social networks and anonymity it affords) was a crucial factor; I wonder, however, whether this emphasis on city subcultures is not itself a product of a particularly male perspective. Not only does urbanization seem to have been far less salient for the formation of lesbian identity, but it does little to account for the erotic practices of people living in rural communities. For excellent renditions of the constructivist view, see David Halperin, "One Hundred Years of Homosexuality," *Diacritics* 16:2 (Summer 1986), pp. 34–45 and "Sex Before Sexuality: Pederasty, Politics, and Power in Classical Athens," *Hidden from History*, pp. 37–53. For useful accounts of the debate between social constructivists and essentialists, see Steven Epstein, "Gay Politics, Ethnic Identity: The Limits of Social Constructionism," *Socialist Review* 93/94 (May–Aug. 1987), pp. 9–54; John Boswell, "Revolutions, Universals and Sexual Categories," *Salmagundi* 58/59 (Fall 1982/Winter 1983), pp. 89–113; Robert Padgug, "Sexual Matters: On Conceptualizing Sexuality in History," *Radical History Review* 20 (1979), pp. 3–23; Gregory A. Sprague, "Male Homosexuality in Western Culture: The Dilemma of Identity and Subculture in Historical Research," *Journal of Homosexuality* 10:3 (Winter 1984), pp. 29–43; John P. de Cecco and Michael G. Shively, "From Sexual Identity to Sexual Relationships: A Contextual Shift," *Journal of Homosexuality* 9:2 (1982–3), pp. 1–26; and Diana Fuss, *Essentially Speaking: Feminism, Nature and Difference* (London: Routledge, 1990), pp. 97–112.

28 For cross-cultural perspectives on homosexuality, see *Hidden From History*; also *The Gay Past: A Collection of Historical Essays*, ed. Salvatore J. Licata and Robert P. Petersen (New York: Harrington Park Press, 1985).

29 See, in particular, the way that appeals to narcissism work in W. Thomas MacCary, *Friends and Lovers: The Phenomenology of Desire in Shakespearean Comedy* (New York: Columbia University Press, 1985); Leonard Tennenhouse, "The Counterfeit Order of *The Merchant of Venice*" and Joel Fineman, "Fratricide and Cuckoldry: Shakespeare's Doubles" in *Representing Shakespeare: New Psychoanalytic Essays*, ed. Murray M. Schwartz and Coppélia Kahn (Baltimore: Johns Hopkins University Press, 1980), pp. 54–109.

30 To my mind, power permeates all aspects of human relations; however, this is not to imply that all relations are based on a sado-masochistic paradigm of dominance and submission. What is important to me is not to *escape* from power (in my mind a hopelessly essentialist fantasy), but to increase our awareness of the positions we occupy and to *use* our power as humanely as possible. Paramount in that attempt is the ability to flexibly maneuver one's position, to exchange roles and positions. Robert Stoller is helpful in detailing the kinds of

roles, positions, and tensions that contribute to the construction of erotic excitement: "I could never list all the polar fields that might make an excitement, but they are such things as: aesthetic/anaesthetic, alive/dead, active/passive, safe/endangered, unmasked/masked, brave/cowardly, loving/hating, loved/hated, kill/be killed, start/not start, move/stop, clever/stupid, strong/weak, secrets kept/secrets exposed, unbound/bound, I/not-I, in control/out of control, free (for example, from deception)/enslaved (by deception), sound/silence, accepted/rejected, broken/whole, triumphant/humiliated, shall I/shan't I, can I/can't I, will I/won't I (refusal), defended/defenseless, familiar/strange, clarity/confusion, movement/paralysis, constancy/inconstancy, time/timelessness, go/stop, permanence/change, knowledge/ignorance, simplicity/ambiguity, tension/relaxation [the list continues]. . . ." (*Observing the Erotic Imagination*, p. 53).

31 Eve Kosofsky Sedgwick, *Between Men: English Literature and Male Homosocial Desire* (New York: Columbia University Press, 1985). Sedgwick has recently come under attack, most notably by David van Leer in "The Beast in the Closet: Homosociality and the Pathology of Manhood," *Critical Inquiry* 15:3 (1989), pp. 587–605. Van Leer identifies "two problematic moves in Sedgwick's analysis of homosocial bonds: her desire to relate homosexuality to 'larger questions' of society and sexuality, and her attempt to thematize homophobia and the homosexual/homosocial bonds that underwrite it as 'homosexual panic,'" (p. 592). Specifically, Van Leer argues that despite Sedgwick's stated project, embedded in her work are homophobic assumptions that foster rather than deconstruct stereotypes of homosexuality: "the unintentional result is to banish from her discourse the category of the healthy, well-adjusted male homosexual while reintroducing two chief myths of gay self-contempt – the fag hag and the closet queen" (p. 598). In this and in the subsequent exchange between Sedgwick and Van Leer ("Critical Response I: Tide and Trust," and "Critical Response II: Trust and Trade," *Critical Inquiry* 15:4 [1989], pp. 745–63) what becomes most clear is that the language by which we analyze homoerotic desire is thoroughly permeated with homophobic and misogynistic associations, irrespective of individual intention. That Van Leer sees this not as a problem of available language, but a problem of Sedgwick's positioning – "as doubly an outsider [neither gay nor male] she is unlikely to delineate 'most authoritatively' a male homosexual tradition" (pp. 600–1) – seems to me a criticism of dubious analytical power. In his efforts to delegitimize Sedgwick, he adopts the untenable position that because she is "unable to speak from within the minority, Sedgwick must perforce speak from within the majority; denied the language of homosexuality, she necessarily speaks heterosexuality" (p. 603). Surely there are more positions than that! Neither homosexuality nor heterosexuality (nor masculinity or femininity, for that matter) are oppositional *essences*; precisely as positions, they are available in varying degrees to us all. Finally, that Van Leer adopts an affirmative gay male rhetoric at the expense of women and feminist theorizing (he calls Sedgwick's comparison of

gay men and women "minimally castrating," p. 601), seems to me an unfortunate step backward from the point of view of both feminism and gay and lesbian theory. At the same time, to the extent that Van Leer argues for the necessity of keeping conceptual categories distinct, and for the reinsertion into the field of analysis the lived experiences of homosexuals, their specific erotic identities and practices, his project and mine are aligned.

32 See, for instance, Joseph A. Porter, "Marlowe, Shakespeare, and the Canonization of Heterosexuality," *South Atlantic Quarterly* 88:1 (1989), pp. 127–47 and *Shakespeare's Mercutio: his History and Drama* (Chapel Hill: University of North Carolina Press, 1988). At the 1989 Shakespeare Association of America Conference, at least fifteen seminar papers dealt with homoeroticism.

33 Joseph Pequigney, for instance, sees his task as securing the "identity" of both Shakespeare and his characters as "homosexual." His impulse to produce "evidence" of "classic male homosexual relationships" works against my thesis in multiple ways. See *Such is My Love: A Study of Shakespeare's Sonnets* (Chicago: University of Chicago Press, 1985), and "The Two Antonios and Same-Sex Love in *Twelfth Night* and *The Merchant of Venice*," unpublished manuscript presented to the Shakespeare Association of America, 1989.

34 The most critically sophisticated analyses of early modern legal discourse on homosexuality are Ed Cohen, "Legislating the Norm: From Sodomy to Gross Indecency," *South Atlantic Quarterly* 88:1 (1989), pp. 181–217, and Bruce Smith, *Homosexual Desire in Shakespeare's England* (Chicago: University of Chicago Press, 1991). Helpful as more general analyses of early modern homoeroticism are Stephen Orgel, "Nobody's Perfect: Or Why Did the English Stage Take Boys for Women," *South Atlantic Quarterly* 88:1 (1989), pp. 7–29, and Jonathan Goldberg, "Sodomy and Society: The Case of Christopher Marlowe," *Southwest Review* 69:4 (Autumn 1984), pp. 371–8. Each is influenced by Foucault as well as by Alan Bray. In addition to the articles listed in note 27, see John Boswell, *Christianity, Social Tolerance and Homosexuality: Gay People in Western Europe from the Beginning of the Christian Era to the Fourteenth Century* (Chicago: University of Chicago Press, 1980); Arthur N. Gilbert, "Buggery and the British Navy, 1700–1861," *Journal of Social History* 10:1 (Fall 1976), pp. 72–98; Caroline Bingham, "Seventeenth-Century Attitudes Toward Deviant Sex," *Journal of Interdisciplinary History* 1:3 (Spring 1971), pp. 447–68; B. R. Burgh, "Ho Hum, Another Work of the Devil: Buggery and Sodomy in Early Stuart England," *The Gay Past*, ed. Licata and Petersen, pp. 69–78; and Guido Ruggiero, *The Boundaries of Eros: Sex Crime and Sexuality in Renaissance Venice* (New York: Oxford University Press, 1985).

35 Bray, *Homosexuality*, p. 92.

36 Goldberg, "Sodomy and Society," p. 371.

37 ibid., p. 376.

38 ibid., p. 372.

39 Adrienne Rich, "When We Dead Awaken: Writing as Re-Vision",

College English 34:1 (Oct. 1972), pp. 18–25; Carroll Smith–Rosenberg, "The Female World of Love and Ritual: Relations between Women in Nineteenth-Century America," *Signs* 1 (Autumn 1975), pp. 1–29. See also Rich's important, if problematic, essay "Compulsory Heterosexuality and Lesbian Existence," *Signs* 5:4 (Summer 1980), pp. 631–60.

40 *A Midsummer Night's Dream* III.ii.198–216; *As You Like It* I.iii.73–4; *Pericles* IV. Prologue 15–40; *The Winter's Tale* I.ii.62–75.

41 James Holstun addresses just this questions in "'Will You Rent Our Ancient Love Asunder?': Lesbian Elegy in Donne, Marvell, and Milton," *ELH* 54:4 (Winter 1987), pp. 835–67. He persuasively argues that these poets employ the technique of "periodizing" to simultaneously acknowledge and master "lesbian" desire: by use of an elegiac structure, "lesbian" sexuality is secured as an event always already in the past. For a further exploration of this question, see my forthcoming "The (In)Significance of 'Lesbian' Desire in Early Modern England," *Erotic Politics: The Dynamics of Desire on the English Renaissance Stage*, ed. Susan Zimmerman (London: Routledge, 1992).

42 Louis Crompton, "The Myth of Lesbian Impunity: Capital Laws From 1270 to 1791," *The Gay Past*, ed. Licata and Petersen, p. 11. See also Brigitte Eriksson (trans.), "A Lesbian Execution in Germany, 1721: The Trial Records," ibid., pp. 27–40; Judith C. Brown, *Immodest Acts: The Life of a Lesbian Nun in Renaissance Italy* (Oxford: Oxford University Press, 1986).

43 Trumbach, "London's Sodomites," p. 13.

44 Crompton, "The Myth of Lesbian Impunity," p. 11.

45 Saslow, "Homosexuality in the Renaissance," p. 95.

46 ibid., p. 96.

47 Katharine Eisaman Maus, "Horns of Dilemma: Jealousy, Gender, and Spectatorship in English Renaissance Drama," *ELH* 54:3 (1987), p. 562.

48 In addition to Howard's far-reaching analysis of cross-dressing and anti-theatricalist rhetoric in "Crossdressing, the Theater, and Gender Struggle in Early Modern England," see Mary Beth Rose, "Women in Men's Clothing: Apparel and Social Stability in *The Roaring Girl*," *ELR* 14:3 (1984), pp. 367–91; and Laura Levine, "Men in Women's Clothing: Anti-theatricality and Effeminization from 1579 to 1642," *Criticism* 28:2 (Spring 1986), pp. 121–43.

49 Saslow disagrees, stating ambiguously that "the perception of female sexual deviance [what kind of deviance?] was conflated with other forms of unorthodoxy, gender and doctrinal," "Homosexuality and the Renaissance," p. 95. Howard suggests that "In the polemical literature women who crossdressed were less often accused of sexual perversion than of sexual incontinence, of being whores . . . in part because the discursive construction of woman in the Renaissance involved seeing her as a creature of strong sexual appetites needing strict regulation" "Crossdressing," p. 424.

50 Lynn Friedli, "'Passing Women': A Study of Gender Boundaries in the Eighteenth Century," *Sexual Underworlds of the Enlightenment*, ed. G. S. Rousseau and Roy Porter (Chapel Hill: University of North Carolina Press, 1988), pp. 234–60.

51 Vera Brittain, *Radclyffe Hall: A Case of Obscenity?* (London: A Femina Book, 1968), p. 21.
52 Saslow, "Homosexuality in the Renaissance," p. 99.
53 This fact becomes increasingly significant as a model for those who theorize sexuality in a contemporary context. Even before the threat of AIDS to gay men, gay and lesbian theorists had begun to move from a paradigm of identity to one of erotic practice. Now, in the global context of AIDS, even conservatives must acknowledge that it is not "who you are" (gay/straight) but "what you do" that is the salient factor in identifying risk. As horrifying as is the impact of AIDS on our individual and collective lives – and I do not mean to trivialize that horror by mentioning it in this theoretical context – it also pressures us to re-examine the paradigms within which we conceive our sexual subjectivities. See Steven Seidman, "Transfiguring Sexual Identity: AIDS & the Contemporary Construction of Homosexuality," *Social Text* (Fall, 1988), pp. 187–203.
54 I am indebted to Peter Stallybrass for helping me to clarify my understanding of early modern heterosexuality.
55 In his nuanced discussion of the transformations of legal discourse over the course of the sixteenth and seventeenth centuries, Bruce Smith also distinguishes between the discourses of acts and desires. See *Homosexual Desire in Shakespeare's England.*
56 Michel Foucault, *The History of Sexuality*, Vol. 1 (New York: Random House, 1978), p. 157.
57 See, in this regard, Luce Irigaray, *This Sex Which Is Not One*, trans. Catherine Porter (Ithaca: Cornell University Press, 1985): "We might suspect the *phallus* (Phallus) of being the *contemporary figure of a god jealous* of his prerogatives; we might suspect it of claiming, on this basis, to be the ultimate meaning of all discourse, the standard of truth and propriety, in particular as regards sex, the signifier and/or the ultimate signified of all desire, in addition to continuing, as emblem and agent of the patriarchal system, to shore up the name of the father (Father)," p. 67.
58 Jonathan Dollimore, "Shakespeare, Cultural Materialism, Feminism, and Marxist Humanism," p. 484.

5 THE HOMOEROTICS OF SHAKESPEAREAN COMEDY

1 Stephen Orgel, "Nobody's Perfect: Or Why Did the English Stage Take Boys for Women," *South Atlantic Quarterly* 88: 1 (1989), pp. 7–8.
2 Stephen Gosson, in *The Schoole of Abuse* (1579; London: The Shakespeare Society, 1841) makes no explicit mention of homoeroticism but initiates the gendered and erotic focus of the anti-theatrical attack by mentioning the theater's "effeminate gesture, to ravish the sense; and wanton speache, to whet desire to inordinate lust." The next year, an anonymous pamphleteer (probably Anthony Mundy) argued that the taking of women's parts by men was explicitly

forbidden by the Law of God, referring to Deuteronomy 23.5. Due to the strength of this biblical authority, denunciation of theatrical cross-dressing became a most effective argument against the stage. In *Playes Confuted in Five Actions* (*Markets of Bawdrie: The Dramatic Criticism of Stephen Gosson*, ed. Arthur Kinney, Salzburg Studies in Literature 4, Salzburg: Institut für Englische Sprache und Literatur, 1974), Gosson takes up the Deuteronomic code and rails against men adopting "not the apparell onely, but the gate, the gestures, the voyce, the passions of a woman." In *The Overthrow of Stage Playes*, John Rainoldes writes: "A woman's garment beeing put on a man doeth vehemently touch and moue him with the remembrance and imagination of a woman; and the imagination of a thing desirable doth stirr up the desire" and "what sparkles of lust to that vice the putting of wemens attire on men may kindle in vncleane affections, as Nero shewed in Sporus, Heliogabalus in himselfe; yea certaine, who grew not to such excesse of impudencie, yet arguing the same in causing their boys to weare long heare like wemen." With Phillip Stubbes' *The Anatomie of Abuses* (1583; Netherlands: De Capo Press, 1972), explicit anxieties about homoeroticism enter the debate: "everyone brings another homeward of their way very friendly and in their secret conclaves they play sodomite or worse. And these be the fruites of playes and Interludes for the most part." The debate culminates in William Prynne's *Histrio-mastix: The Player's Scourge or Actor's Tragedy* (1633; New York: Garland Publishing, 1974), which charges the theaters as being nothing but a pretext for sodomy by listing those who have historically engaged in unnatural acts, including the Incubi, "who clothed their Galli, Succubi, Ganymedes and Cynadi in woman's attire, whose virilities they did oft-time dissect [castrate], to make them more effeminate, transforming them as neere might be into women, both in apparell, gesture, speech, behavior. . . . And more especially in long, unshorne, womanish, frizled haire and love-lockes." For debates about street transvestism, see *Hic Mulier; Or the Man Woman* and *Haec-Vir; Or the Womanish Man* (1620) in *Half Humankind: Contexts and Texts of the Controversy about Women in England, 1540–1640*, ed. Katherine Usher Henderson and Barbara F. McManus (Chicago: University of Illinois Press, 1985), pp. 264–89.

3 Stephen Greenblatt, "Fiction and Friction," *Shakespearean Negotiations: The Circulation of Social Energy in Renaissance England* (Oxford: Clarendon Press, 1988), p. 86.

4 See Orgel, "Nobody's Perfect," pp. 22–9 and Lisa Jardine *Still Harping on Daughters: Women and Drama in the Age of Shakespeare* (Brighton: Harvester Press, 1983), pp. 9–34.

5 C. L. Barber, *Shakespeare's Festive Comedy: A Study of Dramatic Form and its Relation to Social Custom* (New York: Princeton University Press, 1963), p. 6. Barber writes of *Twelfth Night* (and the same presumably would be true of *As You Like It*): "The most fundamental distinction the play brings home to us is the difference between men and women. . . . Just as the saturnalian reversal of social roles need not threaten the social structure, but can serve instead to consolidate it, so

a temporary, playful reversal of sexual roles can renew the meaning of the normal relation" (p. 245). For early feminist analyses, see, for instance, Juliet Dusinberre, *Shakespeare and the Nature of Women*, (New York: Barnes and Noble, 1975), pp. 231–71, and Robert Kimbrough, "Androgyny Seen Through Shakespeare's Disguise," *Shakespeare Quarterly* 33:1 (1982), pp. 17–33.

6 The phrase "traffic in women" was first coined by Emma Goldman in her critique of marriage as a form of prostitution. It gained critical prominence through Gayle Rubin's, "The Traffic in Women: Notes on the 'Political Economy' of Sex," *Toward an Anthropology of Women*, ed. Rayna R. Reiter (New York: Monthly Review Press, 1975), pp. 157–210.

7 I have learned much in this regard from Peter Stallybrass and Allon White, who also critique the reliance on such polarizations. They demonstrate the extent to which binary classifications are always imbued with their others, and argue that the relative radicality of any transgression can only be ascertained by placing it in history. Also helpful is Jonathan Dollimore, "Subjectivity, Sexuality, and Transgression: The Jacobean Connection," *Renaissance Drama* 17 (1986), pp. 53–81.

8 In addition to Jean Howard, "Crossdressing, The Theatre, and Gender Struggle in Early Modern England," *Shakespeare Quarterly* 39:4 (1988), Leah Marcus, "Shakespeare's Comic Heroines, Elizabeth I, and the Political Uses of Androgyny," *Women in the Middle Ages and the Renaissance: Literary and Historical Perspectives*, ed. Mary Beth Rose (Syracuse: Syracuse University Press, 1986), and Laura Levine, "Men in Women's Clothing: Anti-theatricality and Effeminization from 1579 to 1642," *Criticism* 28: 2 (Spring 1986), see Catherine Belsey, "Disrupting Sexual Difference: Meaning and Gender in the Comedies," *Alternative Shakespeares*, ed. John Drakakis (London: Methuen, 1985), pp. 166–90; Phyllis Rackin, "Androgyny, Mimesis, and the Marriage of the Boy Heroine on the English Renaissance Stage," *PMLA* 102 (1987), pp. 29–41; and Karen Newman, "Portia's Ring: Unruly Women and Structures of Exchange in *The Merchant of Venice*," *Shakespeare Quarterly* 38 (1987), pp. 19–33.

9 Orgel, "Nobody's Perfect," p. 13.

10 Sedgwick, *Between Men: English Literature and Male Homosocial Desire* (New York: Columbia University Press, 1985), p. 2.

11 Antonio's marginalization parallels that of Antonio in *The Merchant of Venice*, whose bond to Bassanio is initially honored and redeemed by Portia, but later displaced by her manipulations of the ring plot which, paradoxically, foster her subordination in a patriarchal heterosexual economy.

12 Montrose, "'The Place of a Brother' in *As You Like It*: Social Process and Comic Form," *Shakespeare Quarterly* 32:1 (1981), pp. 28–54.

13 ibid., p. 51.

14 Howard, "Crossdressing," p. 434.

15 ibid., p. 435. Terms can be confusing here, in part due to translation. In Luce Irigaray's formulation, *la mascarade* is "An alienated or false version of femininity arising from the woman's awareness of the man's

desire for her to be his other, the masquerade permits woman to experience desire not in her own right but as the man's desire situates her." Masquerade is the role (playing) required by "femininity." Thus, Rosalind's improvisation is really closer to *mimetisme* (mimicry) which, in Irigaray's terms, is "An interim strategy for dealing with the realm of discourse (where the speaking subject is posited as masculine), in which the woman deliberately assumes the feminine style and posture assigned to her within this discourse in order to uncover the mechanisms by which it exploits her" (*This Sex Which Is Not One*, trans. Catherine Porter, Ithaca: Cornell University Press, 1985, p. 220).

16 Saslow, *Ganymede in the Renaissance: Homosexuality in Art and Society* (New Haven: Yale University Press, 1986), p. 2.

17 Orgel, "Nobody's Perfect," p. 22.

18 Barber, *Shakespeare's Festive Comedy*, p. 231. See also W. Thomas MacCary, *Friends and Lovers: The Phenomenology of Desire in Shakespearean Comedy* (New York: Columbia University Press, 1985).

19 Phyllis Rackin, "Historical Difference/Sexual Difference."

20 Peter Stallybrass helped me with this formulation.

21 Laurie Osborne, "The Texts of *Twelfth Night*," *ELH* (Spring, 1990), pp. 37–61. Osborne's excellent analysis of the manipulation of the placement of the Antonio scenes in eighteenth- and nineteenth-century performance editions suggests that the playtexts themselves indicate changing significations of homoeroticism.

22 The *Oxford English Dictionary*'s first entry for "anxiety," as in "The quality or state of being anxious; uneasiness or trouble of mind about some uncertain event; solicitude, concern," is 1525. The first entry for "jealous," as in "Vehement in feeling, as in wrath, desire, or devotion" is 1382; for "Ardently amorous; covetous of the love of another, fond, lustful" is 1430; and for "Zealous or solicitous for the preservation or well-being of something possessed or esteemed; vigilant or careful in guarding; suspiciously careful or watchful" is 1387.

23 I am indebted to Peter Stallybrass for reminding me of the difference between heterosexual and homoerotic phallic imagery.

24 *Romeo and Juliet* III.i.113–15; *Antony and Cleopatra* I.iv.5–7; and *Coriolanus* IV.v.111–23. I am indebted to Phyllis Rackin for reminding me of some of these instances, and her further amplification in her talk "Historical Difference/Sexual Difference."

25 Randolph Trumbach's historical analysis bears this out; see "The Birth of the Queen: Sodomy and the Emergence of Gender Equality in Modern Culture 1660–1750," *Hidden from History: Reclaiming the Gay and Lesbian Past*, ed. Martin Duberman *et al.* (New York: New American Library, 1989), p. 133.

26 For an analysis of triangular desire, see René Girard, *Deceit, Desire, and the Novel: Self and Other in Literary Structure*, trans. Yvonne Freccero (Baltimore: Johns Hopkins University Press, 1965).

27 Howard, "Crossdressing," p. 432.

28 *Henry IV, part 1*, I.iii.29–69; *Hamlet*, V.ii.82–193 and III.ii.368–9; *King Lear*, II.iv.271–8.

29 Trumbach, "Birth of the Queen," p. 134.

30 Joseph Pequigney, "The Two Antonios and Same-Sex Love in *Twelfth Night* and *The Merchant of Venice*," unpublished manuscript presented to the Shakespeare Association of America, 1989, p. 11.

31 I am following David Bevington's numbering of the sonnets; he follows Thomas Thorpe, the original publisher of the sequence. In "Making Love Out of Nothing At All: the Issue of Story in Shakespeare's Procreation Sonnets," *Shakespeare Quarterly* 41:4 (Winter 1990), pp. 470–88, Robert Crosman takes up the issue of homoeroticism from a sympathetic if rather uninformed historical perspective. Whereas Pequigney argues that the first seventeen "procreation" sonnets record a gradual evolution of the poet's feelings for the young man, Crosman argues that Shakespeare first pretended to fall in love with his patron as a strategy of flattery, and then discovered he was no longer pretending.

32 For an explantion of the repetition compulsion, see Sigmund Freud, *Beyond the Pleasure Principle*, trans. James Strachey (New York: Norton, 1961).

33 Thomas Laqueur, *Making Sex: Body and Gender from the Greeks to Freud* (Cambridge: Harvard University Press, 1990).

34 Stephen Greenblatt, "Fiction and Friction," in *Shakespearean Negotiations: The Circulation of Social Energy in Renaissance England* (Oxford: Clarendon Press, 1988), p. 89.

35 Saslow makes a similar point about Michelangelo's status as a transitional figure; see "Homosexuality in the Renaissance: Behaviour, Identity, and Artistic Expression," in *Hidden From History: Reclaiming the Gay and Lesbian Past*, ed. Martin Duberman, Martha Vicinus, and George Chauncey Jr. (New York: New American Library, 1989), pp. 90–105.

36 See, for instance, Laura Mulvey, "Visual Pleasure and Narrative Cinema," and "Afterthoughts on 'Visual Pleasure and Narrative Cinema' inspired by *Duel in the Sun*," *Feminism and Film Theory*, ed. Constance Penley (London: Routledge, 1988), pp. 57–79; Janet Bergstrom and Mary Ann Doane, "The Female Spectator: Contexts and Directions," *Camera Obscura: A Journal of Feminism and Film Theory* 20/21 (May/Sept. 1989), pp. 5–27; and Irigaray, *This Sex Which Is Not One*, pp. 23–33.

37 Jean Howard alerted me to the fact that class differences are implicated in these erotic differences: as nostalgic pastoral, *As You Like It*'s class hierarchy is diffused and inclusive; *Twelfth Night*, on the other hand, is thoroughly aristocratic and, with the exception of Maria, marginalizes those figures below the rank of "gentleman."

38 Sedgwick, *Between Men*, p. 216.

39 Rackin has initiated such a comparative analysis of transvestism in "Androgyny, Mimesis, and the Marriage of the Boy Heroine on the English Renaissance Stage."

40 Robert Stoller, *Observing the Erotic Imagination* (New Haven: Yale University Press, 1985), p. 15.

AFTERWORD

1 See Peter Stallybrass, "The World Turned Upside Down: Inversion, Gender and the State" and Jean Howard, "Scripts and/versus Playhouses: Ideological Production and the Renaissance Public Stage," *The Matter of Difference: Materialist Feminist Criticism of Shakespeare*, ed. Valerie Wayne (Hemel Hempstead: Harvester Wheatsheaf, 1991), pp. 201–20 and 221–36; Louis Montrose, "Professing the Renaissance: The Poetics and Politics of Culture," *The New Historicism*, ed. H. Aram Vesser (New York: Routledge, 1989), pp. 15–36; and Jonathan Dollimore, "Subjectivity, Sexuality, and Transgression: The Jacobean Connection," *Renaissance Drama* 17 (1986), pp. 53–81.
2 For the constitution of Shakespeare's audience, see Andrew Gurr, *Playgoing in Shakespeare's London* (Cambridge: Cambridge University Press, 1987). For a perceptive analysis of the importance of attending to the material practices of theater-going, see Howard, "Scripts and/Versus Playhouses."

Index